The South China Sea: The Geo-political Epicenter of the Indo-Pacific?

Nguyen Hung Son · Nguyen Thi Lan Anh
Editors

The South China Sea: The Geo-political Epicenter of the Indo-Pacific?

Springer

Editors
Nguyen Hung Son
Diplomatic Academy of Vietnam
Hanoi, Vietnam

Nguyen Thi Lan Anh
East Sea (South China Sea) Institute
Diplomatic Academy of Vietnam
Hanoi, Vietnam

ISBN 978-981-97-8208-6 ISBN 978-981-97-8209-3 (eBook)
https://doi.org/10.1007/978-981-97-8209-3

This project was funded with UK International Development from the UK government
This material has been funded by UK International Development from the UK government; however, the views expressed do not necessarily reflect the UK government's official policies.

This Springer imprint is published by the registered company Springer Nature Singapore Pte Ltd.
The registered company address is: 152 Beach Road, #21-01/04 Gateway East, Singapore 189721, Singapore

Introduction

The South China Sea as the Geopolitical Epicenter of the Indo-Pacific

In recent decades, the South China Sea (SCS) has emerged as the primary geopolitical epicenter of the Indo-Pacific region. Its importance stretches beyond the region, becoming a critical point in the broader global strategic calculus. This maritime zone, rich in resources and brimming with economic and strategic significance, has transformed into one of the most contested areas globally. It is at the intersection of critical economic pathways and mounting geopolitical tensions between regional and global powers.

The South China Sea's significance can be understood on three interconnected levels: economic vitality, geopolitical contestation, and the opportunity for cooperation. The sea's vast resources—both natural and economic—make it essential for the region's prosperity. However, its location and strategic importance to China, the United States, and regional players have made it a flashpoint for geopolitical competition. Despite these tensions, the region offers potential opportunities for collaboration in areas like environmental sustainability, fisheries, and scientific cooperation, provided the competing powers find ways to navigate their overlapping interests.

This book offers a deep dive into the competing strategies in the South China Sea, focusing on the main geopolitical actors, the impact on regional economic prosperity, and the potential for cooperation amidst competition.

The Strategic Importance of the South China Sea

The South China Sea is an expanse that covers approximately 3.5 million square[1] kilometers, bounded by China, Taiwan, Vietnam, the Philippines, Malaysia, Brunei, and Indonesia. The region serves as the primary maritime artery connecting the Indian Ocean to the Pacific, making it a crucial corridor for global trade. It is estimated that around 30% of global maritime trade—valued at over $3.4 trillion annually—passes through its waters.[2] Additionally, around 60% of Japan's and 80% of China's oil imports are transported through this region, underscoring its importance for energy security in East Asia.[3]

This economic significance is mirrored by the South China Sea's abundant natural resources. According to the U.S. Energy Information Administration, 10 billion barrels of petroleum and petroleum products and 6.7 trillion cubic feet of liquefied natural gas (LNG) passed through the South China Sea in 2023.[4] Moreover, the region is a critical hub for the fishing industry, with over 10% of the world's fish stock located within these waters.[5] This combination of economic lifelines and natural wealth has heightened the stakes for the region, transforming it into a highly contested geopolitical space.

Furthermore, the South China Sea serves as a strategic buffer and gateway for regional powers, including China, Japan, and India, as well as external stakeholders like the United States. Its role as a connector between the Indian and Pacific Oceans amplifies its importance in regional security dynamics, particularly in the context of maritime disputes and freedom of navigation operations, shaping the geopolitical landscape of the Indo-Pacific region.

Growing Geopolitical Contestation

The economic importance of the South China Sea is inextricably tied to its geopolitical significance. The region's strategic location makes it a focal point for great power competition, particularly between China and the United States. China claims

---

1 Tang, Danling, Zhen Sun, and Guangjun Sui. "Geological environment in the South China Sea." *Journal of Oceanology and Limnology* 41, no. 2 (2023): 403–408.

2 Bateman, Sam. "Sea lines of communication and safety of navigation." In *Routledge Handbook of the South China Sea*, pp. 46–64. Routledge, 2021.

3 Kaplan, Robert D. "The South China Sea is the future of conflict." *Foreign Policy* 188 (2011): 76.; Uitto, Juha I. "CHINA'S ASIAN DREAM: Empire Building along the New Silk Road/THE SOUTH CHINA SEA: The Struggle for Power in Asia." *Geographical Review* 109, no. 4 (2019): 615–625.

4 U.S. Energy Information Administration. "South China Sea." International Energy Data and Analysis. Last modified February 7, 2017. https://www.eia.gov/international/analysis/regions-of-interest/South_China_Sea.

5 Zhang, Hongzhou. "Fisheries cooperation in the South China Sea: Evaluating the options." *Marine Policy* 89 (2018): 67–76.

nearly the entire sea through its "nine-dash line", a demarcation that overlaps with the Exclusive Economic Zones (EEZs) of several ASEAN countries. The geopolitical ramifications of these claims became starkly apparent following the 2016 Arbitral Tribunal ruling under Annex VII of the United Nations Convention on the Law of the Sea (UNCLOS), in favor of the Philippines, which rejected China's "nine-dash line" claims as having no legal basis. Despite the ruling, China continues to expand its influence through militarization, constructing artificial islands, and deploying military assets, including missile systems and airstrips, to assert control.

The implications of this militarization extend beyond the immediate region. For Beijing, dominance over the South China Sea would provide strategic depth and secure maritime routes crucial for both military and energy needs. Control over the South China Sea would also enhance China's ability to project power into the Western Pacific and protect its Second Island Chain, a key aspect of its broader military strategy. Moreover, the sea provides a vital buffer for China's nuclear deterrent, with its submarine bases on Hainan Island requiring access to the deep waters of the South China Sea to ensure credible second-strike capability.

The book's first part, "*Key Players in the South China Sea Strategic Chessboard*", explores these dynamics. In Chapter 1: "*Geopolitics and the South China Sea*", Leszek Buszynski details how China's rejection of international law and pursuit of its geopolitical ambitions have heightened regional tensions. The chapter further highlights the need for a strategic counterbalance to China's assertiveness to preserve regional stability. In Chapter 2: "*Limits of Cooperation: China's Strategic Intent in the South China Sea and the U.S.-China Security Dilemma*", Sarah Kirchberger focuses on how the U.S.-China rivalry exacerbates existing conflicts in the South China Sea, noting that China's desire for maritime supremacy is unlikely to yield space for genuine cooperation.

As China expands its influence, the United States has sought to reaffirm its commitment to the region through Freedom of Navigation Operations (FONOPs) and alliances with Southeast Asian nations. These operations are designed to challenge China's excessive maritime claims and ensure that vital sea lanes remain open to international shipping. The United States, while having no direct territorial claims in the region, has a vested interest in maintaining regional security and upholding the rules-based international order.

In Chapter 3: "*U.S. Interests in the South China Sea: Defending Norms, not Territory*", Frank Jannuzi articulates how the United States has transitioned from a position of neutrality regarding territorial claims to actively supporting the 2016 international tribunal ruling, which invalidated many of China's claims in the region. Jannuzi emphasizes that the U.S. has no territorial ambitions in the South China Sea but considers the preservation of international maritime law, particularly the principle of freedom of navigation, as central to its strategic interests. Maintaining open sea lanes in the South China Sea is vital not only for global commerce but also for ensuring that no single power, particularly China, dominates the region's maritime routes.

China's maritime ambitions, however, are not solely based on securing its trade routes. As Sarah Kirchberger points out, the sea is integral to China's broader security concerns, particularly its nascent sea-based nuclear deterrence capability. The country has developed an extensive system of artificial islands, military bases, and undersea surveillance networks aimed at monitoring and controlling maritime activity. These installations serve both civilian and military purposes, acting as surveillance points and defensive perimeters for China's strategic submarine fleet based on Hainan Island. The South China Sea, with its deep waters, provides a relatively safe operating environment for China's nuclear submarines, reinforcing its strategic priorities.

ASEAN's Role in Navigating Geopolitical Rivalries

Chapter 4: "*ASEAN Centrality Amidst Indo-Pacific's Geostrategic Environment*" focuses on the critical role of the Association of Southeast Asian Nations (ASEAN) in managing the escalating tensions in the South China Sea. Although several ASEAN member states are directly involved in territorial disputes with China, the organization has traditionally upheld a principle of neutrality. This chapter explores how ASEAN has sought to maintain its centrality by facilitating dialogue between competing powers while avoiding direct confrontation with China or the United States.

In the chapter, Pou Sothirak argues that ASEAN's centrality in the Indo-Pacific hinges on its ability to act as a mediator and a platform for diplomatic engagement. Given the region's growing strategic importance, ASEAN's unity is essential for balancing the influence of external powers and promoting a stable, rules-based order in the South China Sea. The chapter highlights the importance of ASEAN-led multilateral initiatives, such as the long-discussed Code of Conduct (CoC) with China, which aims to establish a framework for managing maritime disputes peacefully. However, achieving consensus among ASEAN members remains a challenge, as economic ties to China and differing security concerns often cause divisions within the bloc.

Economic Prosperity and Regional Connectivity

Beyond the military and strategic importance, the South China Sea plays a central role in ensuring the economic prosperity of the entire Indo-Pacific region. The sea's location connects the Indian and Pacific Oceans, serving as a critical communication line for global shipping and energy supplies. There are estimates that 60% of China's total trade passes through the South China Sea, while Japan, South Korea, and other regional economies rely heavily on its safe passage for energy imports.[6] The sea's

[6] Center for Strategic and International Studies. "How Much Trade Transits the South China Sea?" China Power Project, Accessed September 8, 2024. https://chinapower.csis.org/much-trade-transits-south-china-sea/.

significance to the global economy underscores why its stability is essential for the uninterrupted flow of goods, energy, and capital.

Economic interdependence and regional connectivity make the South China Sea vital for Indo-Pacific development. In Chapter 5: "*India's Reformed Approach Towards the South China Sea Dispute: Is There Scope to Do More?*", Premesha Saha argues that India, while not a direct claimant, has significant interests in ensuring the free flow of trade through the South China Sea. India's increasing involvement in the region, driven by its "Act East" policy and Indo-Pacific vision, further demonstrates how countries outside the immediate neighborhood are deeply invested in the sea's stability.

Cooperation Amidst Growing Competition

Despite the rising tensions and militarization, the South China Sea also presents opportunities for cooperation, particularly in environmental protection, fisheries management, and scientific research. While geopolitical competition often overshadows these areas, regional actors have realized the benefits of collaboration, especially in managing shared resources and addressing environmental challenges.

The book's second part, "*In Search of Cooperation Despite Competition*", examines these opportunities for collaboration. Chapter 6: "*The European Union (EU) and Association of Southeast Asian Nations (ASEAN)—Fields for Cooperation and Convergence of Interests in the Blue Economy in the Twenty-First Century*" highlights the role of the blue economy in fostering economic cooperation between ASEAN and external actors like the EU. As Southeast Asia faces overfishing, marine pollution, and other environmental challenges, cooperation in sustainable marine development offers a pathway to stabilize relations in the region while ensuring the preservation of vital marine ecosystems.

Another area ripe for cooperation is fisheries management, explored in Chapter 7: "*Hook, Line and Cooperate: A Three-Staged Approach to Regional Fishery Cooperation*". Fisheries disputes, particularly illegal, unreported, and unregulated (IUU) fishing, have exacerbated tensions between claimant states, yet they also present an opportunity for collaboration. Given the reliance of millions of people on South China Sea fisheries, joint efforts to manage resources sustainably would benefit all parties involved. The chapter advocates for a staged approach to fisheries cooperation that could gradually build trust and improve governance in contested waters.

The potential for disruption in the South China Sea, whether through conflict, militarization, or blockades, could have a catastrophic impact on global supply chains. This concern is particularly relevant in the context of the semiconductor supply chain, as highlighted in Chapter 8: "*Chips on the Deck: US-China Rivalry and Reorganizing the Supply Chains of Semiconductors*". The chapter explores how the U.S.-China rivalry has forced companies to rethink their supply chains and ensure that critical components like semiconductors, vital for industries ranging from consumer electronics to military hardware, can move freely through the region.

Marine scientific research is another area where regional players can engage in collaborative efforts, as outlined in Chapter 9: *"ASEAN—Important Broker for Marine Scientific Research Cooperation in the South China Sea*". ASEAN, as the central platform for dialogue among Southeast Asian nations, is uniquely positioned to promote scientific research partnerships. ASEAN's efforts in this area can help mitigate tensions by creating a platform for non-military cooperation that addresses shared environmental and scientific challenges.

As tensions persist, Chapter 10*: "The Case for Autonomy: A Military and Legal Option for Creating Capacity to Handle Challenges in the South China Sea"* explores the idea of autonomy for Southeast Asian nations. Rather than solely relying on external powers, the chapter argues that regional countries, particularly Vietnam, the Philippines, and Malaysia, must focus on strengthening their military and legal frameworks. This approach involves enhancing naval capacities to defend territorial waters and using legal avenues such as UNCLOS to uphold their maritime rights. By doing so, these nations can develop a greater degree of self-reliance and stability in dealing with China's assertiveness in the South China Sea.

Chapter 11*: "Emission Reduction from Shipping and Net-Zero Shipping: Institutional Deficiencies and the Way Forward"* shifts attention to the environmental and regulatory challenges in the region, particularly related to shipping emissions. Given the vast amount of maritime traffic passing through the South China Sea, shipping represents a significant source of carbon emissions. The chapter critiques the current institutional frameworks for addressing this issue, arguing that more robust regional cooperation is necessary to ensure sustainable shipping practices. It also outlines potential solutions to achieve net-zero emissions, including technological advancements and stronger regulatory mechanisms.

Lastly, Chapter 12*: "Opportunities and Challenges Associated with Synergy Between Mekong Sub-Regional Cooperation Frameworks and ASEAN-Led Mechanisms"* delves into the potential for closer collaboration between Mekong subregional frameworks and broader ASEAN initiatives. The Mekong sub-region, home to countries like Cambodia, Laos, Myanmar, Thailand, and Vietnam, plays a crucial role in regional development and resource management. The chapter argues that integrating Mekong cooperation efforts with ASEAN's broader strategies could unlock new opportunities for economic development, environmental protection, and regional connectivity. However, it also identifies key challenges, such as differing national interests and the complex influence of external powers like China, which may hinder deeper cooperation.

Navigating a Complex Geopolitical Landscape

The South China Sea embodies the complexity of the Indo-Pacific's geopolitical landscape. As a critical nexus for global trade, economic connectivity, and military strategy, it has become the epicenter of both competition and opportunity. Nations, both regional and global, view the South China Sea through their own strategic lenses, be it China's need for military dominance, the U.S.' commitment to maintaining open sea lanes, or ASEAN's role in fostering dialogue and cooperation.

The chapters in this book offer an in-depth examination of these multifaceted challenges and opportunities. Part One provides a thorough analysis of the strategic competition between the key players, while Part Two explores the avenues for cooperation that remain viable despite rising tensions. Whether through environmental collaboration, shared scientific research, or sustainable fisheries management, there are still possibilities for cooperation in the South China Sea that could serve to de-escalate tensions and promote regional stability.

As the Indo-Pacific continues to gain importance in global geopolitics, the South China Sea will remain a focal point of international attention. This book equips policymakers, scholars, and interested readers with a comprehensive understanding of the dynamics at play in this critical region, emphasizing both the risks of unchecked competition and the potential for cooperative solutions that can ensure long-term stability and prosperity.

Nguyen Hung Son

Contents

Part I
Key Players in the South China Sea Strategic Chessboard

Chapter 1
Geopolitics and the South China Sea

Leszek Buszynski

1. Introduction

This paper examines the impact of geopolitics on the South China Sea maritime dispute and it submits three propositions. First, the resolution of this dispute to achieve long-term stability is through the application of UNCLOS and the accepted norms and rules of international law. However, China rejected a UNCLOS-based resolution of this issue when it repudiated the ruling of the 2016 Arbitral Tribunal of the Law of the Sea and insisted on the validity of its historical rights to the area and the nine-dash line. Chinese commentators have declared that China will not accept Western-derived rules when it comes to its maritime rights or that Chinese historical rights override UNCLOS. The second proposition should be an axiom in international affairs and that a rising power has no incentive or interest in entering into agreements that constrain it. While China is convinced that it is rising power, and the West, the US in particular, is declining, its leaders feel they can brush off UNCLOS in the South China Sea and impose their own settlement of the issues that would secure their claims. In this spirit, China has escalated the geopolitical pressure in the Western Pacific to induce the US, into an accommodation and to obtain ASEAN's acceptance of its maritime claims and its dominant position not only in the South China Sea. The third proposition is that legality requires power for its compliance. That is, if a legal resolution of this and other maritime disputes in the Western Pacific is to be achieved in the face of continued Chinese rejection, there has to be a counterbalance to China or a geopolitical configuration of power that would constrain its ambitions and provide it with an incentive to resolve these issues according to law. Ultimately, there can be no settlement of the South China Sea on the basis of international law without a "strategic equilibrium" in the Western Pacific that would involve the US and its partners in Quadrilateralism, AUKUS, the

L. Buszynski (✉)
Honorary Professor, Australian National University, Canberra, Australia
e-mail: Leszek.Buszynski@anu.edu.au

N. Hung Son and N. Thi Lan Anh (eds.), *The South China Sea: The Geo-political Epicenter of the Indo-Pacific?*, https://doi.org/10.1007/978-981-97-8209-3_1

regional states and NATO members to uphold and strengthen the international legal order and the rule of law.

International Law and Geopolitics

Legal idealists tend to disregard power in their formulation of rules and procedures as though normative principles alone are sufficient to bring about self-enforcement. For them, the rational explication of legality brings about compliance because of its recognised role in resolving disputes, reducing friction between states and enhancing predictability. While that may be the case with reasonable leaders who are willing to submit to law, particularly in the Western or developed world, not all are so constrained. For this reason, neo-realists point out that law requires power for its enforcement and credibility and that the distribution of power is critical for compliance. They contest the claim that law can somehow be self-enforcing and stress that compliance is possible only with the support of state power. If the interests of the most powerful states are affected by any violation of international law, they may act to uphold it. Violations that do not affect those interests, or which are a result of a powerful state's pursuit of its own interests, may go unpunished giving rise to a discrepancy between the law's aspirations and its practical application that has long vexed legal minds. However, the two-way interaction between law and power has long been the subject of legal discussions. The rules and norms set by international law attract support for their predictability and stabilising function and that may bring together the international community in response to a major violation. International law may provide the rationale and basis for a security foundation as it brings together regional and extra-regional states that have a strong interest in upholding its stabilising function and its inherent predictability. Law provides the guidelines and procedures for dispute resolution and settlement, but it can not exist as an abstract notion alone and should be realised and grounded in a security foundation based on geopolitics.

China's Geopolitical Pressure

Does China have a discernible strategy as it engages in geopolitical expansion? The notion of strategy demands consistent direction, planning and oversight towards a particular goal. In China's case, there has been a pattern of repeated pressure and activity directed against neighbouring powers intended to make way for itself in the Western Pacific. China has escalated the pressure and has pushed outwards in the Western Pacific to control the maritime area around Taiwan and to keep the US and its allies at a safe distance from this area. Forcing Taiwanese unification, indeed, is Beijing's main priority as Xi Jinping has constantly reiterated, but this issue is linked inextricably with the South China Sea and what China will do towards Taiwan it would do in the South China Sea. China has the intention to formulate its own rules and to have its claim accepted by the ASEAN claimants in the South China Sea. It wants to settle an outstanding and extensive claim that has been hyped up by patriotic rhetoric in China, but there are strategic issues involved which should not be overlooked. Control over the South China Sea would give China a dominant position over ASEAN and Southeast Asia, detaching it from the US and Japan. It would also provide its navy with unimpeded access to the open sea through the Malacca Strait and to the maritime area around Taiwan through the Bashi channel. With the expected surge of Chinese power, Beijing anticipates that the international community would simply avoid any friction or conflict by making way for it in the South China Sea and the Western Pacific. However, China has geopolitical priorities that go beyond the South China Sea and it has pressed Japan over the Senkaku/Diaoyu islands dispute, sending its maritime militia and coast guard vessels into the Japanese claim area. In June 2020, China staged the Galwan Valley clash with India along the Line of Control in the Himalayas which was regarded as a warning to India to avoid closer security cooperation with the US. In the same year, China imposed trade sanctions on Australia in a pique which was seen as an effort to detach it from the US alliance and bring about its compliance. Why China engaged in this blatant pressure against these countries at the same time requires explanation as countries that may have been well disposed towards China were turned into adversaries. These actions reveal that China's outward expansion is not coordinated or controlled according to some higher plan or schedule and shows signs of opportunism and makeshift adjustment. China's actions brought the US, Japan, Australia and India together in the Quadrilateral Security Dialogue or "the Quad" which demonstrates a lack of strategic calculation in Beijing. It may be that Beijing believes that trade and economics will constrain the Quad members from responding collectively to its assertiveness in the South China Sea and elsewhere. But creating adversaries of the major powers in the Indo-Pacific does not conform to any consistent strategy other than showing that Beijing has engaged in improvised and opportunist geopolitical expansion. This has characterised Beijing's behaviour.

China's naval expansion is at the forefront of its geopolitical expansion and its effort to push back the US naval presence from around Taiwan and the Western Pacific. Xi Jinping's aspiration to achieve unification with Taiwan cannot be achieved while the US naval presence in the Western Pacific remains dominant. Moreover, China seeks to expand its naval access to the Indian Ocean to obtain free access to its naval facilities in Djibouti, Gwador in Pakistan and also transit points in Sri Lanka and Myanmar. China has also been seeking the use of facilities in the South Pacific where it has been assiduously courting the Solomon Islands, Vanuatu and other Pacific countries. China's navy is now the world's largest in terms of naval tonnage and new categories of vessels are being constructed. China's carrier programme reveals the ambition to control the sea around Taiwan and the maritime area up to the first island chain which stretches from Japan and includes the South China Sea and to challenge the Indian navy in the Indian Ocean. Its third aircraft carrier the *Fujian* was launched in June 2022. It joins the *Liaoning* commissioned in 2012 and the *Shandong* which was launched in 2017, both were constructed with ski jumps to launch aircraft based on old Soviet designs. The *Fujian* marks a departure from the old Soviet design and at 72,000 tonnes it will reportedly have electromagnetic rather than steam catapults and will carry the J-35 stealth fighter jet and KJ-600 early warning aircraft.[1] Speculation has it that China plans to build five carriers; the next carrier is expected to be nuclear-propelled.[2] However, China's carrier programme is problematical and reveals that resources and attention are being directed towards it for reasons other than naval strategy, such as prestige and domestic approval. These carriers are highly vulnerable targets for the new technologies that are being developed by the US including hypersonic missiles, Autonomous Unmanned Underwater Vehicles (AUUVs) and long-range robotic drones integrated into networked systems linked by Artificial Intelligence and GPS targeting systems. The irony is that China is also developing these technologies which would put its own carriers at risk.

China's aircraft carriers require access to the open sea without which their usefulness is doubtful, but its constricted maritime geography prevents that. China's carriers are obliged to pass through several straits called choke points, to reach the Pacific Ocean, or through the Malacca Strait to reach the Indian Ocean. The South China Sea is one such outlet and the other is the East China Sea but the access points there are controlled by Japan which has been expanding its naval capability in response to China. To ensure this access to the open sea for its navy without facing the threat of interdiction, China must control the South China Sea or prevent the US and Japan from threatening its movements there. The naval forces deployed in the South Sea Fleet, particularly on Hainan Island are an indication of the importance of the South China Sea in Chinese naval strategy. The carrier *Shandong* has been stationed at the new *Longpo* Naval Base, on Hainan Island. Its mission would be to provide air cover for operations some 800 km further south in the Spratly Islands and for operations to land marines on reefs and atolls currently occupied by Vietnam, Malaysia and the Philippines.

Moreover, the South China Sea is important for China's nuclear strategy which has received conspicuous attention under Xi Jinping. In any conflict over Taiwan, there is the danger of escalation to the nuclear level and if China has a survivable nuclear deterrent that cannot be destroyed by the US it may deter the US and force it to back down. To offset American nuclear superiority, China needs a deployment area for its nuclear missile-carrying submarines (SSBNs) that make up its second-strike nuclear capability in the South China Sea. Two Jin-class SSBNs and two nuclear-powered attack submarines (SSNs) have been docked at Yuling base on Hainan

[1] Sakshi Tiwar, "China's 3rd Aircraft Carrier 'Fujian' To Host AWACS & Large Transport Aircraft For COD & CAP Missions-15 ship-borne fighter jet, early warning aircraft", *Eurasian Times* 1 July 2022 https://eurasiantimes.com/chinas-3rd-aircraft-carrier-fujian-to-host-awacs-large-transport-aircraft/.

[2] "China's Navy Could Have 5 Aircraft Carriers, 10 Ballistic Missile Subs by 2030 Says CSBA Report", *USNI News*, 18 August 2022 https://news.usni.org/2022/08/18/chinas-navy-could-have-5-aircraft-carriers-10-ballistic-missile-subs-by-2030-says-csba-report.

Islands alongside four piers, currently undergoing expansion.[3] China has built a total of six Jin class SSBNs and two variants, which carry the 12 Julang-2 (JL-2) submarine-launched ballistic missile (SLBMs) with a range of 7200–9000 km.[4] These missiles do not have the range to reach the US mainland, so the submarines carrying them would have to move out on patrol into the wider Pacific Ocean to launch them. This means they would have to transit the South China Sea and it becomes imperative for China to control this outlet to the Pacific Ocean. China is reportedly upgrading the Jin class SSBN with the new JL-3 SLBM with a range of around 10,000 km sufficient to strike the West Coast of the US without leaving a deployment zone in the South China Sea.[5] For this purpose, China requires control over South China.

What this means for the ASEAN claimants, Vietnam, Malaysia and the Philippines is greater pressure from China to accept China's dominant position there to ensure that an American naval presence is excluded. China fears that American attack submarines or other vessels traversing the South China Sea could put its SSBN deployment zone at risk. To ensure protection for its SSBN deployment zone, China has constructed three airfields and infrastructure and has stationed anti-ship and anti-aircraft missile systems in the seven reefs it has occupied in the South China Sea. Access to oil and gas reserves and fishing rights are disputed in the South China Sea but these issues can be resolved by agreement and compromise between China and the ASEAN claimants. Ensuring access through the South China Sea for its navy and protection for its SSBNs requires control over the area and cannot be negotiated or conceded, however. Negotiations for the Code of Conduct with ASEAN have been stymied for various reasons relating to its geographic scope, whether it should be legally binding, and also because of the Chinese insistence on excluding foreign military vessels.[6] China continues to press the ASEAN claimants with the intention to nudge them into bilateral negotiations to undermine the 2016 Arbitral ruling which ruled against it and nullified its claims to the South China Sea.

Nonetheless, the ASEAN claimants have resisted China and they have benefited from the presence of the US and Japan in the South China Sea, though they might not acknowledge it publicly, While the US conducts its Freedom of Navigation Exercises (FONOPs) and Japan sends its naval vessels into the South China Sea, China is obliged to bide its time with ASEAN. As the major claimant in the South China Sea, Vietnam has been directly under pressure, its fishing vessels have been captured in

---

[3] "China expands submarine base near South China Sea, satellite images show" *South China Morning Post,* 22 September 2022 https://www.scmp.com/news/china/military/article/3193555/china-expands-submarine-base-near-south-china-sea-satellite.

[4] "A Glimpse of Chinese Ballistic Missile Submarines", Centre for Strategic and International Studies (Washington DC), August 4, 2021 https://www.csis.org/analysis/glimpse-chinese-ballistic-missile-submarines.

[5] Luke Caggiano, China Deploys New Submarine-Launched Ballistic Missiles Arms Control Association, may 2023 https://www.armscontrol.org/act/2023-05/news/china-deploys-new-submarine-launched-ballistic-missiles.

[6] Viet Hoang, "The Code of Conduct for the South China Sea: A Long and Bumpy Road", *The Diplomat,* 28 September 2022.

the Chinese claim area and destroyed by the Chinese Coast Guard some 98 vessels have been destroyed in this way since 2014.[7] Vietnam offers resistance which acts as a major barrier to China's intentions to control the area. Vietnam has fortified its military presence constructing fortifications and infrastructure on the features it occupies in the South China Sea to match China and it has no intention to comply with China's claims.[8] Moreover, Vietnam has developed security cooperation with the US accepting visits by US naval vessels and carriers to its ports which disturbs Beijing. In September 2023, Vietnam hosted a visit by US President Joe Biden, when the relationship was upgraded to a Comprehensive Strategic Partnership to "enhance the collective security of the region".[9] Xi Jinping's visit to Hanoi followed in December 2023 which was an effort to ensure that Vietnam would not go too far in the relationship with the US.[10] Vietnam may extend security cooperation with the US in limited ways but it has no intention of provoking China. In the current situation when China is uncertain about Vietnam's intentions, visits by US Presidents serve to restrain Chinese behaviour. While the US is active/in the region, China is obliged to live with the Vietnamese claims and presence in the South China Sea which it cannot dislodge.

The Philippines is another obstacle to Chinese control over the South China Sea, President Rodrigo Duterte may have expected that he could manage China and negotiate access by Philippine fishermen to Scarborough Shoal which was seized by China in 2012. However, Philippine fishermen have been denied such access and have been regularly harassed by the Chinese Coast Guard. Duterte's Defence Secretary Delfin Lorenzano noted that the presence of Chinese vessels in the Philippine claim area continued unabated.[11] Chinese Coast Guard vessels have resorted to water cannons and dangerous blocking manoeuvres to keep away Philippine Coast Guard and fishing vessels from the area. Floating barriers have been put in place around Scarborough Shoal while around Second Thomas Shoal the Chinese coast guard attempted to block supplies to the small Philippine occupying unit there. Under President Ferdinand Marcos Jr., the Philippines moved to closer security cooperation with the US as a result of Chinese pressure. The Enhanced Defense Cooperation Arrangement (EDCA) which was concluded with the US in 2014 has been expanded to allow the

---

[7] "Vietnam fisherman recounts attacks by China coast guard in South China Sea", South *China Morning Post,* 14 October 2022 https://www.scmp.com/news/asia/southeast-asia/article/3196026/vietnam-fisherman-recounts-attacks-china-coast-guard-south.

[8] Vietnam said to plan military buildup on South China Sea footholds Nikkei Asia YUICHI SHIGA and YUJI NITTA, Nikkei staff writers August 19, 2023, https://asia.nikkei.com/Politics/International-relations/South-China-Sea/Vietnam-said-to-plan-military-buildup-on-South-China-Sea-footholds.

[9] "President Joseph R. Biden and General Secretary Nguyen Phu Trong Announce the U.S.-Vietnam Comprehensive Strategic Partnership", *the White House* 10 September 2023 https://www.whitehouse.gov/briefing-room/statements-releases/2023/09/10/.

[10] "Chinese President Xi Jinping Visits Vietnam", VOA 12 December 2023 https://www.voanews.com/a/chinese-president-xi-jinping-visits-vietnam/7394441.html.

[11] Katrina Hallare 'I am no fool': Lorenzana wants Chinese vessels out of West PH Sea", *Philippine Daily Inquirer* 3 April 2021 https://globalnation.inquirer.net/194803/i-am-no-fool-lorenzana-wants-chinese-vessels-out-of-west-ph-sea.

US Navy access to another four facilities in addition to the original five.[12] Chinese pressure, indeed, arrested Duterte's effort to seek accommodation and brought the Philippines and the US closer than before.

Indonesia does not wish to be regarded as a claimant in the South China Sea and attempted to distance itself from the dispute, but Chinese intrusions into the EEZ around the Natuna islands have dragged it in. As the largest member of ASEAN, Indonesia has steered the organisation away from great power rivalry and a security association with external powers like the US and Japan according to its non-aligned policy. China's pressure confronts Indonesia with a very new situation.[13] The Chinese claim overlaps with Indonesia's EEZ giving rise to clashes in 2016 and 2019, 2020 when Chinese Coast Guard and fishing vessels moved into the area.[14] Beijing insists that Chinese fishermen have the right to access their "traditional fishing area", which Indonesia firmly rejects as being incompatible with UNCLOS. In December 2021, it was revealed that Chinese diplomats protested Indonesia's drilling for oil and natural gas in the disputed maritime territory which opened up another area of dispute with Jakarta.[15] Indonesia's military has turned to security cooperation with the US and also Australia and in August 2022 it joined the US Indo-Pacific Command (INDOPACOM) in what was described as Southeast Asia's largest military exercise called "Super Garuda Shield 2022". This exercise was conducted in various areas including the Natuna Islands and involved forces from 13 countries including Australia, Canada, Japan, Singapore and South Korea.[16]

In its effort to maintain good relations with China, Malaysia has avoided the dispute even though the Chinese claim cuts into its EEZ and its oil and gas field off the coast of Sarawak. Reports of friction with Chinese coast guard and fishing vessels have been downplayed in the media and the public narrative stresses deepening economic and trade ties with China. The Malaysian Maritime Enforcement Agency (MMEA) reports that since 2013, the Chinese Coast Guard has had a permanent presence near Luconia Shoals which are within Malaysia's EEZ and China's

---

[12] "Philippines, U.S. Announce Locations of Four New EDCA Sites", *US Department of Defense* April 3, 2023, https://www.defense.gov/News/Releases/Release/Article/3349257/philippines-us-announce-locations-of-four-new-edca-sites/.

[13] Kornelius Purba "For millions of Indonesians, China's diplomat has crossed the line by openly challenging Indonesia's territorial integrity" "China playing with fire over claim on Natuna waters", *The Jakarta Post*, January 6, 2020 https://www.thejakartapost.com/academia/2020/01/06/china-playing-with-fire-over-claim-on-natuna-waters.html.

[14] "Chinese fishing vessels remain in Natuna amid diplomatic tension: TNI" *The Jakarta Post* January 5, 2020, https://www.thejakartapost.com/news/2020/01/05/chinese-fishing-vessels-remain-in-natuna-amid-diplomatic-tension-tni.html.

[15] Tom Allard, Kate Lamb and Agustinus Beo Da Costa, "China protested Indonesian drilling, military exercises", *Reuters* 2 December 2021, https://www.reuters.com/world/asia-pacific/exclusive-china-protested-indonesian-drilling-military-exercises-2021-12-01/.

[16] Riwan Rahmat, "Indonesia, US conclude massive multinational military exercise with eye on China", *Janes Defence News* 15 August 2022 https://www.janes.com/defence-news/news.

nine-dash line.[17] The Malaysian Auditor-General in July 2020 reported that Chinese vessels had encroached into Malaysian waters 89 times between 2016 and 2019, while the China Coast Guard (CCG) did so 72 times over the same period. The apparent intention was to remind Malaysia of China's presence and to demonstrate its South China Sea claims.[18] While Malaysia's political leaders avoid raising these intrusions with China, the maritime security agencies are increasingly frustrated. Their concern is that China might stake a claim to Malaysia's oil and gas reserves, which would be a red line for the country. Malaysia conducted a joint exercise with the US Coast Guard in the South China Sea.[19] If Chinese pressure continues against Malaysia it may result in expanding security relations with the US in the future.

Indeed, Beijing seems convinced that Chinese control over the South China Sea would be assured but for the US, its presence in the area and its ties with the ASEAN claimants. Chinese commentaries regularly cast the South China Sea dispute as a problem with the US as though the ASEAN claimants have no agency and could be brought into line with its claims. It is for this reason that China marks out the US as the target for its criticism and attempts to present itself as a regional claimant, together with the ASEAN claimants while the US is portrayed as an external power that has no business being there. By presenting itself as a regional state, China seeks to separate ASEAN from the US and also Japan based on its long history of interaction with Southeast Asia and claiming membership rights with ASEAN. In the negotiations for the Code of Conduct over the South China Sea, which have been ongoing for several decades, China insisted on consultation rights as a member of the organisation which was rejected. The problem for China is that it cannot pose as a partner in the ASEAN consultation process while ASEAN calls for a resolution of the issue based on UNCLOS and international law. China wants ASEAN acceptance and legitimisation of its claims while it attempts to impose its own resolution of the South China Sea issue on the organisation. It attempts to separate ASEAN from the US and also Japan, but its actions have only entrenched their presence in the region and their support for the ASEAN claimants.

---

[17] Mike Yeo, "Vietnam strengthens fortifications in disputed South China Sea, satellite images reveal" *Defense News*, 27 February 2021 https://www.defensenews.com/global/asia-pacific/2021/02/26/vietnam-strengthens-fortifications-in-disputed-south-china-sea-satellite-images-reveal/.
"MMEA Miri chief says keeping an eye on China vessel in S. China Sea", *Malay Mail* (Kuala Lumpur) September 24, 2020.

[18] Jason Loh Seong Wei, "South China Sea—Time to display firm resolve—Jason Loh", *Malay Mail* (Kuala Lumpur) July 23, 2020.

[19] Fuad Nizam, "MMEA in joint exercise with US to enhance maritime security in region", *Business Times* August 28, 2023, https://www.nst.com.my/news/nation/2023/08/948310/mmea-joint-exercise-us-enhance.

Strategic Equilibrium

China's outward pressure has stimulated responses from the international community to protect the liberal international order and to ensure maritime security and the rule of law. By rejecting the 2016 Arbitral Tribunals' ruling on its claims to the South China Sea, China has challenged the rule of law which threatens to undermine its applicability to maritime territorial disputes and unravel the fabric of the liberal order. What is required is a counterbalance to China or a strategic equilibrium involving regional and external powers that would dampen China's assertiveness and excessive ambitions and give it an incentive to negotiate the key issues, including the South China Sea. The Quadrilateral security dialogue, or the Quad, brought together Japan, the US with Australia and India to reaffirm maritime security as a direct effort to counter Beijing's assertive moves. Under Prime Minister Shinzo Abe, alarmed by Chinese pressure in the Senkaku/Diaoyu islands and the South China Sea, Japan reached out to India and promoted the Quad as a matter of urgency. What worries the Japanese is that China could gain control over the maritime areas in East China and South China Seas and could interdict Japan's trade lifeline, and its oil and energy supplies and hold it hostage at will. Australia is similarly concerned about China's actions in the South China Sea and is concerned that China would put its trade and the security of its northern approaches at risk. India's involvement has given meaning to the geographic concept of the Indo-Pacific, which the major players including ASEAN have adopted. India has been alarmed by the Galwan Valley clashes with China in 2020 and is apprehensive that China's domination of the South China Sea would facilitate its naval expansion into the Indian Ocean.

The Indo-Pacific has become more closely integrated with NATO. Disturbed by China's threat to the maritime order, key NATO members have indicated their willingness to maintain a naval presence in the Indo-Pacific. France declared its Indo-Pacific strategy in 2018 and has regularly participated in naval exercises in the region. In 2019, it conducted the La Perouse naval exercise with the US, Japan and Australia and in April 2021, France joined the US, Japan, Australia and India in a larger naval exercise in the Bay of Bengal.[20] According to reports, France plans to upgrade its presence in the Indo-Pacific through regular deployment of its nuclear attack submarines (SSNs), an air defence frigate, landing helicopter docks (LHD), and the nuclear-powered aircraft carrier the *Charles de Gaulle*.[21] Germany declared its Indo-Pacific strategy in September 2020 and sent a frigate to the region in 2021 as a demonstration of its interest. In March 2021, Britain's Integrated Review of Security, Defence, Development and Foreign Policy indicated a "tilt" towards the Indo-Pacific. Britain's direct involvement in the Indo-Pacific was declared in September

---

[20] "India joins French-led naval exercise, revealing clues about Quad's plans to contain China in Indo-Pacific, "*South China Morning Post* 4 April 2021 https://www.scmp.com/week-asia/politics/article/3128236/india-joins-french-led-naval-exercise-revealing-clues-about.

[21] Benjamin Felton, "Submarines and Carriers? Upcoming French Deployments To The Pacific", *Naval News*, 18 August 2022 https://www.navalnews.com/naval-news/2022/08/submarines-and-carriers-upcoming-french-deployments-to-the-pacific/.

2021 when it joined the US and Australia in the promulgation of AUKUS. This agreement entailed the transfer of nuclear submarines, probably the Virginia class, to Australia which elevated its strategic significance in the Indo-Pacific as a key player. Some feared that AUKUS would sideline the Quad and ASEAN centrality as well as its Indo-Pacific Outlook, which was declared in 2019. However, Japan, India and despite the controversy some defence officials in ASEAN have welcomed it as a necessary response to China.

Russia's invasion of Ukraine on 24 February 2022 was an ominous reminder of the fragility of international institutions and the confidence that multilateralism could bring stability has been unfortunately broken. Before the invasion on 4 February, Xi Jinping met President Putin and declared a "no limits" friendship with Russia, which tied China closely to the success of the Russian invasion. Many were fearful that Xi Jinping would take the opportunity to invade Taiwan or increase the pressure over this issue and the South China Sea to an intolerable level. Had Russia succeeded in its initial plan to occupy Ukraine, China may have prepared to do so and the situation in the Western Pacific may have been threatening. However, the astonishing incompetence of the Russian military, the strong response of the West and, with massive Western support, the Ukrainian resistance, must make China hesitate. Russia's invasion has galvanised the West and has accelerated the strategic integration of the Indo-Pacific with NATO which invited leaders of Japan, South Korea, Australia and New Zealand to its Madrid Summit in June 2022. Japanese Prime Minister Fumio Kishida was the first Japanese leader to attend a NATO summit and with Australian Prime Minister Anthony Albanese, New Zealand's Prime Minister Jacinda Ardern and South Korean President Yoon Suk-yeol agreed to boost cooperation with NATO.[22] However, because of French opposition, NATO did not agree to open a NATO Liaison Office in Japan, which Kishida had requested. These countries attended the NATO summit in Vilnius in July 2023 which expressed a concern for the defence of the liberal international order in Europe and the Indo-Pacific region.

Conclusion

There can be no legal resolution of the South China Sea according to UNCLOS and international law while China continues with its geopolitical expansion in the Western Pacific. While China is confident that its power is rising and the US is a declining power, it has no incentive or interest to accept a legal resolution that would hinder and impede its access through the South China Sea or to negotiate. Xi Jinping ramps up the pressure over Taiwan and the South China Sea to compel the US to draw back from the Western Pacific and to intimidate the regional states to accept China's position over these issues. China is engaged in a deliberate effort to impose an accommodation on the Indo-Pacific, on the US, Japan and others, which would allow

[22] "Kishida seeks major upgrade of NATO partnership after Russia's war", *Japan Times* 30 June 2022 https://www.japantimes.co.jp/news/2022/06/30/national/fumio-kishida-nato-ties/.

it a free hand over the South China Sea and Taiwan. By provoking alarm, China hopes that others will back down. Distressed by the danger of conflict, Singapore's Senior Minister Tharman Shanmugaratnam called upon the US to give China a greater "role and responsibility" in the multilateral system and to reset the relationship.[23] Some American commentators have called upon the US to negotiate a deal with China as an equal to reduce the danger of conflict. What is not explained, however, is that any such agreement or accommodation would have to recognise Chinese domination in these areas and would be tantamount to surrender for the US and the West after all the effort put into the defence of the liberal order. It would acknowledge the success of China's geopolitical pressure giving it primacy in the Western Pacific. It may be unwelcome to those who call for measures to avoid risk, but only through balanced power in the Indo-Pacific and a strategic equilibrium that includes the Quad, AUKUS and key NATO allies could this situation be stabilised, and China would see that a legal resolution of these maritime issues would be in its interest.

[23] "Tharman: US should give China a bigger role in multilateral system", *Asiaone* 23 September 2022 https://www.asiaone.com/singapore/tharman-us-should-give-china-bigger-role-multilateral-system.

Chapter 2
Limits of Cooperation: China's Strategic Intent in the South China Sea and the U.S.-China Security Dilemma

Sarah Kirchberger

Introduction

This paper argues that an underlying security dilemma between the two great powers China and the U.S. exacerbates existing conflicts of interests and impairs chances for cooperation in the South China Sea (SCS) between China and most other claimants for the foreseeable future. In the current geopolitical context of Russia's war against Ukraine, great-power rivalry has intensified and increasingly focuses on aspects of military security including nuclear posture changes and nuclear deterrence, an area where China traditionally lagged behind the U.S. Given its nuclear ballistic missile submarine (SSBN) base on Hainan Island, China will remain unlikely to compromise with any of its neighbors over conflicting territorial claims in the SCS. Rather, it will continue its project of building up massive multi-domain surveillance infrastructures in the SCS that began roughly since 2012. This encompasses not just the frequently discussed artificial islands, but includes multiple types of networked sensor and communication nodes from the sea bottom through the entire water and air column that could eventually contribute to an advanced multi-domain awareness in the context of a so-called "Ocean Information Network." A demonstrator system seems to have already been built by state-owned defense electronics company China Electronics Technology Group Corporation (CETC) near Hainan.[1] While all the related technical infrastructures are dual-use and contribute simultaneously to civilian research purposes, search-and-rescue, fisheries protection and other non-military functions, another chief aim of this massive construction effort seems centered around the build-up of a novel submarine detection capability. To ensure

S. Kirchberger (✉)
Institute for Security Policy at Kiel University, Kiel, Germany
e-mail: skirchberger@ispk.uni-kiel.de

[1] "Exploring China's Unmanned Ocean Network". 2020. Asia Maritime Transparency Initiative, with J. Michael Dahm, June 16, 2020. https://amti.csis.org/exploring-chinas-unmanned-ocean-network/.

N. Hung Son and N. Thi Lan Anh (eds.), *The South China Sea: The Geo-political Epicenter of the Indo-Pacific?*, https://doi.org/10.1007/978-981-97-8209-3_2

that strategic submarines operating out of Hainan benefit from a security perimeter created through a system of layered defense, China wants the capability to detect submarines to deny an adversary the safe use of the relevant sea areas.[2,3,4] Given China's unwillingness to compromise in matters related to its nascent sea-based nuclear deterrence, the SCS's smaller littoral states will likely discover that coexistence rather than cooperation is the best achievable outcome, although some limited forms of cooperation on mutual issues of concern might be possible.

Chinese Strategic Intent in the SCS: Maritime Geography and the Significance of the First Island Chain

In the view of Chinese naval analysts, Chinese geostrategic interest in the SCS (as well as in the Senkaku/Diaoyu islands and Taiwan) is shaped by China's peculiar maritime geography just as much as by history and politics.[5]

From China's point of view, the U.S. is the most decisive impediment to Taiwan's incorporation into the People's Republic of China—a key goal defined by Xi Jinping in the context of the "China Dream".[6,7] In addition to the political and historical significance attached to the Taiwan unification issue in China, there is an undeniable geostrategic component to this problem: The island of Taiwan is a cornerstone in the so-called "First Island Chain," the string of islands running in a north–south direction in close proximity to China's Eastern coast that essentially consists of Japan, Okinawa, the Senkaku Islands, Taiwan and the Philippines—a natural fence that obstructs China's access to the Pacific Ocean.[8] Ju Hailong 鞠海龙, a professor of International Relations at Jinan University and Executive Director of the China

[2] Bowers, Ian and Sarah Kirchberger. 2021. "Not so disruptive after all: The 4IR, navies and the search for sea control". *Journal of Strategic Studies*, 44 (4): 613-636. https://doi.org/10.1080/01402390.2020.1848819.

[3] Babiarz, Renny. 2017. "China's Nuclear Submarine Force". *Jamestown Foundation China Brief* 17 (10): 17–24. https://jamestown.org/wp-content/uploads/2017/07/CB_17_10.pdf.

[4] "Mei ri qianting de emeng jiang daolai—Zhongguo 20yi ju zi dazao haidi guance wang 美日潜的梦将到来 中国20亿巨资打造海底观测网" (The Nightmare of American and Japanese submarines is Coming, China has Invested Heavily in 2 Billion to Build a Submarine Observation Network). 2017. *Sina.cn*, 31 May. https://jmqmil.sina.cn/wqzb/doc-ifyfqvmh9628274.d.html.

[5] Cf. e.g. Dai 2010, Hu 2012, 217; Zhang 2014; Hu 2015, 6ff; Liu 2015, 180–183; Ju 2015, 223; 231–233.

[6] *Nikkei Asia*. 2022. "Xi Jinping's '37-Year Plan' for Taiwan Reunification," November 1, 2022. https://asia.nikkei.com/static/vdata/infographics/xi-jinpings-37-year-plan-for-taiwan-reunification/.

[7] Ju, Hailong. 2015. *China's Maritime Power and Strategy: History, National Security and Geopolitics*. Singapore: World Scientific.

[8] Erickson, Andrew S. and Joel Wuthnow. 2016. "Barriers, Springboards and Benchmarks: China Conceptualizes the Pacific 'Island Chains'". *The China Quarterly* 225: 1–22. https://doi.org/10.1017/S0305741016000011.

Research Centre for South China Sea issues, calls Taiwan an "indispensable geopolitical pivot of China's maritime power strategy" because it is "the sole island of China that directly connects with open seas, but also a bridge that connects Southeast Asia and Northeast Asia".[9] The impact of geographic factors becomes even clearer when taking bathymetry into account: The entire sea area between China's eastern coast and the First Island Chain is continental shelf—shallow waters whose mean depth is comparable with the Baltic Sea in Europe, another "confined and shallow" body of water that is notoriously complex to navigate, in particular for submarines.[10] Almost three-fourths of the East China Sea is less than 200 m deep. The situation in the Yellow Sea is even more extreme: With a maximum depth of ca. 150 m and a mean depth of only 44 m, it is difficult terrain for submarine operations, in particular for large strategic submarines.[11] In effect, it "forms a flat, shallow, and partly enclosed marine embayment. Most of the sea […] consists of an oval-shaped basin with depths of about 60 to 80 m".[12] Notwithstanding the difficulty of safely operating large submarines in such an environment, China established its first ballistic missile submarine base in the Yellow Sea at Qingdao, likely for lack of a better alternative, before ultimately moving its strategic submarine fleet to the Island of Hainan in the South China Sea about 10 years ago.[13]

The significance of the South China Sea for the PLA becomes apparent when taking its geographic characteristics into account. With a mean depth of more than 1,200m, the South China Sea is the only deep-water sea area that is directly accessible from the Chinese coastline.[14] While Japan, South Korea, Taiwan and the U.S. can all directly access deep Pacific waters from their Eastern coastlines, Chinese vessels have to first pass through any of the First Island Chain's narrow straits that are all heavily monitored by U.S. and allied militaries.[15] Chinese strategists view the U.S. military presence on the First Island Chain with concern because South Korea, the Japanese islands, and Okinawa host multiple U.S. military bases and listening stations that to China are instruments of a military "encirclement" and "containment" that hold not just China's military, but also its main population centers on the east

---

[9] Ju, Hailong. 2015. *China's Maritime Power and Strategy: History, National Security and Geopolitics*. Singapore: World Scientific.

[10] Karlatiras, Stavros. 2016. "The changing nature of naval conflicts in confined and shallow waters (CSW)". In: *Routledge Handbook of Naval Strategy and Security*, eds. Joachim Krause and Sebastian Bruns, 166–176. London and New York: Routledge.

[11] Liu, Xinhua 刘新华. 2015. *Zhongguo fazhan haiquan zhanglüe yanjiu 中国发展海权战略研究 (A Study on China's Strategy of Development of Sea Power)*. Beijing: Renmin chubanshe.

[12] "Yellow Sea". 2014. *Encyclopædia Britannica Online*. http://www.britannica.com/EBchecked/topic/652686/Yellow-Sea.

[13] Babiarz, Renny. 2017. "China's Nuclear Submarine Force". *Jamestown Foundation China Brief* 17 (10): 17–24. https://jamestown.org/wp-content/uploads/2017/07/CB_17_10.pdf.

[14] "Mei ri qianting de emeng jiang daolai—Zhongguo 20yi ju zi dazao haidi guance wang 美日潜的梦将到来 中国20亿巨资打造海底观测网" (The Nightmare of American and Japanese submarines is Coming, China has Invested Heavily in 2 Billion to Build a Submarine Observation Network). 2017. *Sina.cn*, 31 May. https://jmqmil.sina.cn/wqzb/doc-ifyfqvmh9628274.d.html.

[15] Babiarz, Renny. 2017. "China's Nuclear Submarine Force". *Jamestown Foundation China Brief* 17 (10): 17–24. https://jamestown.org/wp-content/uploads/2017/07/CB_17_10.pdf.

coast at risk.[16,17,18] Chinese analysts have also long deplored the vulnerability of China's naval assets in the event of conflict, as they are subjected to extensive U.S. surveillance via satellites, aircraft, ships and land-based listening stations. More than a decade ago, in a 2013 article titled "The current communications electronic warfare situation confronting our navy and analysis of countermeasures," a team of engineers from Wuhan's Naval University of Engineering had concluded that in order to give the Chinese Navy a "life insurance" in the event of conflict with the U.S., China would need to decisively step up the development of its electronic countermeasures to counter the threat of U.S. surveillance assets deployed throughout the region.[19]

With all passageways through the First Island Chain closely monitored by the U.S. and its allies, it remains difficult for Chinese strategic submarine patrols to reach Pacific waters untrailed. This has in the past negatively impacted China's ability to build up a credible sea-based second-strike capability. With their as-yet limited missile range, Chinese SSBNs would need to venture out far into the open Pacific to credibly threaten the entire U.S. mainland.[20,21] This is why Chinese analysts consider the directly reachable SCS the safest operating area for Chinese SSBNs—at least if adversary submarines can be kept at bay there. In a 2017 Chinese newspaper article, Zhou Huaiyang 周怀阳, a professor at the School of Ocean and Earth Sciences of Tongji University was quoted as saying:

> The South China Sea is the only deep-water area around China, and the complex underwater environment is the most suitable hiding place for Chinese submarines. Various types of Chinese submarines go to the open ocean to perform combat readiness patrol missions, the South China Sea is also the safest area to enter and exit. But at the same time, it also allows the submarines of some countries to freely enter and leave the South China Sea, which greatly threatens the security of the Chinese navy and increases the difficulty of conducting defensive operations in the South China Sea.[22]

---

[16] Dai, Xu 戴旭. 2010. *C-xing baowei C形包围* (C-Shaped Encirclement). Shanghai: Wenhui Chubanshe.

[17] Zhang, Wenmu 张文木. 2014. "Ukelan Shijian de shijie yiyi jiqi dui Zhongguo de jingshi 乌克兰事件的世界意义及其对中国的警示 (The Global Significance of the Ukraine Incident and Its Warning to China)". *Guoji anquan yanjiu* 国际安全研究 (Journal of International Security Studies) 2014 No. 4. https://www.guancha.cn/ZhangWenMu/2022_06_22_645753_s.shtml.

[18] Ju, Hailong. 2015. *China's Maritime Power and Strategy: History, National Security and Geopolitics*. Singapore: World Scientific.

[19] Liu, Zhipeng 刘志鹏, Wei Hao 郝威 and Hongjun Zheng 郑红俊. 2013. "Woguo haijun dangqian mianlin de tongxin dianzi zhan xingshi ji duice yanjiu 我国海军当前面临的通信电子战形势及对策研究" (The current Communications Electronic Warfare Situation Confronting Our Navy and Analysis of Countermeasures). *Xinxi tongxin* 信息通信 (Information & Communication) No. 124, 2/2013: 197–198.

[20] Kristensen, Hans M. 2014. "China SSBN Fleet Getting Ready—But For What?". *FAS Strategic Security Blog from the Federation of American Scientists*, 24. April. https://fas.org/blogs/security/2014/04/chinassbnfleet/.

[21] Duchâtel, Mathieu and Eugenia Kazakova. 2015. "Tensions in the South China Sea: The Nuclear Dimension". *SIPRI Commentary*, 27. August 2015. https://www.sipri.org/commentary/essay/2015/tensions-south-china-sea-nuclear-dimension.

[22] "Mei ri qianting de emeng jiang daolai—Zhongguo 20yi ju zi dazao haidi guance wang 美日潜的梦将到来 中国20亿巨资打造海底观测网" (The Nightmare of American and Japanese submarines

The worry expressed here about adversary submarines operating freely in the SCS was echoed in a more recent article by a group of researchers from the Chinese state shipbuilding company CSSC, who wrote that U.S. submarines pose an even greater threat to the PLA than its aircraft carriers:

> The deployments and frequent activities of the world's most advanced submarines in our country's coastal waters are posing an unprecedented threat to our country's coastal security and defense. Its gravity is even more serious than the menace posed by aircraft carrier battle groups on the surface, because the threat of an aircraft carrier battle group is a public one after all. Further, China already has many reliable countermeasures [against carriers] at its disposal.[23]

These geostrategic considerations go a long way to explaining the PLA's focus on subduing Taiwan. The island of Taiwan is separated from the Chinese coastline by only ca. 100nm at its closest point and can, by virtue of its geographic proximity to the Chinese heartland, be used as an "unsinkable aircraft carrier" and as a base for surveillance infrastructures. Conversely, if China were to gain control over Taiwan, this would provide China's navy with a potential "springboard" into the Pacific Ocean: A naval base on Taiwan's eastern coast could greatly aid the PLAN's efforts to conduct nuclear submarine patrols—at least in theory. For this reason, Chinese military strategists have frequently concluded that without an eventual annexation of Taiwan, China can never become a world-class naval power.[24,25,26]

In the absence of control over Taiwan, the current SSBN base on Hainan Island's southern tip is the next best solution, and a longer-range submarine-launched missile than the JL-2 might make it feasible for China to establish an area within the SCS as a kind of "bastion" for the Chinese SSBN fleet from which to threaten the continental U.S. Creating a layered defense around the SSBN base on Hainan, and in particular sealing off access to Hainan from the South, in that scenario becomes an overriding Chinese security priority. The Paracel islands that are disputed between China and Vietnam, but currently under Chinese military control, would play a key role in such a defensive layer protecting the military bases on Hainan. Unsurprisingly, a particular

is Coming, China has Invested Heavily in 2 Billion to Build a Submarine Observation Network). 2017. *Sina.cn,* 31 May. https://jmqmil.sina.cn/wqzb/doc-ifyfqvmh9628274.d.html.

[23] Wang, Wei 王伟, Fujian Yu 于福建 and Junming Zhang 张峻铭. 2022. "Jiyu yun jisuan de tan qian xinxi zonghe chuli xitong jianshe yanjiu 基于云计算的探潜信息综合处理系统建设研究" (Construction Research on Integrated Processing System of Anti-submarine Detection Information Based on Cloud Computing). In: *Shuzi haiyang yu shui xia gongfang* 数字海洋与水下攻防 (*Digital Ocean & Underwater Warfare*) Vol. 5, No. 1 (Feb. 2022), p. 80.

[24] Liu, Xinhua 刘新华. 2015. *Zhongguo fazhan haiquan zhanglüe yanjiu 中国发展海权战略研究 (A Study on China's Strategy of Development of Sea Power).* Beijing: Renmin chubanshe.

[25] Ju, Hailong. 2015. *China's Maritime Power and Strategy: History, National Security and Geopolitics.* Singapore: World Scientific.

[26] Zhang, Wenmu 张文木. 2014. "Ukelan Shijian de shijie yiyi jiqi dui Zhongguo de jingshi 乌克兰事件的世界意义及其对中国的警示 (The Global Significance of the Ukraine Incident and Its Warning to China)". *Guoji anquan yanjiu* 国际安全研究 (Journal of International Security Studies) 2014 No. 4. https://www.guancha.cn/ZhangWenMu/2022_06_22_645753_s.shtml.

Chinese focus seems to lie on constructing undersea sensor installations between Hainan and the Paracel Islands for monitoring intrusions by adversary submarines.[27]

The currently ongoing ambitious Chinese effort to build up a multi-domain anti-submarine detection network within the SCS integrates ASW air assets with unmanned systems, multiple passive and active sonars aboard ships, unmanned vehicles and static arrays on the sea bottom that interlink with manned and unmanned aircraft while relaying all the collected data via satellite uplinks from fixed and floating platforms to computing centers on land that collect and analyze the information in near real-time. Related brochures and analyses by CETC-affiliated Chinese researchers outline a vast ambition of extending such an "ocean information network" (海洋信息网络) gradually from China's near seas along the entire Maritime Silk Road and beyond.[28] This is an extremely costly and technically challenging project, as it requires massive computing power and advanced AI algorithms to comb through vast amounts of collected data in near real-time. Nonetheless, this seems to be precisely the scope of the Chinese ambition in the context of aiming for "information superiority" in the event of potential hostilities.[29] Write the above quoted Wang, Yu and Zhang:

> In order to deal with the threat from an increasing number of ever more advanced submarines in the Asia-Pacific, it is necessary to widely deploy underwater detection forces, and at the same time to improve the transmission and comprehensive processing capabilities of the collected submarine detection information, so it can quickly and effectively guide our combat forces when they set out for defense or attack. It must be a top priority to build an integrated and modernized Chinese comprehensive anti-submarine detection information processing system.[30]

The same article envisages the creation of an "anti-submarine warfare (ASW) information processing cloud" (潜探测信息处理云) that should ideally integrate sensors placed aboard multiple civilian vessels that could then function as nodes within a wide-spread ASW sensor network.[31] For controlling the SCS, China seems to be aiming at "deterrence by detection."

---

[27] Cf. the description of a seemingly already operational demonstration system of such a network deployed in that area by Su, Liu, Yang and Wang, 2020).

[28] Wang, Jipeng 王积鹏, Lei Dai 戴磊, Liwei Zhang 张立伟 and Li Wang王丽. 2019. "Haiyang xinxi wangluo jianshe sikao 海洋信息网络建设思考" (Thoughts on the Construction of the Ocean Information Network). In: *Dianzi kexue jishu 电子科学技术 (Electronic Science & Technology)*, Special issue June 2019, pp. 18–24.

[29] According to J. Michael Dahm (2021, 45), "PLA operational concepts mandate achieving information superiority early in a conflict. The information power capabilities resident on China's SCS outposts mean that PLA forces will likely start from a position of information overmatch, if not superiority, against any intervening force, such as the Philippines or U.S. military.".

[30] Wang, Wei 王伟, Fujian Yu 于福建 and Junming Zhang 张峻铭. 2022. "Jiyu yun jisuan de tan qian xinxi zonghe chuli xitong jianshe yanjiu 基于云计算的探潜信息综合处理系统建设研究" (Construction Research on Integrated Processing System of Anti-submarine Detection Information Based on Cloud Computing). In: *Shuzi haiyang yu shui xia gongfang* 数字海洋与水下攻防 (*Digital Ocean & Underwater Warfare*) Vol. 5, No. 1 (Feb. 2022), p. 80.

[31] Wang, Wei 王伟, Fujian Yu 于福建 and Junming Zhang 张峻铭. 2022. "Jiyu yun jisuan de tan qian xinxi zonghe chuli xitong jianshe yanjiu 基于云计算的探潜信息综合处理系统建设研究" (Construction Research on Integrated Processing System of Anti-submarine Detection Information

U.S. Strategic Intent in the SCS and Adjacent Areas: Defense of Treaty Allies and Taiwan, Freedom of the Global Commons

Despite never having signed up to UNCLOS itself, due to its interest in securing the freedom of the Global Commons for its own armed forces, the U.S. supports its treaty allies and also other South China Sea littoral states that have territorial disputes with China in their advocacy for freedom of navigation and adherence to the UN Convention on the Law of the Sea (UNCLOS). UNCLOS grants ships, including warships, the right to freely operate anywhere outside of any coastal state's 12nm of territorial sea. The U.S. has long rejected China's so-called "historic" rights to sovereignty over large parts of the South China Sea as baseless and its attempts to claim maritime zones around small, artificially enhanced SCS features as excessive, and this legal view was largely supported by the PCA arbitration award of July 2016, which was then in turn rejected by China.[32] The Philippines had taken legal action by submitting a dispute to the Permanent Court of Arbitration (PCA) after China took control of Scarborough Shoal, a feature located within the EEZ of the Philippines that had until then been occupied by the Philippines, in the Spring of 2012.[33]

One particular area of contention between China and the U.S. are the latter's frequently conducted "freedom of navigation operations" (FONOPs) in the disputed sea areas. U.S. naval vessels in such FONOPs make it a point to transit through maritime zones claimed by China in excess of the rights granted via UNCLOS. According to the 2016 arbitration award (*PCA Case No. 2013–19*), none of the SCS features actually qualify as "islands" in the sense of Art. 121, UNCLOS, and therefore none are entitled to a 200nm EEZ—it follows that littoral states can only claim an EEZ emanating directly from their own coastlines regardless of their claimed sovereignty over any islets, reefs or other features in the SCS. Further, the PCA award categorized only naturally high-tide features, such as Itu Aba, Scarborough Shoal or Fiery Cross Reef as "rocks" in the sense of the UNCLOS definition, which are consequently entitled to a territorial sea of 12nm, but no EEZ. Many SCS features, however, were classified by the PCA merely as "low-tide elevations" (such as Mischief Reef, Subi Reef or Hughes Reef), which means they do not even generate a territorial sea, regardless of whether they were artificially enhanced with reclaimed land or not.[34]

Based on Cloud Computing). In: *Shuzi haiyang yu shui xia gongfang* 数字海洋与水下攻防 (*Digital Ocean & Underwater Warfare*) Vol. 5, No. 1 (Feb. 2022), p. 80.

32 Office of Ocean and Polar Affairs, U.S. Department of State. 2022. "People's Republic of China: Maritime Claims in the South China Sea", *Limits in the Seas* No. 150, https://www.state.gov/wp-content/uploads/2022/01/LIS150-SCS.pdf.

33 De Castro, Renato Cruz. 2016. "Facing Up to China's Realpolitik Approach in the South China Sea Dispute: The Case of the 2012 Scarborough Shoal Stand-off and Its Aftermath". *Journal of Asian Security and International Affairs* 3(2): 157–182. https://doi.org/10.1177/2347797016645452.

34 Permanent Court of Arbitration. 2016. "Press Release: The South China Sea Arbitration". The Hague, July 12, 2016. https://pcacases.com/web/sendAttach/1801.

The key rationale of the—according to China—"provocative" American FONOPs in the SCS is to put forth a challenge to unlawful maritime claims around such features in order to prevent a situation where unlawfully declared maritime zones would gradually become customary law over time when in practice respected by others over a longer period of time. Notably, the U.S. conducts FONOPs not just within the SCS and not only against unlawful claims made by China; rather, it conducts them in various parts of the world where freedom of the sea lanes is challenged by claims beyond the rights granted by UNCLOS, including against claims made by various U.S. treaty allies. The U.S. Freedom of Navigation program has existed since 1979, is conducted in accord with the U.S. Oceans Policy of 1983, and all FONOPs are documented publicly in annual "Freedom of Navigation (FON) Reports" published by the U.S. Department of Defense.[35] According to the FON Report that covers the period between 1 Oct 2020 and 30 Sept 2021, in that year the U.S. "challenged 37 excessive maritime claims of 26 claimants" which included claims by U.S. treaty allies South Korea, Japan and Italy; by Taiwan; India; various Caribbean, Indian Ocean and MENA countries, as well as SCS littoral countries Vietnam, Indonesia and Cambodia, in addition to China. Against Chinese claims, five FONOPs were conducted that year, among them four in the SCS.[36] Although the U.S. is not actually itself a party to UNCLOS, it voluntarily adheres to its provisions, and its policy of conducting FONOPs in support of UNCLOS is long-standing and transparent. By comparison, other Western navies seem to typically avoid sailing through the 12nm zones around China's artificial island features even if they in principle reject the legality of those claims.[37] China on its part in practice regularly violates the rights of other SCS claimant states granted by UNCLOS, for instance when conducting economic activities within the EEZs of other states that emanate directly from their coastlines—despite being a voluntary party to UNCLOS.[38,39]

In addition to its extensive treaty alliance commitments in the region, the U.S. has security concerns on account of its own territories in the Western Pacific, in

[35] All Freedom of Navigation Reports by the U.S. DoD since 1991 can be viewed at https://policy.defense.gov/OUSDP-Offices/FON/.

[36] *U.S. Annual Freedom of Navigation Report, Fiscal Year 2021*. https://policy.defense.gov/Portals/11/Documents/FON%20Program%20Report_FY2021.pdf.

[37] Bachelier, Jérémy and Céline Pajon. 2023. "France in the Indo-Pacific: The Need for a Pragmatic Strategic Posture". IFRI Focus Stratégique No. 117. https://www.ifri.org/sites/default/files/atoms/files/ifri_bachelier-pajon_france_in_the_indo-pacific_oct2023.pdf.

[38] Huong, Le Thu. 2019. "China's Incursion into Vietnam's EEZ and Lessons from the Past". Asia Maritime Transparency Intiative, AMTI Update 8 August 2019. https://amti.csis.org/chinas-incursion-into-vietnams-eez-and-lessons-from-the-past/.

[39] According to the PCA's Press Release on its 2016 Award, the PCA "found that China had violated the Philippines' sovereign rights in its exclusive economic zone by (a) interfering with Philippine fishing and petroleum exploration, (b) constructing artificial islands and (c) failing to prevent Chinese fishermen from fishing in the zone. The Tribunal also held that fishermen from the Philippines (like those from China) had traditional fishing rights at Scarborough Shoal and that China had interfered with these rights in restricting access. The Tribunal further held that Chinese law enforcement vessels had unlawfully created a serious risk of collision when they physically obstructed Philippine vessels" (Permanent Court of Arbitration Press Release 2016, 2).

particular Guam, and in terms of its nuclear balance with China. Since it is not in the U.S. interest to see China successfully turn parts of the SCS into a closed-off safe haven for SSBN patrols, a voluntary back scaling of U.S. naval operations in that body of water is not to be expected. Likewise, it is not in the U.S. national security interest to let Taiwan be annexed by force and turned into a Chinese "springboard" into the Pacific, as that could lead to the implosion of the entire American "hub and spokes" system of bilateral security alliances in the Western Pacific that has existed since WWII while at the same time massively improving the geopolitical situation of China.[40] The Chinese strategic goal of expelling the U.S. military from the Western Pacific and the U.S. goal of preserving its status as a resident power in the Western Pacific and the hub of an extensive alliance system are therefore mutually incompatible and result in a security dilemma.[41]

Against the backdrop of an ever more assertive China under Xi Jinping and a deepening Russian-Chinese "unlimited friendship" despite Russia's war against Ukraine, the stable status quo between China and the U.S. in Asia since the Korean War is now at risk of disintegration. This is mainly due to Chinese attempts at unilaterally changing the military power balance in the Taiwan Strait and in the South China Sea. Efforts to bolster deterrence on both sides unfortunately have the potential to lead into a deterrence trap.[42] Under these circumstances, the SCS's smaller littoral states should carefully analyze their own ability to protect their maritime interests, while overall acting in a stabilizing rather than disruptive way.

Conclusion

Maritime geography, when coupled with an understanding of the long-term geostrategic goals of the rivaling great powers U.S. and China, holds the key for understanding why there is currently a higher risk of conflict and lower prospects for reducing tensions in the SCS and adjacent Western Pacific than in previous decades. That situation is unlikely to improve in the near to medium term. In summary, the U.S. military presence in the Western Pacific; its guardian role toward Taiwan, Japan and the Philippines; and the U.S. advocacy for freedom of the Global Commons through FONOPs in the South China Sea and Taiwan Strait are all thorns in the side of the PRC. The Chinese preference would be for the U.S. to ultimately dissolve its alliances with Japan, South Korea and the Philippines, end its guardian relationship with Taiwan, and greatly reduce its military footprint in the Western Pacific overall. This is not in the interest of U.S. treaty allies, though, and ultimately, the credibility

[40] Brzezinski, Zbigniew. 1997. *The Grand Chessboard: American Primacy and Its Geostrategic Imperatives.* New York: Basic Books.

[41] Holslag, Jonathan. 2015. *China's Coming War with Asia.* Cambridge: Policy Press.

[42] Culver, John K. and Sarah Kirchberger. 2023. "US-China Lessons from Ukraine: Fueling More Dangerous Taiwan Tensions". Atlantic Council. June 15, 2023. https://www.atlanticcouncil.org/wp-content/uploads/2023/06/Fueling-more-dangerous-Taiwan-tensions.pdf.

and deterrent effect of the entire U.S. alliance system, not just in the Western Pacific, hinges upon its willingness and capability to fulfill its commitments toward them in case of a contingency. Unless the U.S. decides to voluntarily abdicate its preeminent position in the world, a withdrawal from the Western Pacific as envisaged by China is not in the U.S. interest, which means that the underlying security dilemma between China and the U.S. will remain difficult to alleviate. The stable, decades-long status quo between China and the U.S. has become increasingly brittle since the beginning of the Xi Jinping administration, and the Chinese military has been focused on gaining quantitative superiority while exploiting new and emerging technologies to find new attack angles and for leapfrogging over stages of development that other militaries had to slowly pass through. At the same time, the U.S. sees China's strong performance in various future technologies as a direct threat to the foundations of its national prosperity, and thus ultimately also to its military supremacy.[43]

The "pivot to Asia" announced under U.S. President Barack Obama gained additional momentum under Trump, and the election of Joe Biden in 2020 did not change the fundamental direction of this policy. Rather, the Biden administration maintained most of the previous administration's measures toward China. The American perception of China as an existential threat to the economic and security interests of the U.S. has actually become one of the very few issues on which there is bipartisan agreement in Washington D.C. The U.S. military will therefore likely continue to challenge China's "excessive" and "unlawful" claims by conducting FONOPs in the disputed areas of the SCS, as it is not in the U.S. security interest to accept limitations on the freedom of movement of American warships anywhere, much less in this particular sea area, and because they offer the U.S. navy a chance to gather intelligence on China's military development. China will continue to protest against this, and also against American involvement in the Taiwan issue through various means, including via calibrated military exercises and various forms of coercion directed against Taiwan and other U.S. allies in the SCS.

The shifting military balance between the great powers has lately caused concern in the U.S. over the strengthening of China's nuclear deterrence posture. Since China's sea-based nuclear deterrence hinges upon its ability to establish a sea denial capability in at least some parts of the SCS, it is hard to see how in the context of a steadily deepening security dilemma, and given the massive Chinese investments in surveillance infrastructures around contested SCS island territories, China could be brought round to compromising with its smaller neighbors regarding its maritime claims. This concerns e.g. the Paracel Islands disputed between China and Vietnam, which now form an integral part of the layered defense that the Chinese military has been building up around Hainan for guarding its SSBN operations there.

Although there is presumably a shared interest on all sides—including China and the U.S.—to avoid accidental escalation, there remains a risk that a further deepening

[43] Wray, Christopher. 2020. "The Threat Posed by the Chinese Government and the Chinese Communist Party to the Economic and National Security of the United States". Remarks delivered on July 7, 2020 at the Hudson Institute. https://www.fbi.gov/news/speeches/the-threat-posed-by-the-chinese-government-and-the-chinese-communist-party-to-the-economic-and-national-security-of-the-united-states.

of China-U.S. tensions over Taiwan with increasingly robust competition could pave the way for great-power conflict. At the same time, China's military modernization effort, in particular the massive PLAN fleet expansion and the installation of various types of detection infrastructures in the SCS area are about to change the playing field for all actors in the area. Littoral states and rival claimants need to analyze the impact of these changes for their own defensive postures and respond adequately, while holding the door open for China and the U.S. to engage in bilateral and multilateral efforts to create risk-mitigation mechanisms and trust-building measures that could help avoid accidental escalation from any minor incident.

Chapter 3
U.S. Interests in the South China Sea: Defending Norms, not Territory

Frank Jannuzi

Introduction

The South China Sea is a region of growing significance where great power rivalries—principally the contest between China and the United States for hegemony in East Asia—threaten to undermine peace and stability to the detriment of all the parties involved. In addition to its economic importance, the South China Sea holds geo-strategic value not only as a "choke point" for the flow of energy from the Middle East to energy-hungry East Asian oil importers but also as the potential passageway for naval forces responding to any contingency in the Taiwan Strait. Given these realities, it is no wonder that many nations—not only China and those ASEAN states in the immediate vicinity who claim territory in the South China Sea but also the United States, Japan, the Republic of Korea, England, and the countries that comprise the European Union—are all monitoring the situation closely. After all, all of them have a stake—whether direct or indirect—in how overlapping claims to territory and resources are ultimately resolved.

In this short paper, I lay out why the South China Sea matters to the United States and why the United States has chosen to engage so concertedly in a region so far from U.S. shores. The United States has long placed a high priority on the *process* by which the disputes in the South China Sea are resolved, while downplaying the significance of any particular outcome. In taking this approach, the United States had essentially echoed its posture on the future of Taiwan. The United States often cares more about the method—one that follows the rule of law and is free of any coercion or use of force—than it does about the ultimate resolution arrived at by the disputants.

But when it comes to the South China Sea, the United States has significantly shifted its posture in the past few years from one of emphasizing process to one that

F. Jannuzi (✉)
Maureen and Mike Mansfield Foundation, Washington, DC, USA
e-mail: fjannuzi@mansfieldfdn.org

N. Hung Son and N. Thi Lan Anh (eds.), *The South China Sea: The Geo-political Epicenter of the Indo-Pacific?*, https://doi.org/10.1007/978-981-97-8209-3_3

also explicitly rejects many of China's more expansive territorial claims. The United States can no longer truly be considered a neutral party, having aligned itself with the Philippines and the ruling by an international tribunal rejecting China's maritime claims. The United States and its allies are also helping Vietnam upgrade its maritime patrol capabilities and have increased the frequency of multilateral naval exercises in the region. This more assertive stance suggests that U.S.-China tensions over the South China Sea will remain a fixture for years if not decades to come.

Finally, I will share some insights on how small satellites and big data might improve transparency in the realm of Maritime Domain Awareness (MDA) in the South China Sea, and why such transparency is not necessarily a neutral public good.

South China Sea: Why it Matters

The South China Sea is rich in natural resources. More than half of the world's fishing vessels are in the South China Sea, and millions depend on these waters for their food and livelihoods. The waters are estimated to hold 10% of the world's fishery resources. In addition to its fish, the South China Sea holds about 190 trillion cubic feet of natural gas and 11 billion barrels of oil in proved and probable reserves, according to the U.S. Energy Information Agency. The U.S. Geological Survey in 2012 estimated that there could be another 160 trillion cubic feet of natural gas and 12 billion barrels of oil undiscovered in the South China Sea.[1]

Perhaps more important than the resources contained in the region is its significance as a passageway for global trade. Roughly 30% of all maritime trade passes through the South China Sea on its way to the busy ports of Southeast Asia. The Strait of Malacca at the western entrance to the South China Sea is one of the most vital shipping lanes in the world, seeing the passage of nearly 100,000 vessels each year, including tankers transporting roughly 25% of all the oil carried at sea. This oil from the Persian Gulf is vital to the economies of China, Japan, and the Republic of Korea; three of the world's top ten economies.

Given its fisheries, proven and potential fossil fuel deposits, and strategic location, the South China Sea has long attracted the attention of neighboring and distant states. China, Taiwan, Philippines, Malaysia, Vietnam, and Brunei lay claim to some of all of the South China Sea and its major island features. China's claims are the most expansive, relying on explorations by Chinese sailors dating back to the Song Dynasty (960–1279 CE), as well as on a map first published by China's Nationalist government in 1947 outlining China's territorial influence (the so-called "nine-dashed line" map). In addition to China, Malaysia, the Philippines, and Vietnam lay claim to part of the Paracel and Spratly Island chains which lay in the heart of the South China Sea.

Several of the claimant states have established outposts or military bases to bolster their claims and defend their interests. In recent years, China has dredged extensively

[1] https://amti.csis.org/south-china-sea-energy-exploration-and-development/ accessed on November 11, 2022.

and dramatically expanded its presence, constructing airfields and port facilities. Despite initial promises not to militarize its possessions, China has deployed military aircraft, air defense weaponry, and surface-to-surface missiles, underscoring its determination to defend its expansive territorial claims.

U.S. Stake: Beyond Process

The United States does not have any territorial claims in the South China, and for decades, the United States avoided formally taking a position on how the competing claims of Brunei, Indonesia, Malaysia, the People's Republic of China, the Philippines, Taiwan, and Vietnam should ultimately be resolved. The U.S. position on the South China Sea flows in part from its treaty commitments to the Philippines and in part from its interest in maintaining freedom of navigation for both commercial vessels and the U.S. Navy. Having little direct stake in who controlled territory in the region—its tiny islands and shoals held little military significance, and its petroleum reserves were, until recently, largely theoretical—the U.S. long maintained that the claimant states should submit to UN arbitration to settle their disputes peacefully in accordance with international norms.

This U.S. posture—process over outcome—came under strain when China began to build out its holdings and adopted a more assertive posture toward other claimant states, including U.S. ally the Philippines. In 2010, then Chinese Foreign Minister Yang Jiechi told his ASEAN counterparts that China's claims should hold more weight than those of other nations, saying, "China is a big country and other countries are small countries and that is just a fact." China followed this diplomatic broadside with a campaign of island-building—enhancing features that were barely above sea level (if that) into significant island outposts with ports and airfields. President Obama responded to China's more assertive tone and island-building by increasing the frequency of so-called "FONOPS (Freedom of Navigation Operations)" by the U.S. Navy, while his Secretary of State, John Kerry, urged all parties to respect the "status quo" and avoid taking actions to change the balance of power unilaterally. These entreaties by Secretary of State Kerry were largely ignored by China.

Still, throughout the Obama Administration's term in office, the United States avoided taking a clear position on the competing claims to exclusive economic zones, undersea resources, and territory in the South China Sea. Even when the Philippines filed a suit at the International Court of Justice contesting Chinese maritime claims, the United States remained largely on the sidelines (in part because the United States has not ratified the UN Convention on the Law of the Sea). The US did, however, sign an agreement with the Philippines in 2014 to strengthen bilateral ties, including security links. President Obama mostly focused on trying to bolster unity among the nations of ASEAN to negotiate a binding Code of Conduct with China to govern activities in the region. Under the rubric of its "Pivot to Asia," the Obama administration also began to court closer relations with Vietnam and Indonesia to counter China's growing military presence and hedge against potential aggression by China.

It was not until July 2020 that the United States abandoned its fence-sitting position and came down squarely in support of the ICJ's 2016 ruling in favor of the Philippines and against China. In a blistering statement, Secretary of State Pompeo lambasted China for its "might makes right" approach, stating, "The PRC's predatory world view has no place in the twenty-first century." Although the U.S. statement technically does not apply to land features that are above sea level, Pompeo for all intents and purposes sided squarely with the Philippines, Brunei, Indonesia, Malaysia, and Vietnam, all of which oppose Chinese assertions of control over various islands, shoals, reefs, and fisheries.

Pompeo's statement was unequivocal and is quoted at length below because it remains the most authoritative elaboration of U.S. policy on the competing claims in the South China Sea:

"As the United States has previously stated, and as specifically provided in the Convention [UNCLOS], the Arbitral Tribunal's decision is final and legally binding on both parties. Today we are aligning the U.S. position on the PRC's maritime claims in the SCS with the Tribunal's decision. Specifically:

The PRC cannot lawfully assert a maritime claim—including any Exclusive Economic Zone (EEZ) claims derived from Scarborough Reef and the Spratly Islands—vis-a-vis the Philippines in areas that the Tribunal found to be in the Philippines' EEZ or on its continental shelf. Beijing's harassment of Philippine fisheries and offshore energy development within those areas is unlawful, as are any unilateral PRC actions to exploit those resources. In line with the Tribunal's legally binding decision, the PRC has no lawful territorial or maritime claim to Mischief Reef or Second Thomas Shoal, both of which fall fully under the Philippines' sovereign rights and jurisdiction, nor does Beijing have any territorial or maritime claims generated from these features.

As Beijing has failed to put forth a lawful, coherent maritime claim in the South China Sea, the United States rejects any PRC claim to waters beyond a 12-nautical mile territorial sea derived from islands it claims in the Spratly Islands (without prejudice to other states' sovereignty claims over such islands). As such, the United States rejects any PRC maritime claim in the waters surrounding Vanguard Bank (off Vietnam), Luconia Shoals (off Malaysia), waters in Brunei's EEZ, and Natuna Besar (off Indonesia). Any PRC action to harass other states' fishing or hydrocarbon development in these waters—or to carry out such activities unilaterally—is unlawful.

The PRC has no lawful territorial or maritime claim to (or derived from) James Shoal, an entirely submerged feature only 50 nautical miles from Malaysia and some 1000 nautical miles from China's coast. James Shoal is often cited in PRC propaganda as the 'southernmost territory of China.' International law is clear: An underwater feature like James Shoal cannot be claimed by any state and is incapable of generating maritime zones. James Shoal (roughly 20 m below the surface) is not and never was PRC territory, nor can Beijing assert any lawful maritime rights from it."

Not surprisingly, China rejected not only the tribunal's ruling but also the United States' support for it. Through its Embassy in Washington, China said it was firmly opposed to Washington's assertions over its claims in the South China Sea and rejected as "completely unjustified" the allegation that Beijing had bullied its neighbors. "The United States is not a country directly involved in the disputes. However, it has kept interfering in the issue. Under the pretext of preserving stability, it is flexing muscles, stirring up tension, and inciting confrontation in the region," the Chinese embassy said. China also took the opportunity to impose sanctions on Lockheed Martin for its role in upgrading Taiwan's Patriot air defense missile system, implicitly linking the U.S. policy shift in the South China Sea with Beijing's grievances about Washington's support for Taiwan.

That linkage, of course, is not difficult to fathom. Not only is Taiwan a claimant state, the United States insistence on freedom of navigation in the South China Sea is linked to its commitment to maintain its ability to intervene in a Taiwan conflict, if necessary. Although the U.S. severed its mutual defense treaty with Taiwan in 1979 as part of a deal establishing formal diplomatic relations with Beijing, the Taiwan Relations Act of that year obligates the United States to provide Taiwan with such defense goods and services as it may require to maintain an "adequate" self-defense capability, and further obligates the United States to sustain its own ability to respond to a Taiwan contingency. Taiwan remains today the one issue over which the United States and China could plausibly find themselves in military conflict.

South China Sea in Strategic Context of US-China Rivalry

When President Biden came into office, he inherited a tense U.S.-China relationship. Consistent with his focus on the American middle class and his long-held faith in the value of U.S. alliance relationships in Europe and Asia, Biden announced his intention to compete with China across many dimensions—economic, security, and values. He crafted legislative proposals to strengthen U.S. infrastructure, accelerate the development of critical technologies (AI, quantum computing), and speed the transition to renewable forms of energy as a means of combatting climate change. To the surprise of some pundits, he kept in place the key pillars of his predecessor's approach to China, namely:

Enhancing security and economic ties with "like-minded" states, especially Australia, Japan, and the ROK;
Hedging against China by expanding functional multilateral groups such as the QUAD.
Sustaining tariffs on Chinese goods and selective "decoupling" from China's economy on certain high technologies.

Biden went further, deepening strategic cooperation with Australia through the AUKUS nuclear-powered submarine agreement, forming a strategic partnership with Taiwan on semiconductor supply chain resiliency, and countering China's RCEP regional trade arrangement with its own Indo-Pacific Economic Framework (IPEF), an admittedly tepid effort to bolster the rules-based international economic order while not offering new access to U.S. markets. At home and abroad, the Biden Administration put in place a policy framework designed to win a competition with China for global leadership.

Biden's moves over his first two years in office set the stage for his first in-person meeting with President Xi in Bali on November 14, 2022. Working from what he hopes will prove to be an enduring position of strength—bolstered by better-than-expected mid-term election results at home, and improving trilateral ties among Japan-ROK-U.S.—Biden reached out to President Xi with a spirit of calm realism.

Biden, who long has resisted efforts to demonize or "sanitize" China, sought to emphasize points of common interest over differences. "As leaders of our two nations, we share responsibility, in my view, to show that China and the United States can manage our differences, prevent competition from becoming anything ever nearing conflict and to find ways to work together on urgent global issues that require our mutual cooperation," Biden said as the talks got underway.

In response to a reporter's question about the overall direction of US-China relations: "I'm not suggesting this is kumbaya, but I do not believe there's a need for concern, as one of you raised a legitimate question, of a new Cold War."

Biden said following his meeting with Xi: "He was clear, and I was clear that we will defend American interests and values, promote universal human rights and stand up for the international order and work in lockstep with our allies and partners," Biden said. "We're going to compete vigorously but I'm not looking for conflict."

Although the two leaders issued no formal joint statement, the overall tone of the meeting was businesslike and without drama. On Taiwan, Biden chose to underscore continuity rather than change, while pouring cold water on the notion circulating in some circles in Washington that a Chinese military move against Taiwan was in the offing. Moreover, Biden announced that he is sending Secretary of State Blinken to Beijing, and the two nations are set to resume formal talks on climate change, suspended following Pelosi's visit to Taiwan.

The relatively reassuring tone of the Biden-Xi meeting, however, cannot completely mask the fact that so long as the United States and China remain at loggerheads over China's claims in the South China Sea, there will be plenty of opportunity for tension arising from Chinese and U.S. military moves, including various unilateral and multilateral military exercises and FONOPS which are becoming routine. Biden and Xi seem poised to accept such tension as part of a new normal; hoping to prevent any miscalculation or escalation through enhanced dialogue and frankness. The success of the United States in managing similar tensions with the Soviet Union gives reason for cautious optimism, provided only that the China–Taiwan relationship remains stable.

Enhancing Transparency: Small Satellites and Big Data

Against this backdrop of great power competition, the introduction of new technologies—small earth observation satellites tethered to big data analytics—promises to transform the world's ability to monitor the situation in the South China Sea in real time. The launch of new large constellations of optical and infrared imaging satellites promises to provide nations and even NGOs with an unprecedented maritime domain awareness, tracking the movement of thousands of vessels on the world's oceans and determining their activities using algorithms and artificial intelligence.

Capitalizing on these new technologies, the Biden Administration announced in Tokyo in May the launch of the Indo-Pacific Maritime Domain Awareness initiative, under the auspices of the QUAD. The IPMDA will share commercially available satellite data and alert smaller Southeast Asian states if there are territorial intrusions or if ships carry out illicit activity such as illegal fishing, smuggling, or piracy in waters within their maritime boundaries. "This initiative will transform the ability of partners in the Pacific Islands, Southeast Asia, and the Indian Ocean region to fully monitor the waters on their shores and, in turn, to uphold a free and open Indo-Pacific," the White House statement said.

The data on vessel movements will be shared with participants in four "information fusion centers" located in India, Singapore, the Solomon Islands, and Vanuatu. The trove of near real-time data that's available under the program will include ship identification numbers or call signs, their locations, potential paths, their port of origin, and final destinations.

Such transparency on "dark shipping" would appear at first glance to constitute a clear "public good." It is hard to see how any nation could legitimately object to efforts to reduce illegal fishing, drug smuggling, trafficking in persons, piracy, and other illicit activities. But, of course, the IPMDA will also provide an unprecedented window into the so-called "gray zone" activities by China's fishing fleet, which ranks high on indices of illegal fishing according to the IUU and has also been used by Beijing at times to bolster its territorial claims or even to obstruct movements by vessels by other states claiming territory in the South China Sea.

Best case, the IPMDA will shine a spotlight on all illicit shipping, and better equip nations to police their own waters and hold other nations accountable. "This initiative really isn't military so much as law enforcement in nature," said Gregory Poling, director of the Southeast Asia Program and Asia Maritime Transparency Initiative at the Center for Strategic and International Studies told CNBC. "It will help small island and coastal developing states in the Indian and Pacific Oceans monitor and enforce laws in their own waters. By helping deliver public goods like this, the Quad does far more to compete with China than if it were to take explicitly anti-Chinese measures."[2]

Worst case, transparency might actually exacerbate tension between China—intent on expanding its regional military and political influence—and the nations

---

[2] https://www.cnbc.com/2022/06/09/quads-maritime-initiative-could-spur-militarization-of-indo-pacific.html accessed November 11, 2022.

of the Quad. The QUAD, after all, is a Japan-inspired construct implicitly, if not explicitly, configured to check China's reach and reinforce the rules-based liberal democratic order against China's brand of authoritarian state-led capitalism.

By "democratizing" access to information and analysis once reserved to space-faring nations equipped with robust analytic capabilities, the IPMDA will, at a minimum, ensure that no state's actions in the disputed South China Sea can be carried out absent the knowledge and scrutiny by all interested parties, a development that should empower previously marginalized players to assert their rights and hold major powers accountable. It's a potential "game-changer," the full implications of which will play out over the next few years as the fluid security situation in the South China Sea continues to evolve.

Chapter 4
ASEAN Centrality Amidst Indo-Pacific's Geostrategic Environment

Pou Sothirak

At the outset, I would like to express my sincere appreciation to Dr. Pham Lan Dung, Acting President, the Diplomatic Academy of Vietnam, for her kind invitation extended to me to attend the 14th South China Sea International Conference under the theme of "Peaceful Sea—Solid Recovery," from 16 to 17 November, 2022, in the beautiful city of Da Nang, Vietnam.

My presentation attempts to first address ASEAN's Relevance amidst fierce competition between the United States and China in the Indo-Pacific theater and discuss how this rivalry continues to affect ASEAN relevance.

Second, I will discuss implications born out of the United States and China's relentless quest for dominance in the Indo-Pacific region.

And at the end, I will give concluding remarks with a set of recommendations to enhance ASEAN Centrality to safeguard the region of Southeast Asia from the unyielding influence by external powers.

ASEAN's Relevance Amidst the United States and China Rivalry

From the time of its inception in 1967 to the full 10 membership of all Southeast Asia countries in 1999, ASEAN has evolved in stages, step-by-step, on the basis of consensus, non-interference, and at a pace comfortable to every member state.

ASEAN's hallmarks include the creation of the Treaty of Amity and Cooperation in Southeast Asia (TCA) which was signed in 1976; the ASEAN Charter which entered into force in 2008, setting out the governing principles on how ASEAN intends to conduct its affairs; the ASEAN Community Blueprints; the adoption of

P. Sothirak (✉)
Cambodian Institute for Cooperation and Peace, Phnompenh, Cambodia
e-mail: pousothirak@gmail.com

N. Hung Son and N. Thi Lan Anh (eds.), *The South China Sea: The Geo-political Epicenter of the Indo-Pacific?*, https://doi.org/10.1007/978-981-97-8209-3_4

the ASEAN Community Vision 2025, and the ASEAN Political-Security Community (APSC) Blueprint 2025 all of which are design to build a more cohesive ASEAN Community.

Capitalizing on ASEAN Centrality, these ASEAN trademarks are designed to pick up more steam for the sake of navigating through a period of strategic and political haphazard and economic stagnations as well as concern and uncertainty from the relentless major power competitions, regional and global flashing points and the unyielding outbreak of the pandemic.

Moving forward, the regional grouping must constantly remind all its 10 members to remain united or else suffer outside powers inference that can undermine "ASEAN Centrality" affecting ASEAN's traditional modus operandi and its fundamental cohesion.

Security and stability in the Asia Pacific region are increasingly affected by strategic competition for influence between the United States and China over a handful of strategic regional and global issues. It is clear that China's aspiration to become a dominant global player, as a strategic equal to the United States which resists unsympathetically Beijing's ambition has resulted in an intense competition between the two great powers. This competition significantly affects Southeast Asia as they try to avoid the spillover effects regarding their relations with the two superpowers.

Let Us Review Briefly What at Stake Between the United States and China

In recent times, Washington has realized that the Indo-Pacific region, which is regarded as the US global strategic orientation, faces mounting challenges, particularly from the People's Republic of China. The United States believes that only the PRC with combining economic, diplomatic, military, and technological might can rival the American preeminent position in the long run as China continues to rise and seeks to become the world's most influential power.

With the Indo-Pacific Strategy, the United States seeks out strategic competition with the PRC to defend the interests and vision for the future that Washington holds dear and shares with others by strengthening the liberal international system, keeping it grounded in shared values to overcome the twenty-first-century challenges. The objective is not to change the PRC but to shape the strategic environment in which it operates, building a balance of influence in the world that is maximally favorable to the United States as Washington seeks to manage competition with the PRC responsibly, at least this is what US policymakers have mentioned.

On the other hand, since taking power in 2012, Chinese President Xi Jinping has been relentless in developing China's economic, diplomatic, and political influence on a global scale as well as building up its military strength and power projection capabilities. At the 2017 party congress, President Xi said China will become a global leader by the middle of the century and amplified policies to accelerate the growth of China's comprehensive national power in support of the country's "great rejuvenation" by 2049 through the assertive use of all instruments of national power, including both economic and military.

Beijing's strategic priorities will inevitably challenge US economic and military might as China aspires to become a global power, changing the unipolar world toward a multipolar or bipolar structure in which it will be the other superpower through strengthening its power projection capacity in the region and by expanding its economic and military power globally in order to achieve its strategic objectives and protect its core interests. However, Beijing has repeatedly denied this ambition.

It is in this context that the Association of Southeast Asian Nations (ASEAN) must remain vigilance, creative, and bold so as to ensure ASEAN's continued relevance, viability, and vitality.

The ASEAN Way in creating norms which have been embedded in an open, inclusive regional architecture, creating a multi-layered structure of institutional frameworks with ASEAN at the center, must not constrain ASEAN space for action to achieve desirable results. ASEAN must endeavor to bring to the table a strategic agenda that can boost its foreign policy and reassure the bloc's credibility. ASEAN's principle of neutrality, non-interference, and the ASEAN Way must not come at the expense of ASEAN relevance for action to work out suitable and necessary arrangements that can lead to the reduction of tensions caused by big power competition.

Implications for ASEAN

The United States and China in recent days compete fiercely against each other in all fields. Their bilateral relationship is arguably the world's most consequential relationship, impacting the global world and ASEAN included.

When dealing with the United States and China, ASEAN faces multiple implications. These implications involve the different views these two powers see each other through ideological principles, choice of political system in their respective countries, how the international system supposed to work in the global, regional, and individual country basis, as well as the believes and values each of the two powers adhere to and not to mention how they conduct their foreign policy between them and bilaterally with individual countries in the Indo-Pacific region.

The current international liberal system of which the United States had put in place since WWII is now shaken up by China which seems to be dissatisfied with the existing international order, but for different reasons. For Beijing, the current order is ill-equipped to address twenty-first-century challenges on terms with which China can accept. It is with this choice of international order that sparks the relentless confrontation between the two biggest powers and without an appropriate mechanism at hand, conflicts are eminent, affecting every country in the world.

The intensification of United States and China rivalry flared up acutely during the last round of the Shangri-La Dialogue where the American and Chinese defense leaders offered their respective visions for the future of the region. Broadly speaking, US Defense Secretary Lloyd Austin articulated America's positive vision for the region, while his Chinese counterpart, Defense Minister General Wei Fenghe, focused on how China will be important to the future of Asia and why it would be a mistake for any country to impede on Chinese core interest.

While emphasizing how the United States views the Indo-Pacific as the strategic center of gravity for American interests in the twenty-first century, Secretary of Defense Lloyd Austin's presentation focuses on the revitalization of the alliance system to tighten their bonds to deal with Chinese assertiveness which the United States and its allies perceive as detrimental to the liberal international system.

Secretary Austin distinctively expressed American superiority against the notions that China would command the future of the world order that the United States have brought about at the end of WWII. He spoke eloquently about the US Department of Defense's determination to remain at the top of technological innovation with huge resources and capacity pooling with the allies and partners to undertake cutting-edge research and development to co-produce new and emerging technologies that are more potent and lethal. He emphasized that America's goal is to protect each country's ability to pursue its own interests and guard allies and partners from any perceived security threat from a bigger power. However, he advocated for the maintenance of open channels with Beijing to manage tensions. Washington will not force countries to choose between the United States and China.

Chinese Defense Minister Gen. Wei Fenghe's presentation, on the other hand, was more acute, stressing that China's rise and its continued development cannot be stopped and China cannot be isolated or excluded from the region. Gen. Wei warned that American attempts to form exclusive blocs (e.g., through the Quadrilateral Security Dialogue or the AUKUS pact) would split the region and undermine the interests of all. He appealed to participants at the Shangri-La Dialogue to resist American plans to seek to encircle and contain China. Gen. Wei also identified a series of security challenges confronting China, including Taiwan, the South China Sea, North Korea, Ukraine, and the formation of exclusive groupings that challenged China's rise. For China, the United States have been the trouble marker standing in the shadow of each of these challenges. He told the participants that the People's Liberation Army would fight to the end and warned that China would "crush" any efforts to achieve Taiwan independence. Nonetheless, Gen. Wei reassured that "peaceful unification" remains China's utmost goal on Taiwan and that China hopes for "sound, steady development" of relations with the United States.

As the United States and China push-and-shove one another in order to extend their spheres of dominance globally, all countries are inescapably drawn into the complexities of this global power play. International stability now hinges on whether the world order will be reshaped toward a more China-centric, downgrading US influence. The distribution of the capabilities of both countries, both soft and hard, will be determined by their relentless rivalries, signaling the arrival of a new bipolar world. The drivers for such bipolarity world led by both the United States and China can be seen unmistakably in the post-Covid-19 crisis world where both Washington and Beijing exert, uncompromisingly, their bilateral diplomacy in the multilateral sphere, i.e., the UN, G20, APEC, EU, or ASEAN.

During G20 Meeting in Bali, Indonesia, President Joe Biden and President Xi Jinping exhibit positive body language given the impression that the tensions between their countries are easing up as they are contesting for influence in Asia and beyond. However, they remain blunt with each other over the issues of Taiwan, Korean Peninsula, and Ukraine.

By attending the G20, President Xi intends to recharge China's diplomacy and promotes China leadership role in finding solution to the world's problems. President Biden, on the other hand, seeks no conflict with Beijing, assuring that there will be no "new Cold war" with China. The two leaders engage in direct talk on strategic and sensitive issues that define their relationship.

President Biden brought up various hot issues including raising the US objections to China's "coercive and increasingly aggressive actions toward Taiwan," Beijing's "non-market economic practices," and human rights practices in "Xinjiang, Tibet, and Hong Kong, more broadly."

At the opening session of the G20, President Xi describes the US-led security alliance as a "Cold War mentality" and such security formation will only divide the world, and hinder global development and human progress. As for Taiwan, China refers to it as the "first red line" that must not be crossed in US-China relations. In response, Biden assures Xi that US policy on Taiwan, which has for decades been to support both Beijing's "One China" stance and Taiwan's military. At the G20, President Biden has been quite pronouncing that the United States would reinforce its traditional leadership and remain more "prepared than any country in the world, economically and politically, to deal with the changing circumstances around the world."

Consideration to Enhance ASEAN Centrality in Navigating the United States and China Rivalry

At present, cooperation between United States and China is nearly impossible as mounting domestic and international pressures confine both states to remain at odds with one another over trade tensions, technological rivalries, strategic issues such as flash points related to the Korean peninsula, Cross-Strait relations, the South China Sea problems, and the outbreak of war in Ukraine. They also differ staggeringly when it comes to the crisis in Myanmar and the Ream naval base in Cambodia perceived as a Chinese military base.

The risks of conflict in the Indo-Pacific between the United States and China standouts and constantly lurks behind ASEAN apprehension.

ASEAN has struggled to maintain collective duty to manage one of the most difficult tasks in handling great power relations so as to maintain peace, stability, and prosperity in the region at the same time maintaining collective strategic autonomy as well as safeguarding the independence of each individual state in the regional bloc.

To prevent any unwarranted implications created by the United States and China's tussle for dominance in this region and in a global world and for ASEAN Centrality to transpire as a viable mechanism to balance effectively big power's rivalry in the Indo-Pacific, here are some of my thoughts:

1- ASEAN must assess accurately the shifting of the geostrategic environment being unfolded in the post-Covid-19 world order. While continuing to ride on China's economic might, it is also important for ASEAN to recognize that the United States still remains the dominant extra-regional power in Southeast Asia. ASEAN must avoid leaning too deep into China's economic bounty and the need to continue to open the region for the U.S. military presence in the region to guarantee regional stability and security and to ensure that China's growing power is indeed peaceful.
2- ASEAN needs to exhibit a bolder strategy to engage both powers smartly but prudently by not circumventing one power against the other. In managing external relations with the two biggest powers, SEAN should maintain its credibility as being a neutral partner and masterful at balancing big powers' competition to prevent ASEAN as a whole from taking sides with one power or the other. Doing so is considered as ceding the initiative to manage ASEAN destiny to an outside power and will weaken ASEAN bargaining power with that power in the protection of its own regional interest.
3- ASEAN needs to maintain a comfortable distance and not to get entwine with the manner through which the United States and China compete with each other while going after their national interest respectively nor provoke them to go against one another on how to resolve hard security issues such as the SCS issues, the Myanmar crisis, the Ukraine war, the Cross-Strait relations or how they intend to assist countries to recover swiftly from Covid-19. Doing so allows ASEAN to play a role as a credible interlocutor in engaging the two powers in a strategic dialogue, building trust between them, and working together instead to resolve those security challenges.
4- On the strategic issue of the Code of Conduct in the South China Sea, ASEAN and China need to focus on resolving challenges for a binding and credible code. In my view, these challenges are: first, the geographical scope has not been defined and agreed upon; second, COC's legal status remains undefined. While most ASEAN members desire that the COC should be legally binding, but China appears reluctance on this aspect; third, the applicability of international norms for the COC remains doubtful, and without effective monitoring mechanism to reinforce international law and norms the COC may end up like the ineffective DOC; and the fourth challenge is the lack of mutual cooperation and trust among the claimant states and other stakeholders. All claimant states, except China, want to be reassured that China does not try to impose its unjust "claim" over others,

i.e., the nine-dash lines. The United States wants the code not to obstruct the American's freedom of navigation through sea-lane communications.

5- To appease the anxiety surrounding potential conflicts between the United States and China, ASEAN must find suitable multilateral mechanisms to constrain or help manage their behavior. Multilateral cooperation is the only way to temper United States and China rivalry. ASEAN must strike a balance between having multilateral cooperation that leans toward weak organizational structures that emphasize consensus-building, with the alternative practice of an effective multilateralism exercised through EU style with legally binding commitments within overarching institutional structures.

6- ASEAN should continue its attempts to engage the United States and China through existing frameworks, even if there are limitations in terms of what can be accomplished. Washington and Beijing are keen to court ASEAN and to pay some consideration to its wishes when framing their respective policies toward Southeast Asia. How much clout ASEAN has in this regard will depend on its ability to forge unity and centrality—hence there is a need to seriously push forward for a more effective ARF, the ADMM Plus processes, and the East Asia Summit (EAS).

7- While engaging China in security dialogue, ASEAN should capitalize on its strategic role to encourage China to adhere to the promise that its rise is indeed peaceful and beneficial to the region and urge China to work toward collective resolve to find a peaceful solution to the South China Sea issues according to the principles and norms of the international law and on the need to lean on relevant multilateral instruments as often prescribed by the ASEAN Chairman's Statement.

8- Likewise, when reaching out to the United States, the first thing ASEAN should do is to let Washington know that the bloc is at the core of US Indo-Pacific strategic and economic interests and that Southeast Asia welcomes the US presence in this region as a reassuring stabilizing force. The bloc should encourage the United States to invest with confidence in ASEAN Centrality to meet Washington's demanding interest in securing greater strides in leading the Indo-Pacific strategy in resolving flashpoints that derive from US-China competition such as the flaring up such as cross-strait tension, the South China Sea issue, the lingering denuclearization of the Korean Peninsula, the future prospect of the International rules-based order with the rise of China and its impact on other regional powers such as the EU, Australia, Japan, and Korea. In addition, it would be wise for ASEAN to pay due consideration to US foreign policy deriving from the adherence to the rule of law, democracy, human rights, individual freedom, and good governance in order to induce the United States to be more forthcoming in helping Southeast Asian countries meet their physical and human development need.

Chapter 5
India's Reformed Approach Towards the South China Sea Dispute: Is There Scope to Do More?

Premesha Saha

Introduction

The territorial and maritime disputes along the South China Sea (SCS) remain unresolved and continue to impede the path to peace and security in the Indo-Pacific region. Extra-regional countries like India and the United States also have stakes in securing the SCS. India, while not a South China Sea littoral state, is invested in the maintenance of the rules-based order and freedom of navigation in these sea lanes of communication (SLOCs). Recent statements from the Ministry of External Affairs illustrate that India intends to move away from its historical "balanced" approach towards China and the SCS disputes, and play a more proactive role, guided by its Act East policy, in particular, as well as its overall Indo-Pacific vision. While India intends to maintain its neutrality when it comes to the issue of sovereignty in these disputes, New Delhi has become more vocal in the recent months, primarily after the June 2020 Galwan Valley clash between Indian and Chinese troops. There is no doubt that there has been a palpable shift in India's approach to the disputes along the South China Sea. This tilt may not be a significant one, and it remains to be seen whether it is merely symbolic or more substantial. However, a certain momentum is visible in India's stance, and such a shift, albeit slight, can be a facilitator for new policy initiatives and actions on the part of India in the SCS and the broader Indo-Pacific. India can engage in a substantial course of action to help the ASEAN littorals. This will show India's regard for Southeast Asia as the fulcrum connecting the Indian the Pacific Oceans, thereby enlivening the principles underlined in its Indo-Pacific policy.

The rationale and implications of India's strategies and responses *vis-à-vis* the SCS dispute will have an impact and bearing on its overall "Act East" initiative and in the successful advancement of India's Indo-Pacific vision as well.

P. Saha (✉)
Strategic Studies Programme, Observer Research Foundation, New Delhi, India
e-mail: premesha.saha@orfonline.org

N. Hung Son and N. Thi Lan Anh (eds.), *The South China Sea: The Geo-political Epicenter of the Indo-Pacific?*, https://doi.org/10.1007/978-981-97-8209-3_5

India's stakes in the South China Sea can be viewed as economic and diplomatic. Both these aspects impinge on India's "Act East Policy". The economic factor is driven by the presence of energy resources and trade that plies between India and the nations in the region. The energy factor is significant given the reported energy potential of the region. Diplomatically India would like to be seen as a responsible growing power that advocates healthy relations between nations, thereby ensuring a secure regional architecture wherein nations settle their differences amicably. For very long in standing with this approach, India has adopted a neutral stance, has requested nations to sort out their differences peacefully, and has even refrained from making statements that might irk the Chinese sentiments. India has further requested the nations to establish a code of conduct that would ensure "freedom of navigation" and "access to resources".[1]

According to experts like Abhijit Singh, Senior Fellow at the Observer Research Foundation, New Delhi, "A tendency to view the region through a prism of geopolitics and "balance of power" makes Indian decision makers wary of taking a stand on China's aggressive posturing. Yet the costs of saying and doing nothing are rising for India as China's firming grip over disputed territories in the South China Sea portends greater power projection in the Eastern Indian Ocean."[2] Even though, India still intends to maintain its neutrality when it comes to the issue of sovereignty in this dispute. But in recent times, a shift is noticeable in India's stance as is clear from statements like "actions and incidents in the South China Sea erode trust and the ongoing negotiations on the proposed code of conduct should not be prejudicial to legitimate interests of third parties and should be fully consistent with the UN Convention on the Law of the Sea (UNCLOS)",[3] by External Affairs Minister, S. Jaishankar at the 15th East Asia Summit convened on November 14, 2020. This bold statement from the External Affairs Minister that might upset the Chinese sentiments is reflective of a change in the thinking of the elite and the upper echelons of the Indian diplomatic community that this "long adhered balanced approach towards China and regarding the SCS dispute" is reaping no benefits for India and how India is now prepared to play a more proactive role in this region under the aegis of its Act East policy in particular and its Indo-Pacific vision in general.

The aim of this paper is to look into this shift in India's stand on the SCS dispute. Firstly, what are the push factors that have led to this shift? Secondly, India's maritime engagements and activities in the region; thirdly, analyse the implications of India's stance on the Association of Southeast Asian Nations (ASEAN), five member-states of which (Brunei, Indonesia, Malaysia, the Philippines, and Vietnam) are involved

---

[1] S.S. Parmar, "What is at stake for India in the South China Sea? What has been India's stand in that conflict so far?", https://idsa.in/askanexpert/stakeforIndiaintheSouthChinaSea.

[2] Abhijit Singh (2020), "China tightens grip over the South China Sea—should India worry?", published April 25, 2020, https://www.orfonline.org/expert-speak/china-tightens-grip-over-the-south-china-sea-should-india-worry-65181/#:~:text=India's%20position%20on%20the%20South,and%20doing%20nothing%20are%20rising.

[3] Rezaul H Laskar (2020), "India concerned over situation in South China Sea that 'erode trust'", published November 14 2020, https://www.hindustantimes.com/india-news/india-concerned-over-situation-in-south-china-sea-that-erode-trust/story-gAdrIY3UugAeOhi9g7YRQJ.html.

in territorial disputes with China in the SCS, and lastly, what will be the impact on India's Indo-Pacific vision will be delved into as well—whether it will get the much-needed push?

What is at Stake for India in the SCS?

Although India does not claim any territory in the South China Sea, the region gains salience for India in the context of the safety and security of its maritime trade that transits through these waters. It also has economic interests in the region and is engaged in joint development of energy resources which are critical for its economic vitality.[4] David Scott rightly points out that, "The South China Sea is becoming a factor in India's own strategic calculations and strategic debates, and India is becoming a factor in the strategic calculations of South China Sea states."[5] India is an extra-regional power that operates and impacts the region through regular naval deployments, visits, and exercises in these waters, through established and growing strategic-military partnerships with various South China Sea littoral states, through involvement in oil exploitation in these waters, and through diplomatic discussions on this issue in various regional forums.[6]

The South China Sea is in the middle of the maritime stretch running from the Eastern Indian Ocean to the Western Pacific.[7] With the Indo-Pacific concept gaining a lot of traction in the recent past, the importance of the SCS cannot be relegated. Given that the Indian Navy also operates in the Western Pacific, in cooperation with the United States and Japanese navies, then a secure access through the intervening waters of the South China Sea becomes all the more important an interest for India.[8] India's growing interest in the Indo-Pacific is already known and India views, "the Indo-Pacific as an integrated and organic maritime space with the ASEAN at its centre."[9] ASEAN and the far-eastern Pacific are the primary focus areas of Modi's

---

[4] Vijay Sakhuja and Pankaj Jha (2016), "India and the South China Sea" in C.J. Jenner and Trang Truong Thuy (eds.) *The South China Sea: A crucible of Regional Cooperation or Conflict-making Sovereignty Claims*, Cambridge University Press, p. 118.

[5] David Scott (2013), "India's Role in the South China Sea: Geopolitics and Geoeconomics in Play", *India Review*, Volume 12 Number 2, p. 51.

[6] David Scott (2013), "India's Role in the South China Sea: Geopolitics and Geoeconomics in Play", op.cit.

[7] David Scott (2013), "India's Role in the South China Sea: Geopolitics and Geoeconomics in Play", op.cit.

[8] David Scott (2013), "India's Role in the South China Sea: Geopolitics and Geoeconomics in Play", op.cit.

[9] Rezaul H Laskar (2020), "India concerned over situation in South China Sea that 'erode trust'", op.cit.

Act East policy, the Southeast Asian commons are a "vital facilitator of India's future development."[10]

Unconventional maritime concerns and the escalation of the SCS territorial dispute are creating rifts and divergences among ASEAN countries over the territorial claims of some of the islands in the SCS. Thereby, leading to greater friction towards the effective functioning of security mechanisms in Asia and severe effects in the realm of international security. China-ASEAN relations are under strain and India seems eager to fill the void as a responsible regional stakeholder. As a leading power, India intends to play a larger role in settling the SCS dispute and to stabilise the situation. Although India is not a claimant state, it wishes to enter the stage in order to meet its own interests. India is not a competitor and rather wishes to play the role of an external balancer in the SCS maritime territorial dispute. The SCS is a crucial (sea line) for Indian trade and the expansion of its Indo-Pacific initiative. Additionally, it has the potential to enhance regional growth and further India's engagement with Southeast Asia.[11]

Most notably, the SCS occupies a significant geostrategic position in terms of international shipping. New Delhi's economic vitality rests on an assured supply of energy and safe and secure trading routes in the region including the Straits of Malacca. It has high stakes in keeping the sea lanes open in the SCS. The majority of shipments of energy and raw materials pass through it. India and many other countries have an interest in protecting the sea lanes that run through the area, as they consider open and stable maritime commons essential to international trade and prosperity. The SCS is an important junction for navigation between the Pacific and Indian Oceans and an important maritime gateway. India's maritime strategic interests in the region are well established, including the fact that almost 55 per cent of India's trade with the Indo-Pacific region passes through these waters.[12]

India has also been pursuing joint energy development opportunities with Vietnam in waters that both Hanoi and China claim. India signed an agreement with Vietnam in October 2011 to expand and promote oil exploration in the South China Sea and then reconfirmed its decision to carry on despite the Chinese challenge to the legality of Indian presence.

By accepting the Vietnamese invitation to explore oil and gas in blocks 127 and 128, India's state-owned OVL, not only expressed New Delhi's desire to deepen its friendship with Vietnam but also ignored China's warning to stay away.[13]

---

[10] Abhijit Singh (2016), "India's Strategic Stakes in the South China Sea", *Asia Policy*, Number 21, p.17.

[11] Deshika Elapata (2020), "India: A Growing Presence in the South China Sea", *European Institute for Asian Studies Briefing Paper*, https://www.eias.org/wp-content/uploads/2019/07/Briefing-Paper_India-Maritime-Security_DeshikaElapata-1.pdf.

[12] Rajeev Ranjan Chaturvedy (2015), "South China Sea: India's Maritime Gateway to the Pacific", *Strategic Analysis*, Volume 39 Number 4, p.364.

[13] Harsh V. Pant (2012), "Understanding India's Interest in the South China Sea: Getting into the Seaweeds", *CSIS Commentary*, https://www.csis.org/analysis/understanding-india%E2%80%99s-interest-south-china-sea-getting-seaweeds.

With the rise of Chinese activities in the SCS, China's growing footprints in the Eastern Indian Ocean are also clearly visible, particularly in Chinese research and survey vessel presence. In September last year, an Indian warship expelled the Shiyan 1, a Chinese research vessel found intruding into the exclusive economic zone off the coast of India's Andaman and Nicobar Islands. Chinese Dongdiao class intelligence-gathering ships now can be seen operating in the waters of the Eastern Indian Ocean, close to the eastern sea border near the Andaman and Nicobar Islands last year. Further to add on to India's concerns, China's mining operations in the Southern Indian Ocean have also increased exponentially, as also has the presence of Chinese fishing boats in areas close to India's territorial waters.[14]

India's Response to the South China Dispute

Diplomatic Standing

India has long been involved on the margins of the South China Sea issue. Delhi has always tried to balance these very real interests with its predilection to not offend China by wading too deeply into South China Sea affairs, mostly out of the fear that such a move could prompt Beijing to deepen its own naval operations in the Indian Ocean. Nonetheless, the Indian Navy first deployed to the South China Sea in 2000, and, in a pointed message to China, it has at times threatened to send naval assets to the region to protect its energy investments in the waters near Vietnam.[15]

India's position on the South China Sea was indicated in the joint ASEAN-India Vision Statement in December 2012. It stressed, "India's role in ensuring regional peace and stability, and for that we agree to promote maritime cooperation to address common challenges on maritime issues," and that "we are committed to strengthening cooperation to ensure maritime security and freedom of navigation, and safety of sea lanes of communication for unfettered movement of trade in accordance with international law, including UNCLOS."[16] Furthermore, at the 8th East Asia Summit (EAS) in Brunei Darussalam on 10 October 2013, former Prime Minister Manmohan Singh observed that "a stable maritime environment is essential to realize our collective regional aspirations. We should reaffirm the principles of maritime security, including the right of passage and unimpeded commerce, in accordance with international law, and peaceful settlement of maritime disputes. We welcome the collective commitment by the concerned countries to abide by and implement the 2002 Declaration on the Conduct of Parties in the South China Sea and to work towards the adoption

[14] Abhijit Singh (2020), "China tightens grip over the South China Sea – should India worry?", op.cit.

[15] Zachary Keck (2014), "India Wades Into South China Sea Dispute", *The Diplomat*, published March 12 2014, https://thediplomat.com/2014/03/india-wades-into-south-china-sea-dispute/.

[16] Nandini Jawli (2016), "South China Sea and India's Geopolitical Interests", *Indian Journal of Asian Affairs*, Volume 29 Number 1/2, p.89.

of a Code of Conduct in the South China Sea on the basis of consensus. We also welcome the establishment of the Expanded ASEAN Maritime Forum for developing maritime norms that would reinforce existing international law relating to maritime security."[17]

It is clear from the above statements that New Delhi's stand in the diplomatic ambit had been carefully tailored, where the issue of freedom of navigation and the establishment of a mutually agreed COC had been raised, but still, the thin line of not impinging the Chinese sentiments had been cautiously maintained.

Naval Posturing

The Indian Navy has embarked on a series of deployments since the year 2000. India has also increased its maritime deployments in the South China Sea, signalling a desire for an expanded security role in the Western Pacific. These deployments include unilateral appearances by the Indian Navy, bilateral exercises, friendly port calls, and transit through these waters. Some naval deployments are part of bilateral SIMBEX exercises with the Singapore Navy. Friendly port calls to littoral countries such as Brunei, Malaysia, Indonesia, the Philippines, and, above all, Vietnam also bring the Indian Navy into these disputed waters. This is why Raja Mohan identified that "New Delhi's Look East policy has acquired a distinct naval dimension. The traditional clear distinctions, then, between the Indian Ocean and the Pacific are beginning to blur. India is now looking beyond the Strait of Malacca to include the South China Sea in its national security calculus."[18] Indian deployments have been maintained over the years in more than nominal strength. For example, the deployments of a five-ship flotilla (two Kashin class destroyers, INS Ranjit and Ranvijay; the frigate Godavari; the missile corvette Kirch; the offshore patrol vessel Sukanya; and the fleet tanker Jyoti) in 2004 to the South China Sea. India's establishment in July 2012 of deep water maritime facilities in Campbell Bay (INS Baaz), the most southerly point of the Andaman Islands, enables India to conduct surveillance operations over the South China Sea.[19]

On May 18, 2016, four ships of the Indian Navy's Eastern Fleet were sent on a two-and-half month long operational deployment to the South China Sea and North Western Pacific. In a demonstration of its operational reach and commitment to India's "Act East" Policy, the Indian Navy's Eastern Fleet was sent to the seas, according to a press release of the Ministry of Defence. The naval force consisted of the 6,200-tonne Shivalik-class guided-missile stealth frigates Satpura and Sahyadr armed with super-sonic anti-ship and land-attack cruise missiles; the 27,550-tonne

---

[17] Vijay Sakhuja and Pankaj Jha (2016), "India and the South China Sea", op.cit. p.p. 119-120.

[18] David Scott (2013), "India's Role in the South China Sea: Geopolitics and Geoeconomics in Play", op.cit.

[19] David Scott (2013), "India's Role in the South China Sea: Geopolitics and Geoeconomics in Play", op.cit.

Deepak-class fleet tanker Shakti, one of the largest surface warships in the Indian Navy; and the 1,350-tonne Kora-class guided-missile corvette Kirch, armed with sub- and super-sonic anti-air and anti-ship missiles. The purpose of the deployment was to strengthen military-diplomatic ties and enhance inter-operability with other navies. The Indian warships made port calls at Cam Rahn Bay in Vietnam, Subie Bay in the Philippines, Sasebo in Japan, Busan in South Korea, Vladivostok in Russia, and Port Klang in Malaysia. The visits to each port lasted four days and were aimed at strengthening bilateral ties and enhancing cooperation between the navies.[20]

Is There a Shift in India's Stand on the SCS in the Offing?

India can now be seen publicly stating its discomfort with China's growing assertiveness in the SCS. While India has always emphasised the need to ensure freedom of navigation and overflight in the South China Sea, a more vocal stand is now being taken, with the South China Sea being declared as "the global commons,"[21] wherein all disputes should be settled in accordance with international law. The Indian Navy has reportedly deployed one of its frontline warships in the South China Sea after the June 15 clash with Chinese PLA troops in the Galwan Valley.[22] Though there are speculations if this was just a part of the routine naval deployments, which the Navy has been carrying out in the region, the message it sends out is unmistakable. Additionally, the Indian Navy also deployed its frontline vessels along the Malacca Straits near the Andaman and Nicobar Islands and the route from where the Chinese Navy enters the Indian Ocean Region to keep a check on any Chinese naval activity. It is a crucial sea trade route for China. The Navy also held exercises in the Andamans and has deployed MiG-29 K fighters in the islands.[23] Last year in May 2019, the Indian Navy conducted a joint sail in the South China Sea with the navies of the United States, Philippines, and Japan to demonstrate the presence of like-minded parties in the South China Sea region amid suggestions by the Philippines Defence Minister that "India has expressed its intent to carry out navigation activities in the

[20] Nandini Jawli (2016), "South China Sea and India's Geopolitical Interests", op.cit. p.90.

[21] "South China Sea part of global commons: India", *Times of India*, July 17, 2020, https://timesofindia.indiatimes.com/india/south-china-sea-part-of-global-commons-india/articleshow/77009643.cms.

[22] "Indian Navy deploys warship in South China Sea after Galwan clash", *Deccan Chronicle*, Published on August 31, 2020, https://www.deccanchronicle.com/nation/current-affairs/310820/indian-navy-deploys-warship-in-south-china-sea-after-galwan-clash.html#:~:text=Indian%20Navy%20deploys%20warship%20in%20South%20China%20Sea%20after%20Galwan%20clash,-DECCAN%20CHRONICLE.&text=New%20Delhi%3A%20The%20Indian%20Navy,talks%20between%20the%20two%20nations.

[23] "Indian Navy deploys warship in South China Sea after Galwan clash", *Deccan Chronicle*, op.cit.

South China Sea."[24] From a seemingly ad hoc approach which didn't go beyond India deciding to explore energy resources with Vietnam in the past, today New Delhi is relatively more relaxed in adopting a more robust defence posture in concert with other like-minded countries in the region.

At the virtual summit between Prime Minister Modi and Vietnamese Prime Minister Nguyen Xuan Phuc in December 2020, according to Ministry of External Affairs then secretary (East) Riva Ganguly Das, both leaders spoke of the importance of a "rules-based order in the region including by upholding international law, especially the UNCLOS. A peaceful, stable, secure, free, open, inclusive and rules-based region is in the common interest of all countries. Prime Minister stressed that the Code of Conduct negotiations on the South China Sea should not prejudice the interest of other countries in the region."[25] Similar stance was reiterated by External Affairs Minister, Jaishankar at the 15th East Asia Summit in November 2020 that "the Code of Conduct negotiations should not be prejudicial to legitimate interests of third parties and should be fully consistent with UNCLOS."[26]

In a statement issued by the Japanese Defence Ministry after the December 2020 meeting between the Indian and the Japanese Defence Ministers, it mentioned, "the two nations wanted to send "a clear message that they strongly oppose any attempts to unilaterally change the status quo by coercion or any activities that escalate tension."[27] It also claimed the two ministers "shared the view on highlighting the importance of a free and open maritime order based on the rule of law."

The basic principles—freedom of navigation, peaceful resolution of disputes, respect of international laws which have underlined India's South China Sea approach has remained the same. But the fact that the realisation that "the aggressiveness with which China has sought to protect its turf in the South China Sea has led Indian strategists to believe that, unless sustained pressure is brought to bear upon China, a negotiated solution to the dispute is unattainable."[28] Initially, the lurking fear that any statement which might even slightly reflect the side India is on with regard to this dispute would clearly show that India has let go off its neutrality as a show of its strategic support for the United States which has been the forerunner in raising its voice and conducting FONOPs in response to Chinese unilateralism in the South China Sea. After the release of the new official position of the U.S. on the SCS in July 2020, India has also been seen to release official statements with

[24] Dipanjan Roy Choudhury, "India is interested in navigation in the South China Sea region: Philippines", *The Economic Times*, published July 7, 2020, https://economictimes.indiatimes.com/news/defence/india-is-interested-in-navigation-in-the-s-china-sea-region-philippines/articleshow/76825668.cms?from=mdr.

[25] "South China Sea Code of Conduct Negotiations Shouldn't Discriminate: India to Vietnam", op.cit.

[26] "15th East Asia Summit", *Ministry of External Affairs Press Release*, published November 14 2020, https://www.mea.gov.in/press-releases.htm?dtl/33194/15th+East+Asia+Summit.

[27] Clive Hammond (2021), "South China Sea: India and Japan's joint pact sparks Beijing anger as tensions rise", published January 4 2021, https://www.express.co.uk/news/world/1379390/south-china-sea-news-india-japan-beijing-world-war-3-east-china-sea-conflict-spt.

[28] Abhijit Singh (2016), "India's Strategic Stakes in the South China Sea", op.cit. p.15.

phrases such as "eroding of trust", "the COC should not step on the interests of any third party or external not directly involved in the dispute". Positive development in India's SCS policy is clearly visible. Some have attributed this shift to the Galwan Valley clash- Since May 2020, Chinese and Indian troops have been involved in a confrontation along the disputed Himalayan border with New Delhi suggesting that Chinese transgressions of the LAC have occurred at four places: Pangong Tso, Galwan Nalah, and Demchok in Ladakh and at Naku La in Sikkim.[29] This is perhaps the biggest crisis in the relations between the two countries in decades.

With growing concerns in India about China's expansionist tendencies, India is ready to embark on a more proactive role in the region, reflected in a range of policy choices New Delhi has made in recent times, both vis-à-vis the region and China.

Push Factors for the Shift in India's Approach Towards the South China Sea Dispute

India's Act East Policy is Gaining Momentum

China's unilateral attempts to claim and dominate the SCS have been discussed at ASEAN and related summits, such as the East Asia Summit (EAS) in early November 2019. Due to India's lack of direct interest in the region and its prominence as a benign neighbour, Vietnam and other ASEAN nations have requested its assistance in engaging in and stabilising naval cooperation in the region—and to balance China's assertiveness in the South China Sea. ASEAN nations have long called on India to deepen its involvement in the South China Sea issue. Laura Q. Del Rosario, the Philippines' former deputy minister for international economic relations, had once stated that "India should go East, and not just Look East."[30]Furthermore, as much as the Southeast Asian countries are keen on partnering with India and establishing stronger economic and strategic ties, India has its own agenda in attempting to curtail China's dominance and aspirations to become a regional security power in the SCS. In view of ASEAN nations seeking ways to respond to and prevent a China-driven East Asian security order, engaging India as an extra-regional power could serve as a constructive step. China's rise and increasing trade with ASEAN underscores India's need to increase its collaboration with ASEAN. India is seizing the opportunity to utilise its regional standing for setting up collaborations and functional frameworks with like-minded ASEAN countries and thereby exert its influence. It is thereby assuring the deterrence of unilateral authoritativeness by diffusing tension

[29] Rohan Venkataramakrishnan, "'Wuhan spirit' to LAC skirmishes: What you need to know about the India-China stand-off", Scroll.in, published May 26 2020, https://scroll.in/article/962875/wuhan-spirit-to-lac-skirmishes-what-you-need-to-know-about-the-india-china-stand-off.

[30] Zachary Keck (2014), "India Wades Into South China Sea Dispute", op.cit.

and preventing the potential of an armed conflict, working towards creating a stable environment in Southeast Asia.[31]

It has been rightly pointed out recently by former Foreign Secretary, Vijay Gokhale, "India too have to be responsive to ASEAN's expectations. While strategic partnerships and high-level engagements are important, ASEAN expects longer-lasting buy-ins by India in their future. They have taken the initiative time and again to involve India in Indo-Pacific affairs. It is not as if our current level of trade or investment with ASEAN makes a compelling argument for them to automatically involve us. They have deliberately taken a longer-term view."[32]

India's defence links have increased overtime, in particular, in the naval domain. With countries like Vietnam, India has been deepening its defence cooperation since the 1990s. In December 2020, during the virtual meeting between Prime Minister, Modi with his Vietnamese counterpart, Nguyen Xuan Phuc, seven agreements were inked. The seven agreements inked include one on implementing arrangements on defence industry cooperation and another on nuclear cooperation between India's Atomic Energy Regulatory Board and Vietnam Agency for Radiation and Nuclear Safety. The summit provided an opportunity to hand over one high-speed guard boat to Vietnam, the launch of two other vessels manufactured in India, and keel-laying of seven vessels being manufactured in Vietnam under the $100-million defence Line of Credit extended by India to that country. The two sides also agreed to explore new and practical collaborations to build capacities in blue economy, maritime security and safety, marine environment and sustainable use of maritime resources, and maritime connectivity.[33] India has deepened bilateral and multilateral engagement on various levels with Southeast Asian countries. Mutually supporting each other in the South China Sea and the Bay of Bengal, has allowed the ASEAN nations and India to sustain and bolster relations, such as port calls to friendly countries and transits. The relations between India and ASEAN have evolved over recent times. It is only a matter of time before India's naval capabilities, maritime infrastructure, closer naval partnerships and capacity-building progresses into stronger cooperative partnerships in this region. The collaborative interests between the ASEAN countries and India are further evident through the prioritisation of freedom of navigation and overflight in the South China Sea—which were key aspects discussed at the ASEAN-India Summit in November 2019.[34]

---

[31] Deshika Elapata (2020), "India: A Growing Presence in the South China Sea", op.cit.

[32] Vijay Gokhale (2020), "How the South China Sea situation plays out will be critical for India's security", *The Indian Express*, published June 16 2020, https://indianexpress.com/article/opinion/columns/south-china-sea-dispute-asean-countries-relations-vijay-gokhale-6460680/.

[33] "South China Sea Code of Conduct Negotiations Shouldn't Discriminate: India to Vietnam", *The Wire*, published December 22 2020, https://thewire.in/diplomacy/south-china-sea-code-of-conduct-negotiations-shouldnt-discriminate-india-to-vietnam.

[34] Deshika Elapata (2020), "India: A Growing Presence in the South China Sea", op.cit.

China's Growing Assertiveness in the South China Sea

In the first half of 2020 alone, Chinese naval or militia forces have rammed a Vietnamese fishing boat, "buzzed" a Philippines naval vessel, and harassed a Malaysian oil drilling operation, all within their respective EEZs. Since 2015, China has built a runway and underground storage facilities on the Subi Reef and Thitu Island as well as radar sites and missile shelters on Fiery Cross Reef and Mischief Reef. The Chinese have conducted ballistic missile tests in the South China Sea in June 2019 and continue to enhance naval patrols to enforce area denial for others. The South China Sea is effectively militarised. [35] In April 2020, Beijing declared new administrative districts in the Paracel and Spratly Islands, the latest step in China's bid to legitimise effective control over these areas. The Vietnamese Ministry of Foreign Affairs reported in April 2020 that a Chinese Coast Guard vessel "rammed and sunk" a Vietnamese fishing boat carrying eight Vietnamese fishermen in the Paracel Islands in the South China Sea. It maintained that this violates "Vietnam's sovereignty over the Paracel Islands, causes property losses and endangers the lives, safety and legitimate interests of the Vietnamese fishermen." [36] There have been incidents involving Chinese fishing vessels and the Chinese Coast Guard with Indonesian fishing vessels in waters around the Natuna Sea as well. In February 2020, Chinese fishing boats flanked by Chinese Coast Guard vessels dropped their trawl nets yet again. China's illegal fishing near the Natuna Sea carries global consequences, reminding regional governments of Beijing's expanding claims to the South China Sea through which one-third of the world's maritime trade flows. Besides these incidents, there were satellite images showing a Chinese military plane landing on Kagitingan Reef in the West Philippine Sea in late March. There are also reports that China recently opened a research station on Kagitingan and Zamora Reef, also in the West Philippine Sea, to gather data on the ecology, geology, and environment in the Spratlys.[37]

Reformed Attitude of Claimant Countries

Philippine President Rodrigo Duterte decided not to suspend the long-standing Visiting Forces Agreement with the U.S.—a move widely seen as a shift in strategy because of Beijing's aggression in the disputed South China Sea. Beijing's artificial island-building in the South China Sea, military drills belligerent approach to diplomacy, and a deepening rift with Washington have led to countries like Vietnam

---

[35] Vijay Gokhale (2020), "How the South China Sea situation plays out will be critical for India's security", op.cit.

[36] Harsh V Pant and Premesha Saha (2020), "Fishing in troubled waters during a pandemic", *The Hindu*, published April 24 2020, https://www.thehindu.com/opinion/lead/fishing-in-troubled-waters-during-a-pandemic/article31417974.ece.

[37] Harsh V Pant and Premesha Saha (2020), "Fishing in troubled waters during a pandemic", op.cit.

and Malaysia seeking closer security ties with each other and with the U.S.[38] As the most vocal claimant in the South China Sea dispute, Vietnam is also seeking to strengthen security ties with countries like Japan, Australia, and India. Malaysia, Philippines, Indonesia, and Vietnam have all been submitting notes verbale to the UN rejecting China's nine-dash line and its claims to "historic rights" in the South China Sea to be inconsistent with UNCLOS. These countries have been highlighting the 2016 ruling.[39] Even Brunei issued its first statement on the South China Sea and referenced the ruling.[40] The ASEAN countries released a vision statement in June 2020 where they underlined the need for China to abide by international law and to fast-track the conclusion of the Code of Conduct for the South China Sea.[41]

Early this year in January 2020, Jakarta promptly summoned China's ambassador and issued a formal diplomatic protest. In the meantime, the Indonesian military deployed ten naval ships to the area and four F-16 fighters to Natuna Island. Indonesian President Joko Widodo even flew to the island to survey the situation.[42] The Indonesian patrol ship KN Pulau Nipah 321 had been deployed for such patrols in Indonesia's western maritime zone until November 2020.[43] Traditionally, Indonesia has tried to sidestep its maritime row with China. Emphasising the lack of a "territorial dispute" between the two countries, Indonesia has frequently offered to act as a neutral mediator between China and its Southeast Asian neighbours in their perennial dispute over the Spratly Islands. But today, China's burgeoning maritime forces and newly built military facilities in the Spratly archipelago have greatly expanded its reach in the South China Sea. As a result, China seems to have resumed its southward push through the South China Sea. Using "salami tactics"—actions designed to incrementally overcome opposition—China has already put the Philippines on its heels and seems on its way to doing the same to Malaysia and, perhaps, even Vietnam and Indonesia.[44]

---

[38] Kristin Huang, "Indo-Pacific strategy gains support as China's assertiveness fuels fears", *South China Sea Morning Post*, published on September 26 2020, https://www.scmp.com/news/china/diplomacy/article/3102894/indo-pacific-strategy-gains-support-chinas-assertiveness-fuels.

[39] On July 12, 2016, the Permanent Court of Arbitration ruled in favour of the Philippines and also ruled that China has 'no historical rights based on the nine dashed line map'.

[40] Ian Storey, "As US-China tensions rise, what is the outlook on the South China Sea dispute in 2020-21?", *South China Sea Morning Post* , published on September 8 2020, https://www.scmp.com/week-asia/opinion/article/3100563/us-china-tensions-rise-what-outlook-south-china-sea-dispute-2020.

[41] "ASEAN Leaders' Vision Statement on a Cohesive and Responsive ASEAN: Rising Above Challenges and Sustaining Growth", published on June 26 2020, https://asean.org/asean-leaders-vision-statement-cohesive-responsive-asean-rising-challenges-sustaining-growth/.

[42] Felix K. Chang (2020), "The Next Front: China and Indonesia in the South China Sea", *Foreign Policy Research Institute*, published January 27 2020, https://www.fpri.org/article/2020/01/the-next-front-china-and-indonesia-in-the-south-china-sea/.

[43] "Indonesian patrol confronts Chinese ship in economic zone near disputed South China Sea", *The Economic Times*, published on September 16 2020, https://economictimes.indiatimes.com/news/international/world-news/indonesian-patrol-confronts-chinese-ship-in-economic-zone-near-disputed-south-china-sea/articleshow/78138691.cms?from=mdr.

[44] Felix K. Chang (2020), "The Next Front: China and Indonesia in the South China Sea", op.cit.

Stronger Stand from Other Extra-Regional Players

On 13 July 2020, the United States Secretary of State, Mike Pompeo released a statement, which reflects the hardening of the US policy in a "vital, contentious part of the Indo-Pacific region which is the South China Sea." The statement claims that "Beijing's claims to offshore resources across most of the South China Sea are completely unlawful, as is its campaign of bullying to control them" is clearly symbolic of a shift in the official position of the United States. The US' new policy is in line with the 2016 International Arbitration Tribunal ruling which was in favour of the Philippines and the Chinese historical claims to the maritime resources were declared "unlawful" and beyond the purview of the United Nations Convention on the Law of the Sea (UNCLOS). Though the United States has in the past come up with statements showcasing support and giving a nod to the Tribunal ruling, but taking an official stand on Beijing's maritime claims in the SCS and spelling out that "PRC has no lawful territorial or maritime claim to Mischief Reef or Second Thomas Shoal (off the Philippines), Vanguard Bank (off Vietnam), Luconia Shoals (off Malaysia), waters in Brunei's EEZ, and Natuna Besar (off Indonesia)" is clearly a departure from the neutral stand on the issue of "territorial claims" as well. [45] Additionally, the United States is all set to establish a USD 2.2 billion Pacific Deterrence Initiative, aimed at enhancing America's deterrence and defence posture; increasing readiness and capability in the Indo-Pacific region; and deepening cooperation with allies and partners including India, Australia, and Japan, amid China flexing its muscles in the region. The bipartisan Congressional conference report on National Defence Authorisation Act for the fiscal 2021 has budgeted USD 2.2 billion to establish the Pacific Deterrence Initiative (PDI), which, lawmakers said, sends a strong signal to China and any potential adversaries, as well as to its allies and partners, that America is deeply committed to defending its interests in the region.[46]

In November 2020, Japan and Australia agreed on a breakthrough defence pact allowing reciprocal visits for training and operations and voiced concern over the disputed South China Sea, where China is extending its military influence. The Reciprocal Access Agreement strengthens defence ties between the two countries at a time when China is asserting its role in the region and the United States is going through a messy leadership transition. The pact allows Japanese and Australian troops to visit each other's countries and conduct training and joint operations and was agreed in principle by Japanese Prime Minister Yoshihide Suga and his Australian counterpart, former Prime Minister Scott Morrison, who was visiting Tokyo at the time. In the statement issued after their meeting, the two leaders also expressed concern about "recent negative developments and serious incidents in the South

[45] "U.S. Position on Maritime Claims in the South China Sea", https://www.state.gov/u-s-position-on-maritime-claims-in-the-south-china-sea/.

[46] Lalit K. Jha (2020), "US to establish Pacific Deterrence Initiative to counter China", *Outlook*, published December 7 2020, https://www.outlookindia.com/newsscroll/us-to-establish-pacific-deterrence-initiative-to-counter-china/1989121.

China Sea, including militarisation of disputed features, dangerous coercive use of coast guard vessels."[47]

India's Options

There is no doubt that there has been a palpable shift in India's approach to the disputes along the South China Sea. This tilt may not be a significant one, and it remains to be seen whether it is merely symbolic or more substantial. However, a certain momentum is visible in India's stance, and such a shift, albeit 15 Challenges and Options for India slight, can be a facilitator for new policy initiatives and actions on the part of India in the SCS and the broader Indo-Pacific. In the short term, it will not be feasible for India to have a military role and it has also wisely chosen to stay clear of any involvement in a possible confrontationist scenario. It has conveyed its unwillingness to participate in joint patrols or FONOPS with the US Navy in the South China Sea. Since this is a regional issue and given the prevalent opinion that "ASEAN centrality and unity" is waning, the Southeast Asian countries will want to handle the disputes at the ASEAN platform. However, there remain ways where India can show its Southeast Asian neighbours that even while it is aware that it has a limited role in the military domain, given their sensitivity to the idea of foreign military operating in their sovereign waters, India can still engage in a substantial course of action to help the ASEAN littorals. This will show India's regard for Southeast Asia as the fulcrum connecting the Indian the Pacific Oceans, thereby enlivening the principles underlined in its Indo-Pacific policy.

- India is fully committed to a Free and Open Indo-Pacific and to ensuring a rules-based international order. To that extent, it is fully supportive of initiatives in this regard in the entire region. It participates in numerous bilateral and multilateral naval exercises in the region; it is usually the first responder in any Humanitarian Assistance and Disaster Relief (HADR) operation; and it is an active participant in various regional security forums. India can, in the various bilateral, CORPAT exercises it undertakes with the Southeast Asian navies, introduce the aspect of information-sharing, and networking among national agencies of this region towards providing HADR as well as Search and Rescue operations during natural calamities. This has been done in the past under the aegis of the ASEAN Regional Forum and can be re-started, or else introduced in the Samudra Shakti and SIMBEX exercises.
- Effective maritime enforcement capacity begins with strong maritime domain awareness (MDA), defined as the ability to gather, process, analyse, and share real-time information about what is occurring at sea. This capacity is vital for promoting marine safety, responding to vessels in distress, stopping illegal activity,

[47] "Anti-China alliance: Japan, Australia reach security pact amid fears over South China Sea row", *Zee News*, published November 18 2020, https://zeenews.india.com/world/anti-china-alliance-japan-australia-reach-security-pact-amid-fears-over-south-china-sea-row-2325225.html.

tracking at-sea transshipments, and protecting waters from illegal incursions by foreign vessels. Most countries must rely on multilateral information sharing. India's Indian Ocean Region Information Fusion Centre (IOR-IFC) can work with the IFC in Singapore, the Indonesian Maritime Information Centre, and Malaysia's International l India-Indonesia bilateral joint maritime exercise 16 Challenges and Options for India Maritime Bureau to exchange and share information on illegal incursion and movement of Chinese fishing and naval vessels in the disputed waters of the SCS.

- India has already been engaged in capacity-building initiatives with countries like Vietnam and the Philippines. India and Vietnam pursue naval cooperation which includes composite training programmes in the field of submarines, aviation, and dockyard training. In 2015, both countries' coast guards signed an MOU for the establishment of collaborative relationships to combat transnational crime and for sharing best management practices and augmenting operational-level interactions. In 2016, India and Vietnam upgraded their ties to the level of a "comprehensive strategic partnership." The two have signed an agreement to exchange white shipping information. India is also exploring the possibility of selling warships to the Vietnamese Coast Guard.
- In 2017, India and the Philippines signed an MOU on defense cooperation and logistics. In 2019, they signed another MOU on the sharing of white shipping information. Their coast guards regularly conduct bilateral maritime exercises. Such initiatives should be undertaken with other claimant countries like Indonesia. Moreover, the Indian Coast Guard can provide training to the Vietnamese, Filipino, and Indonesian Coast Guards. Coast Guard exchange programmes can be initiated and exercises can be conducted to provide training in handling cases of illegal fishing vessels, especially Chinese fishing boats entering the disputed waters. Given that the Chinese fishing vessels encroaching on the disputed waters have become a regular occurrence and the coast guards are the first responders, besides naval training and exchange, coast guard training and contributing to their capacity building also need to be considered.
- India had been exploring international markets in Southeast Asia and elsewhere to sell the Brahmos missile system. Among the ASEAN countries, Vietnam was the first country that was offered these missiles. India proposed a US$ 100-million line of credit to the Philippines for the purchase of military hardware. It has also offered the Philippines its Akash missile systems (25 kms, mid-range surface-to-air missile system) that can intercept and destroy hostile aerial platforms. Recently, India's BrahMos Aerospace and the Philippines signed a deal worth almost $375 million for the Philippine Marines to acquire three batteries of the BrahMos cruise missile, a shot in the arm for New Delhi's efforts to emerge as an exporter of major defence hardware. India should now consider signing similar deals with countries like Vietnam and Indonesia.

- Some claimant countries like Indonesia are keen on infrastructure development of the islands around the disputed waters (for example, in the Natuna Sea). Indonesia is seeking to invite the United States to invest in the development of the Riau Islands' Natuna regency, which is a part of Indonesia's outer islands in the southern part of the contested South China Sea. This is where India and its other Quad partners can come in. India can push the United States, Japan, and Australia to invest in the infrastructure development in Southeast Asia, and by extension, in the ASEAN Masterplan on Connectivity 2025.
- Extra-regional players like India, the United States, Japan, and Australia can constantly voice the need for upholding international law in the SCS on the part of China and for the faster conclusion of the COC on terms which would be acceptable to China as well as the claimant ASEAN countries. This can help create pressure on the Chinese leadership in various global platforms.
- Besides the platform of Quad, India can work with other countries in other forums. For instance, most of the naval activity in the South China Sea is dominated by the Asian and Pacific powers. The recent announcements by European navies to operate in the SCS, directly challenging China's expansive claims and supporting freedom of navigation at sea, are causing concern for Beijing. India can consider joining such activities. The United States has plans to set up a "numbered fleet"—i.e., the First Fleet which could be operating in the crossroads between the Indian and the Pacific oceans and based in Singapore. Apparently, US allies and partners such as India, Singapore, and Japan may have endorsed its utility and agreed to support it.
- India has launched the Indo-Pacific Oceans' Initiative which mostly deals with the Blue Economy and sustainable use of marine resources. Countries like Vietnam and Indonesia are already a part of this initiative. There should be a push from India's end to include the other claimant countries as well and hold regular dialogues to come up with measures of how efficient and sustainable resource extraction can happen in the disputed waters in the SCS and these measures can then be incorporated in the final Code of Conduct signed with the PRC.

The key is to start with such soft security issues in the immediate term and draw out proposals that will be immediately acceptable to the ASEAN member-states. This will help India gain the trust of its ASEAN partners: that India truly is an advocate of ASEAN centrality and that Southeast Asia is the cog of its Indo-Pacific policy. Even the Quad members, the European countries like France, as well as the UK, can work alongside India and the other like-minded countries in the Indo-Pacific on these non-conventional areas.

Part II
In Search of Cooperation Despite Competition

Chapter 6
The European Union (EU) and Association of Southeast Asian Nations (ASEAN)—Fields for Cooperation and Convergence of Interests in the Blue Economy in the Twenty-First Century

Tomasz Lukaszuk

The chapter aims to analyze the activities of the two most prominent regional organizations in the blue economy in the world—EU and ASEAN, finding the similarities and differences in the context of their cooperation opportunities. Both have maritime character, with the sea area under their jurisdiction more extensive than the total land area.[1] Half of their population lives less than 50 km from the sea,[2] and the blue

[1] *EU part of the regional sea surface area (km2) and the area covered by MPAs in 2016 (dark colour and in %)*, European Environment Agency, 11.12.2019, https://www.eea.europa.eu/data-and-maps/figures/eu-part-of-the-regional/eu-part-of-the-regional, access 25.02.2020; D. Fallin et al., *Oceans of Opportunity: Southeast Asia's Shared Maritime Challenges*, Center for Strategic and International Studies, September 10, 2021, https://www.csis.org/analysis/oceans-opportunity-southeast-asias-shared-maritime-challenges, access 25.02.2020.

[2] *Eurostat regional yearbook 2011*, European Commission, https://ec.europa.eu/eurostat/documents/3217494/5728589/KS-HA-11-001-13-EN.PDF/c0dd33ed-0db2-4d8b-ae03-26d9bf3e57fc?version=1.0#:~:text=In%202008%2C%20around%20205%20million%20people%20lived%20in,44%20%25%20of%20the%20coastal%20Member%20States%E2%80%99%20population., access 20.03.2022.

T. Lukaszuk (✉)
University of Warsaw, Warsaw, Poland
e-mail: t.lukaszuk@uw.edu.pl

N. Hung Son and N. Thi Lan Anh (eds.), *The South China Sea: The Geo-political Epicenter of the Indo-Pacific?*, https://doi.org/10.1007/978-981-97-8209-3_6

economy plays a significant role in their overall development.[3] The EU introduced the Integrated Maritime Policy in 2007,[4] intending to make interconnected sea-based activities more coherent and sustainable development goals oriented. ASEAN countries started to implement primary elements of common fishery policy in 2016,[5] recognizing the significance of the blue economy in its strategic documents and following the advice and good practices of the European Union. The chapter argues that the experience of the EU served as a model for ASEAN countries, helping them attain several goals in sustainable maritime development. Despite different approaches toward the blue economy, both regional organizations found a common language and interests. The chapter starts with a theoretical explanation of the blue economy and an analysis of differences in approaches between ASEAN and the EU in defining the blue economy. Then, the activities in the blue economy of both regional organizations are explored. The final section highlights their existing and possible development of joint efforts in the blue economy.

Blue Economy—Definitions, Similarities and Differences in Approaches Between ASEAN and the European Union

Blue economy occurred as a new term, being a part of the process of formation of maritime governance concept in the last decade of the twentieth century. Maritime governance is defined in this chapter as a complex and dynamic process at global, regional, and national levels, regulating and monitoring all spheres of state and non-state actors' activity at seas and oceans.[6] Maritime governance itself is considered a result of deepening processes of globalization at sea. The development of maritime studies, technological progress in shipping, and the discovery of oil and gas deposits in the continental shelves resulted in a change of perception of different areas of

---

[3] *€566 billion and growing: the EU blue economy is thriving*, EU Science Hub, European Commission, 27 June 2018, https://joint-research-centre.ec.europa.eu/jrc-news-and-updates/eu-blue-economy-thriving-2018-06-27_en#:~:text=The%20EU%27s%20blue%20economy%20%E2%80%93%20all%20economic%20activities,and%20creates%20jobs%20for%20nearly%203.5%20million%20people., access 20.02.2024; I. M. Ramli and T. Waskitho, *Blue Economy Initiatives in South-East Asia: Challenges and Opportunities*, Economic Research Institute for ASEAN and East Asia (ERIA), Research Project Report FY2023 No. 17, Jakarta, November 2023, https://www.eria.org/uploads/media/Research-Project-Report/RPR-2023-17/Blue-Economy-Initiatives-in-South-East-Asia.pdf, access 20.01.2024.

[4] *Integrated Maritime Policy of the European Union*, Fact Sheets on the European Union—2023, https://www.europarl.europa.eu/ftu/pdf/en/FTU_3.3.8.pdf#:~:text=The%20Integrated%20Maritime%20Policy%20%28IMP%29%20of%20the%20European,interlinked%20activities%20related%20to%20oceans%2C%20seas%20and%20coasts., access 25.03.2022.

[5] *Strategic Plan of Action on ASEAN* Cooperation *on Fisheries 2021-2025 Final*, ASEAN Sectoral Working Group on Fisheries, https://asean.org/wp-content/uploads/2021/12/FAFD-16-SPA-Fisheries-202528ASWGFi.pdf, access 25.02.2021.

[6] T. Łukaszuk, *The Concept of Maritime Governance in International Relations*, Stosunki Międzynarodowe—International Relations, number 4 (v. 54), Warsaw 2018, p.143.

activities in the maritime domain, allowing for a more holistic view. The cognitive process of maritime studies was deepened and broadened within and on the sidelines of the Third Conference of Law of the Sea 1973–1982, which resulted in the signing of 1982 and coming into force in 1994 of the United Nations Convention of Law of the Sea (UNCLOS). UNCLOS triggered the development of studies, perceptions, and terminology of components of maritime governance related to legal, environmental, and especially economic issues. The twenty-first century has contributed to the progress of research on maritime economic activities through sustainable development goals with cross-cutting globalization interdependence at all horizontal and vertical levels within and beyond national jurisdiction at sea. The main goals include improving human well-being and social equity and decoupling socio-economic development from environmental degradation. In this regard, the efficiency and optimization of natural marine resources within ecological limits becomes paramount. It includes sourcing and using local raw materials and, where feasible, utilizing "blue," low-energy options to realize environmental benefits.

Blue economy became "a buzzword in the maritime economic realm and is about increasing human well-being through the sustainable development of ocean resources, while significantly reducing environmental risks and ecological scarcities."[7] It is "a widely used term around the world with three related but distinct meanings—the overall contribution of the oceans to economies, the need to address the environmental and ecological sustainability of the oceans, and the ocean economy as a growth opportunity for both developed and developing countries."[8] It was developed conceptually in the first two decades of the twenty-first century, mainly through debate within and on the sidelines of activities in the United Nations system. It has different definitions and descriptions.

As an ocean economy, ocean governance, and oceans governance, the blue economy has been applied since 1992 to describe the broadly apprehended development of maritime economy discussed at different conferences related to Rio de Janeiro "Earth Summit"[9] and covering among others:

- fishery;
- offshore renewable energy;
- aquaculture and mariculture;
- seabed extractive activities.[10]

---

[7] S. Bateman, R. Gamage, and J. Chan, *ASEAN and the Indian Ocean: the Key Maritime Links*, S. Rajaratnam School of International Studies, Research Report, Singapore Jul. 1, 2017, p.12, http://www.jstor.com/stable/resrep05888.5, access 02.02.2024.

[8] *Introduction to the Blue Economy*, Center for the Blue Economy, Middlebury Institute of International Studies, Monterey, https://www.middlebury.edu/institute/academics/centers-initiatives/center-blue-economy/about/history, access 31.01.2024.

[9] *United Nations Conference on Environment and Development, Rio de Janeiro, Brazil, 3–14 June 1992*, United Nations Conferences, https://www.un.org/en/conferences/environment/rio1992, access 28.02.2024.

[10] M. Haward, J. Vince, *Oceans Governance in the Twenty-first Century. Managing the Blue Plane*t, Edward Elgar, Cheltenham 2008, p.9.

The term "oceans economy" was utilized in the UNCTAD report "The Oceans Economy: Opportunities and Challenges for Small Island Developing States" in 2014, including sustainable fishing and aquaculture, renewable marine energy, marine bioprospecting, maritime transport and open ship registration, marine, and coastal tourism.[11]

The terms "blue growth," "ocean economy," and "marine economy" have been used as synonyms for "blue economy" by different states and organizations, as discussed by Rosa María Martínez-Vázquez, Juan Milán-García, and Jaime de Pablo Valenciano,[12] in their comprehensive comparative study. They tried to identify the origins of differences in terminology, showing that various states "addressed the importance of different sectors and the interest of governments in promoting it for the development of their national economies."[13]

According to the World Bank, the blue economy constitutes the "sustainable use of ocean resources for economic growth, improved livelihoods, and jobs, and ocean ecosystem health."[14] UNEP found the blue economy as the sustainable ocean economy "recognized as a multifaceted and cross-cutting concept that drives economic growth and innovation while ensuring ocean sustainability and rule-based ocean governance."[15] UNEP looks at oceans are spaces for development where "spatial planning integrates conservation, sustainable use, oil and mineral wealth extraction, bioprospecting, sustainable energy production, and marine transport."[16] That kind of approach occurred as a consequence of UNCLOS and shifted maritime countries' activities from purely coastal, "brown water" endeavors, to oceanic, in terms of responsibilities, benefits, economic modeling, and decision-making processes.[17] Both the continuation and confirmation of UNCLOS oceanic and joint responsibility attitude was the High Seas Treaty, adopted in 2023 by the Intergovernmental Conference on Marine Biodiversity of Areas Beyond National Jurisdiction (BBNJ), with the aim of "protecting, caring for, and ensuring the responsible use of the marine

[11] *The Oceans Economy: Opportunities and Challenges for Small Island Developing States*, UNCTAD/DITC/TED/ 2014/5, UNITED NATIONS PUBLICATION, p.2, https://unctad.org/system/files/official-document/ditcted2014d5_en.pdf, access 02.02.2024.

[12] R. M. Martínez-Vázquez, J. Milán-García, and J. de Pablo Valenciano, *Challenges of the Blue Economy: evidence and research trends*, Environmental Sciences Europe, Springer Open Access, 202, 33:61, p.3, https://doi.org/10.1186/s12302-021-00502-1, access 06.02.2024.

[13] Ibidem.

[14] *Blue Economy*, World Bank Group, www.worldbank.com/oceans, access 15.09.2021.

[15] *Advancing the Sustainable Blue Economy in ASEAN Region*, Webinar 30.06.2022, United Nations Environment Programme, https://www.unep.org/events/webinar/advancing-sustainable-blue-economy-asean-region#:~:text=In%20the%20Declaration%2C%20the%20Blue%20Economy%20is%20defined,and%20ecosystems%20for%20economic%20growth%20across%20various%20sectors., access 20.10.2022.

[16] *Blue Economy Concept Paper*, UNEP, (2012), p.3, https://www.unep.org/resources/report/blue-economy-concept-paper, access 20.10.2022.

[17] Ibidem.

environment, maintaining the integrity of ocean ecosystems,"[18] including sustainable management of fish stocks.

The European Union sees the blue economy as the set of sectors of the economy covering fisheries, aquaculture, coastal tourism, maritime transport, port activities, and shipbuilding.[19] The scope of the sectors considered as a part of EU blue economy has been increasing since the first publication of the Blue Economy Report in 2018,[20] as a result of the progress in maritime-related research, rise in spending on investments, and implementation of integrated maritime policy programs. 2023 Report considered seven established sectors: marine living resources, marine non-living resources, marine renewable energy, port activities, shipbuilding and repair, maritime transport, and coastal tourism; and two emerging sectors: emerging marine renewables (floating wind energy, floating solar photovoltaic energy) and blue biotechnology (algae sector).[21] The European Union utilizes the term "Blue Growth" as a description of the long-term strategy to support sustainable growth in the marine and maritime sectors as a whole.[22]

ASEAN defines blue economy as "the sustainable, resilient and inclusive use, governance, management and conservation of oceans, seas as well as marine and coastal resources and ecosystems for economic growth across various sectors such as fishery, aquaculture, maritime transport, renewable energy, tourism, climate change, and research and development while improving human well-being and social equity."[23] In addition, Southeast Asian nations emphasized in its 2021 Declaration that the blue economy is "a multifaceted and cross-cutting concept that involves all three pillars of the ASEAN Community,"[24] which means that security issues are included, especially related to navigation of merchant fleet.[25]

---

[18] United Nations News, 19 June 2023, https://news.un.org/en/story/2023/06/1137857, access 06.02.2024.

[19] F. Scholaert (Editor), *The blue economy. Overview and EU policy framework. In-depth analysis*, European Parliament, Brussels (January 2020), p.1, https://www.europarl.europa.eu/RegData/etudes/IDAN/2020/646152/EPRS_IDA(2020)646152_EN.pdf, access 30.10.2022.

[20] *The 2018 Annual Economic Report on EU Blue Economy*, Directorate-General for Maritime Affairs and Fisheries (European Commission), Joint Research Centre (European Commission), Brussels 2018, https://op.europa.eu/en/publication-detail/-/publication/79299d10-8a35-11e8-ac6a-01aa75ed71a1, access 09.02.2024.

[21] *The EU Blue Economy Report 2023*, Directorate-General for Maritime Affairs and Fisheries (European Commission), Joint Research Centre (European Commission), Brussels 2023, https://op.europa.eu/en/publication-detail/-/publication/9a345396-f9e9-11ed-a05c-01aa75ed71a1, access 09.02.2024.

[22] *Blue Growth. Supporting sustainable growth of the marine and maritime sectors*, European Commission, Brussels 2022, https://s3platform.jrc.ec.europa.eu/blue-growth, access 09.02.2024.

[23] *ASEAN Leaders' Declaration on the Blue Economy*, Brunei Darussalam ASEAN Summit, October 26, 2021, https://asean.org/asean-leaders-declaration-on-the-blue-economy/, access 20.10.2022.

[24] Ibidem.

[25] Three pillars of ASEAN Community are: ASEAN Political-Security Community (APSC), the ASEAN Economic Community (AEC) and the ASEAN Socio-Cultural Community (ASCC).

EU and ASEAN share many similarities in their concept of the blue economy in line with UN conventions and sustainable development programs. The differences in approaches of both regions toward the blue economy are related mainly to security issues stemming from four factors:

1. the size of the maritime domain in Southeast Asia is three times larger than that in Europe[26];
2. the significance of the waters of the Eastern Indian Ocean, South China Sea, and West Pacific Ocean in the context of Sea Lines of Communication is more significant than the Mediterranean—with 40% of the world trade passing through straits and Exclusive Economic Zones of ASEAN countries[27];
3. activities of big-size trawlers owned by regional[28] and extra-regional players,[29] equipped with sophisticated food processing devices;
4. the number of unsolved territorial disputes over continental shelves in the South China Sea and the rise of China's assertiveness in the maritime domain in the twenty-first century.

The blue economy is essential for both regions as it directly employs over 5.4 million people in the EU, accounts for 1.3% of EU GDP,[30] and generates a gross added value of almost €500 billion a year.[31] In the case of ASEAN, there are two biggest archipelagos of the world (Indonesia and the Philippines), and "more than half of the world's fishing vessels are in the South China Sea."[32] Southeast Asia is responsible for "15% of worldwide fish production, 33% of seagrass meadows,

---

[26] J. Bradford and B. Strating, *Maritime Governance Policy and Priorities in Southeast Asia*, Asia Maritime Transparency Initiative, November 21, 2023, https://amti.csis.org/maritime-governance-policy-and-priorities-in-southeast-asia/, access 01.03.2024; *EU part of the regional sea surface area (km2) and the area covered by MPAs in 2016 (dark colour and in %)*, European Environment Agency, 11 Dec 2019, https://www.eea.europa.eu/data-and-maps/figures/eu-part-of-the-regional, access 01.03.2024.

[27] *ASEAN Maritime Outlook*, Jakarta, August 2023, https://asean.org/wp-content/uploads/2023/08/20231011_AMO-Report-COMPLETE.pdf, access 02.11.2023.

[28] P. Suuronen et al, *A Path to a Sustainable Trawl Fishery in Southeast Asia*, Reviews in Fisheries Science & Aqua culture, Volume 28, 2020—Issue 4, Taylor and Francis Online, pp. 499–517, https://doi.org/10.1080/23308249.2020.1767036, access 02.02.2024.

[29] P. Chalk, *Illegal Fishing in Southeast Asia: Scope, Dimensions, Impacts, and Multilateral Response*, China Brief Volume: 23 Issue: 13, July 21, 2023, https://jamestown.org/program/illegal-fishing-in-southeast-asia-scope-dimensions-impacts-and-multilateral-response/, access 02.03.2024.

[30] F. Scholaert (Editor), *The blue economy. Overview and EU policy framework. In-depth analysis*, European Parliament, Brussels (January 2020), p.1.

[31] *Blue Economy Development Framework. Growing the Blue Economy to Combat Poverty and Accelerate Prosperity*, https://thedocs.worldbank.org/en/doc/446441473349079068-0010022016/original/AMCOECCBlueEconomyDevelopmentFramework.pdf, access 02.11.2022.

[32] L. Hartman, *The importance of the South China Sea*, Bureau of Global Public Affairs, U.S. Department of State, 11.07.2019, https://share.america.gov/importance-of-south-china-sea/#:~:text=The%20importance%20of%20the%20South%20China,waters%20for%20their%20food%20and%20livelihoods.&text=The%20importance%20of%20the,their%20food%20and%20livelihoods.&text=of%20the%20South%20China,waters%20for%20their%20food.

territorial waters comprise an area three times the land area."[33] Like in the majority of ASEAN members, the blue economy constitutes an essential part of the Vietnamese economy as the marine sector contributes 47% to GDP and is expected to contribute up to 70% by 2030.[34] All the ASEAN countries made a significant progress in the twenty-first century in their Maritime Potential Index (MPI) and the Maritime Economy Index (MEI).[35] However, there is still an enormous potential to utilize it in a sustainable way. The following section discusses how the European Union and ASEAN tried to optimize their maritime potential in the second decade of the twenty-first century.

The European Union and ASEAN Activities in Blue Economy Policy

The EU is the only international organization serving as the contracting party to the UNCLOS. The European Commission also played an essential role at the Earth Summit in Rio de Janeiro in 1992, encouraging other countries to conclude binding agreements on measures to prevent further pollution of oceans, including the Convention on Biological Diversity.[36] From the very beginning of its existence, it dealt with the sustainable use of living resources in the form of a common fisheries policy.[37] Member countries agreed in 1983 to establish a new generation of regulatory instruments under the Common Fisheries Policy—the concept of relative stability and conservatory management measures based on total allowable catches and quotas.[38]

The Policy has been reformed several times to adjust it to the dynamics of the global market and growing challenges to environmental protection. The further enlargement of the EU also contributed to transformation and adjustments in regulations. More considerable attention was extended to the social dimensions of fisheries with a focus on changes in the profession of the coastal population with movement from fishery into the tourism sector as a result of the strategy of fish stock management

[33] M. J. Spalding, *The Role of ASEAN in Addressing Global Ocean Issues*, The Asia Foundation, February 22, 2017, https://asiafoundation.org/2017/02/22/role-asean-addressing-global-ocean-issues/, access 20.10.2022.

[34] Minh Vu, *Blue economy—indispensable path for Vietnam to tap potential*, Hanoi Times 5.11.2021, https://hanoitimes.vn/blue-economy-indispensable-path-for-vietnam-to-tap-potential-319197.html, access 31.10.2022.

[35] H.-D. Evers and A. Karim, *The Maritime Potential of ASEAN Economies*, *Journal of Current Southeast Asian Affairs*, volume 30, no 1, (2011), pp. 117–124, https://journals.sagepub.com/doi/pdf/10.1177/186810341103000105, access 31.10.2022.

[36] *Convention on Biological Diversity*, United Nations, 1992, https://www.cbd.int/doc/legal/cbd-en.pdf, access 05.10.2022.

[37] *Treaty of Rome* (1957, Art. 38-43), European Parliament, https://www.europarl.europa.eu/about-parliament/en/in-the-past/the-parliament-and-the-treaties/treaty-of-rome, access 02.10.2020.

[38] T. Lukaszuk, "Normative Powers in Maritime Affairs: India—EU Cooperation in the Indian Ocean Region," *The Copernicus Journal of International Studies*," No.1 (2020), p.70.

at maximum sustainable yield for all managed stocks. The Commission continued applying of multiannual plans (MAPs) to manage fisheries in different sea-basins. The regionalized approaches were applied to allow EU countries with a management interest to propose detailed measures in the context of fleet capacity ceilings per country in combination with the obligation for EU countries to ensure a stable and enduring balance between fishing capacity and fishing opportunities over time.[39]

The critical issue in implementing the Policy was that small-scale fisheries represent 80% of the EU fishing fleet contributing to 48% of employment in EU fisheries. To make the Policy effective at all levels, especially in the Mediterranean, the small-scale fleet was exempted from several obligations applied to larger vessels, such as fishing authorizations. In addition, the European Commission also provides financial support to the sector under the European Maritime, Fisheries, and Aquaculture Fund (EMFAF). Small-scale coastal fishing can be supported with a rate of public aid and exempted from accurately reporting their catches and their position while fishing. It created limitations in implementing the Policy making some of the steps in the Mediterranean region counter-productive. At the same time, 70% of stocks in the North East Atlantic, where the fisheries had more prominent and more modern ships at their disposal, became managed in a sustainable manner.[40]

The further effort of the EU in introducing the blue economy as a part of the concept of integrated ocean governance, introduced by the UN 1992 Earth Summit and developed at the Global Oceans Fora in 2001 and 2005, was the creation of the Integrated Maritime Policy. The integrated ocean governance was identified in Chapter 17 of Agenda 21 as a holistic approach toward ocean governance, and the EU applied such an approach in 2007 in the Integrated Maritime Policy.[41]

Understanding that the Policy needed not only to be holistic, dealing with all areas of human activities and environmental context but also transparent and inclusive for all parties, the Commission made governmental and non-governmental institutions related to the maritime domain involved in the creation of the document. A one-year consultation period with such a broad scope of stakeholders helped to prepare also the Action Plan.[42] Both documents were designed to improve the coordination of policies related to interdependent areas of activities in the oceans, seas, islands, coastal regions, and maritime sectors to foster the sustainable development of all sea-based activities and coastal regions. Strengthening of seaports and enhancing

---

[39] *Common fisheries policy (CFP)*, European Commission, https://oceans-and-fisheries.ec.europa.eu/policy/common-fisheries-policy-cfp_en, access 20.09.2017.

[40] *EU Common Fisheries Policy*, Federal Ministry of Food and Agriculture, Federal Republic of Germany, https://www.bmel.de/EN/topics/fisheries/fisheries-policy/eu-common-fisheries-policy.html#:~:text=EU%20Common%20Fisheries%20Policy%201%20Sustainable%20management%20of,...%206%20Fishing%20effort%20and%20technical%20measures%20, access 31.10.2022.

[41] *An Integrated Maritime Policy for the European Union*, Communication from the Commission, Public Register of Documents, COM_COM(2007)0575 / FULL / EN15/10/2007, https://www.europarl.europa.eu/RegistreWeb/search/simple.htm?references=COM_COM(2007)0575&languages=EN&sortAndOrder=DATE_DOCU_DESC, access 20.09.2018.

[42] *Action plan for an integrated maritime policy*, European Commission 2007, https://eur-lex.europa.eu/legal-content/EN/TXT/HTML/?uri=LEGISSUM:l66049, access 20.08.2018.

maritime transport competitiveness, accompanied by endeavors to maritime safety and security, were among the priorities. The Plan showed the urgency of developing cross-cutting tools at all layers—from regional through national up to local. The Integrated Maritime Policy (IMP) was introduced at the regional level and incorporated into member countries' domestic laws. Furthermore, based on the national regulations, every administrative unit was obliged to prepare the executive program for the IMP at the local level.

As an institutional part of the IMP, the European Commission changed the name of its Directorate General for Fisheries (DG FISH) to Maritime Affairs and Fisheries (DG MARE). DG Mare continued to conduct stakeholder consultations on "seabed mining, marine biotechnology, maritime surveillance, seabed mapping and forecasting, tourism and ocean energy, to overcome the problems with fragmented sectoral policy-making."[43] In order to address the specific needs and conditions of different sea-basins, the European Commission prepared custom-made strategies—COM (2008) 763 for the Arctic,[44] COM (2009) 248 for the Baltic Sea[45] and COM (2009) 466 for the Mediterranean region.[46]

ASEAN members, like the EU, adopted Ministerial Understanding on Fisheries Cooperation at an early stage of their integration in 1983, within the ASEAN Committee on Food, Agriculture, and Forestry (COFAF) established in 1977. ASEAN Ministers of Agriculture and Food (AMAF) agreed to exchange information and expertise; coordinate action in resources research activities; undertake appropriate action in the evaluation and management of shared stocks and migratory species in the ASEAN region; engage for the rational utilization of fisheries; share and transfer of technology at all levels to improve the socio-economic status of the fishermen and fish farmers.[47]

The Strategic Plan of Action for ASEAN Cooperation on Fisheries (2016–2020) focused on enhancing trade and market access, production using sustainable technologies, ensuring food security and safety, increasing resilience to climate change

---

[43] Jan-Stefan Fritz and John Hanus, "The European Integrated Maritime Policy: The next five years," *Marine Policy*, vol.53 (2015):2.

[44] *Communication from the Commission to the European Parliament and the Council the European Union and the Arctic Region*, Commission of the European Communities, Brussels, 20.11.2008 COM(2008) 763 final, https://eur-lex.europa.eu/LexUriServ/LexUriServ.do?uri=COM:2008:0763:FIN:EN:PDF, access 02.09.2018.

[45] *EU Strategy for the Baltic Sea Region*, COM(2009)248—Communication, EU Monitor, Brussels 10 June 2009, https://www.eumonitor.eu/9353000/1/j9vvik7m1c3gyxp/vikqhnlmstze, access 02.09.2018.

[46] *Towards an Integrated Maritime Policy for better governance in the Mediterranean*, COM(2009)466—Communication, EU Monitor, Brussels 11 September 2009, https://www.eumonitor.eu/9353000/1/j9vvik7m1c3gyxp/vikqhntmolyw, access 02.09.2018.

[47] *ASEAN Ministerial Understanding on Fisheries Cooperation*, Singapore, 22 October 1983, https://www.asean.org/wp-content/uploads/images/2012/Economic/AMAF/Agreements/ASEAN%20Ministerial%20Understanding%20On%20Fisheries%20Cooperation.pdf, access 20.10.2022.

and natural shocks, and assisting small producers in increasing competitiveness.[48] ASEAN became a major producer of fish and other fisheries products. The 10 ASEAN countries accounted for a quarter of global fish production, and four of them — Indonesia, Thailand, Vietnam, and the Philippines are among the world's top ten largest fish producers.[49]

Fishery constitutes a major part of the blue economy activities of ASEAN countries, but tourism also plays a critical role as the fastest-growing sector in the blue economy.[50] Being aware of the diversity and "the complementary nature of the region's tourist attractions,"[51] and "the valuable role of tourism in narrowing the development gap among member states,"[52] they agreed in 2012 "to enhance the development and promotion of ASEAN as a single tourism destination to establish an integrated network of tourism and travel services."[53] At the same time, there was an understanding of the interdependence between tourism and harmonizing the objectives of tourism development with the implementation and observance of environmental protection standards, with the goal of the adoption of certification programs for sustainable tourism. The crucial role of local communities in environmentally sensitive areas was emphasized as well.

In their first joint declaration on the blue economy, announced on the occasion of the 38th ASEAN Summit on 26 October 2021, the regional leaders also pointed to the significance of joint actions in such areas of the blue economy as maritime transport and renewable energy.[54] They decided to task the ASEAN Coordinating Council (ACC) to develop a regional action plan for cooperation on the blue economy.

ASEAN and the EU are at different stages in implementing sustainable, resilient, inclusive maritime policy in the blue economy. The following section discusses how they tried to and could cooperate in the blue economy in terms of different conditions and challenges faced by both organizations.

---

[48] *Fisheries Cooperation*, ASEAN Secretariat, https://asean.org/our-communities/economic-community/enhanced-connectivity-and-sectoral-development/asean-food-agriculture-and-forestry/fisheries-cooperation/, access 31.10. 2022.

[49] *Fisheries. Where to invest*, ASEAN, https://investasean.asean.org/index.php/page/view/fisheries, access 31.10.2022.

[50] Mark J. Spalding, *The Role of ASEAN in Addressing Global Ocean Issues*, The Asia Foundation, February 22, 2017, https://asiafoundation.org/2017/02/22/role-asean-addressing-global-ocean-issues/, access 20.10.2022.

[51] *ASEAN Tourism Agreement*, ASEAN Secretariat, Jakarta May 11 2012, https://asean.org/asean-tourism-agreement/, access 02.11.2022.

[52] Ibidem.

[53] Ibidem.

[54] *ASEAN Leaders' Declaration on the Blue Economy*, Brunei Darussalam ASEAN Summit, October 26, 2021, https://asean.org/asean-leaders-declaration-on-the-blue-economy/, access 20.10.2022.

ASEAN—EU Cooperation in Blue Economy

Security serves as a vital part of the framework of the blue economy cooperation in Southeast Asia, especially in the South China Sea and Sea Lines of Communication context. "The EU Strategy for Cooperation in the Indo-Pacific" and "The ASEAN Outlook on the Indo-Pacific" became the conceptual basis for the security area since 2021 in order to reinforce synergies and strengthen mutually beneficial cooperation between the two organizations.[55] "Plan of Action to Implement the ASEAN-EU Strategic Partnership (2023–2027)"[56] played the role of the executive road map of the cooperation. It emphasized the significance of the consequent continuation of the ASEAN-EU High-Level Dialogue on Maritime Security Cooperation. The document also highlighted efforts aimed at strengthening cooperation on maritime domain awareness and maritime safety, including on passenger ship safety and seafarer training and welfare, search and rescue (SAR). In this context, the significance of implementation of the ASEAN Declaration on Cooperation in Search and Rescue of Persons and Vessels in Distress at Sea[57] was emphasized.

The EU appreciates ASEAN's commitment to effective multilateralism and supports the principle of ASEAN centrality, its efforts to build a rules-based regional maritime architecture, and the multilateral anchor that it provides. The EU also "supports the ASEAN-led process toward an effective, substantive and legally binding Code of Conduct in the South China Sea, which should not prejudice the interests of third parties."[58] EU-ASEAN cooperation also covers a wide range of security issues, including activities through the ASEAN Regional Forum (ARF)[59] like the Inter-Sessional Meeting on Maritime Security (ISM on MS). The EU started to respond institutionally to ASEANs expectations in security earlier. It initiated EU-ASEAN High-Level Dialogues (HLD) on Maritime Security in 2013. The first HLD was held in Indonesia. There was a political will in the EU to "exploit the convergence of interests with ASEAN and to continue making security related to

---

[55] *Philippines: first subcommittee on maritime cooperation with the European Union takes place in Brussels*, European External Action—the Diplomatic Service of European Union, Brussels 27.09.2023, https://www.eeas.europa.eu/eeas/philippines-first-subcommittee-maritime-cooperation-european-union-takes-place-brussels_en, access 10.02. 2024.

[56] *Plan of Action to Implement the ASEAN-EU Strategic Partnership (2023-2027)*, The ASEAN Secretariat, August 4, 2022, https://asean.org/plan-of-action-to-implement-the-asean-eu-strategic-partnership-2023-2027/, access 10.02. 2024.

[57] *ASEAN Declaration on Cooperation in Search and Rescue of Persons and Vessels in Distress at Sea*, ASEAN Secretariat, Summit related documents, Ha Noi, 27 October 2010, https://asean.org/asean-declaration-on-cooperation-in-search-and-rescue-of-persons-and-vessels-in-distress-at-sea/, access 10.02.2024.

[58] *South China Sea: Statement by the Spokesperson on challenges to peace and stability*, European External Action—the Diplomatic Service of European Union, Brussels 24.04.2021, access 02.02.2024.

[59] *Joint Communication to the European Parliament and the Council. The EU strategy for cooperation in the Indo-Pacific*, European Commission, High Representative of the Union for Foreign Affairs and Security Policy, Brussels, 16.9.2021, p.5, https://www.eeas.europa.eu/sites/default/files/jointcommunication_2021_24_1_en.pdf, access 10.10.2021.

economy issues a dynamic vector of bilateral cooperation."[60] In an effort to make the dialogue an effective instrument ASEAN and the EU focus on maritime safety, counter-piracy efforts, environmental protection, and regional stability. The Critical Maritime Routes program, created in 2009 and concentrated on the security and safety of essential maritime routes, constitutes another form of maritime security cooperation. It consists of five projects, with the aim to link them up progressively in the near future, thus contributing to create trans-regional synergies and increase maritime security and safety of critical maritime routes. Among those projects is CMR Indian Ocean (CRIMARIO I and II), with a goal of enhancing maritime domain awareness, through cooperation actions in the Indian Ocean.[61] Additionally, a Maritime Operational Coordination and Communications platform (IORIS) was launched in 2018, which enhances interagency collaboration at national and regional levels.[62] IORIS major activities are focused on alerts in native languages, advanced mapping, vessel intercept, satellite-based data feeds. As implementation of CRIMARIO and IORIS, as the first ASEAN member and the second Asian state after South Korea, Vietnam concluded with the EU in 2019 an agreement on participation in the EU crisis management operations.[63] Singapore-based Information Fusion Centre (IFC) started cooperation with CRIMARIO on information sharing on maritime security in the Western Indian Ocean in 2020. The EU and Indonesia conducted the first joint naval exercise in the Arabian Sea in 2022, concentrating on the mitigation of pirate activities and acts of armed robbery at sea, threatening the security of Sea Lines of Communication (SLOCs).[64]

The role of security of SLOCs in the context of the EU–ASEAN blue economy cooperation gained further significance after the Ukraine war outbreak in 2022. It had an essential impact on shipping distances, regularity of sailing, and chain of food supply at the intercontinental level.[65] The new chapter of the Israel-Palestinian conflict, which started in 2023, accompanied by Houthis attacks on merchant fleet

---

[60] *Blue Book 2016. EU-ASEAN Development Cooperation in 2015*:12–13, https://www.eeas.europa.eu/sites/default/files/eu-aseanbluebook2016hr.pdf, access 18.10.2022.

[61] *CRIMARIO—Critical Maritime Routes Indo-Pacific*, European Commission, Service for Foreign Policy Instruments, Brussels, 04.08.2022, https://fpi.ec.europa.eu/projects/crimario-critical-maritime-routes-indo-pacific_en, access 07.02.2024.

[62] *Indo-Pacific Regional Information Sharing (IORIS) Platform*, European Union, CRIMARIO, https://www.crimario.eu/wpcontent/uploads/2023/09/IORIS_Factsheet_A4_V6.pdf, access 10.12.2023.

[63] *Agreement between the European Union and the Government of the Socialist Republic of Viet Nam establishing a Framework for the Participation of Viet Nam in European Union Crisis Management Operations*, European Union External Action Service—The Diplomatic Service of the European Union, EU/VN/CRISIS MANAGEMENT/en2, Brussels, 17.10.2019, https://www.eeas.europa.eu/sites/default/files/viet_nam_fpa.en19.with_date_in.pdf, access 07.02.2024.

[64] *EU-Indonesia—Joint press release on First Joint Naval Exercise*, Delegation of the European Union to Indonesia and Brunei Darussalam, 16.08.2022, https://www.eeas.europa.eu/eeas/eu-indonesia-joint-press-release-first-joint-naval-exercise_en?s=168, access 06.02.2024.

[65] *Review of Maritime Transport 2023*, UNCTAD, 27 September 2023, https://unctad.org/publication/review-maritime-transport-2023, access 02.02.2024.

traffic between the EU and ASEAN in the Red Sea,[66] deepened those phenomena with the addition of the return of COVID pandemic period container shipping high insurance costs.[67] The EU extended assistance to Ukraine through Solidarity Lanes considered a key to global, especially Indian Ocean littorals food security[68] and launched a special mission EUNAVFOR ASPIDES to protect vessels from Houthi attacks in the Red Sea.[69]

Another area where the EU and ASEAN found mutual benefit, was food safety, the reduction of environmental impact, and the increase in overall sustainability. In 2017, a new platform, EURASTIP (Europe Asia Science and Technology Innovation Platform), was launched with the support of EATIP (European Aquaculture Technology and Innovation Platform) to reinforce cooperation with aquaculture-producing countries—in particular, Thailand and Vietnam. EURASTIP was also tasked to establish business-to-business brokerage events on standards for aquaculture site planning, animal health, food product safety, and farm governance.[70] There are six essential pillars of the program: 1. Establish and Strengthen National Pilot Platforms (NPP) in Asia; 2. Innovative Education, Training and Capacity Building; 3. Aligning Standards and Certification; 4. Increase the amount of strategic collaborations between European and SE-Asian aquaculture; 5. Dissemination, Legacy, Impact Management; 6. Project Coordination and Administration.[71] The program has been implemented through Memorandums of Understanding, joint courses and co-location between states and exchanges and internal capacity building between entrepreneurs. EU-funded vocational education projects such as Aqua-tnet, WAVE, VALLA, and BlueEDU, existing since 1996, were extended and European Skills, Competences, Qualifications, and Occupations (ESCO) program was implemented in Indonesia, Malaysia, Thailand, and Vietnam through trainings, mobility programs, and internships.[72]

---

[66] *Security and freedom of navigation in the Red Sea: Council launches EUNAVFOR ASPIDES,* Council of the EU, Press Release, 19 February 2024, https://www.consilium.europa.eu/en/press/press-releases/2024/02/19/security-and-freedom-of-navigation-in-the-red-sea-council-launches-new-eu-defensive-operation/#:~:text=In%20close%20cooperation%20with%20like-minded%20international%20partners%2C%20ASPIDES,of%20navigation%2C%20especially%20for%20merchant%20and%20commercial%20vessels., access 21.02.2024.

[67] *Review of Maritime Transport 2023*, UNCTAD, 27 September 2023.

[68] *EU-Ukraine Solidarity Lanes*, European Commission, 11 September 2023, https://eu-solidarity-ukraine.ec.europa.eu/eu-assistance-ukraine/eu-ukraine-solidarity-lanes_en, access 29.02.2024.

[69] *Security and freedom of navigation in the Red Sea: Council launches EUNAVFOR ASPIDES,* Council of the EU, Press Release, 19 February 2024.

[70] *Blue Book 2017. EU-ASEAN Development Cooperation in 2016*, European Union External Action Service, https://www.eeas.europa.eu/sites/default/files/euidnbluebook2017_0.pdf, access 18.10.2022.

[71] *EURASTIP—Promoting Multi-Stakeholder Contributions to International Cooperation on Sustainable Solutions for Aquaculture Development in South-East Asia*, Founded by the European Union Horizon 2020 Programme, https://eurastip.eu/exchanges/, access 07.02.2024.

[72] EURASTIP Best Practice Case Studies: Aquaculture Training and Capacity Building Collaborations Between Europe and Southeast Asia, EURASTIP 2019, p.16, https://eurastip.eu/wp-content/uploads/2019/08/Eurastip-Report-FINAL_web.pdf, access 15.02.2024.

Apart from aquaculture, the EU has also supported ASEAN in its policy on Illegal, Unreported, and Unregulated (IUU) fishing by arranging a series of dialogues to improve existing monitoring, control, and surveillance tools, and mitigate IUU fishing in ASEAN waters. Utilizing the Enhanced Regional EU-ASEAN Dialogue Instrument (E-READI), the EU facilitated the first and second ASEAN dialogue with the EU on the issue of IUU in 2019.[73] The EU also established direct cooperation with individual ASEAN members like Thailand,[74] aimed at the implementation of sustainable and legal exploitation of fish stocks tailored to individual necessities. The assistance extended to Thailand plays a critical role in fisheries in the whole region of Southeast Asia as Thailand is "the world's biggest exporter of prepared or preserved tuna comprising 29% of the world's exports."[75] Indonesia and the Philippines are among the top five tuna producers as well.[76] The EU inspired, encouraged, and helped Thailand to modernize its fisheries sector, including the establishment of the Command Centre for Combatting Illegal Fishing (CCCIF) and the enactment of the Fisheries Act in 2015, replacing regulations from 1947.[77]

The efforts to "reduce, re-use and recycle to protect the marine environment and coral reefs"[78] were also among the top priorities of EU-ASEAN cooperation. Building resilience against and mitigating the impact of climate change on the marine and coastal environment[79] play a crucial role in developing the blue economy of archipelagic and littoral states in Southeast Asia. Seeking synergies between political frameworks in climate change mitigation efforts—the European Green Deal and the ASEAN Community Vision 2025—both strategic partners decided in 2021 to introduce a program Green Team Europe Initiative granted by the EU in areas of climate action, environmental and biodiversity protection, at national and regional levels in Southeast Asia.[80] Starting 2019, EU-ASEAN High-level dialogue (HLD) on Environment and Climate Change gathers every year to discuss and plan projects on cooperation also in the maritime domain like biodiversity, waste management,

---

[73] *Blue Book 2021. EU-ASEAN Development Cooperation in 2020*, p.48.

[74] A. Tavornmas and K. Cheeppensook, *Shaping ocean governance: a study of EU normative power on Thailand's sustainable fisheries*, https://link.springer.com/article/10.1007/s10368-020-00475-1, access 25.02.2024.

[75] L. Hasnan, *Southeast Asia's lucrative tuna industry*, The ASEAN Post, 6 September 2019, https://theaseanpost.com/article/southeast-asias-lucrative-tuna-industry, access 25.02.2024.

[76] Ibidem.

[77] Y. Naiki and J. Rakpong, *EU–Third Country Dialogue on IUU Fishing: The Transformation of Thailand's Fisheries Laws*, Transnational Environmental Law, 11:3 (2022), Cambridge University Press, p.642, https://doi.org/10.1017/S2047102522000206, access 25.02.2024.

[78] *Blue Book 2021. EU-ASEAN Development Cooperation in 2020*: 25, https://euinasean.eu/wp-content/uploads/2021/04/Blue-Book-2021.pdf, access 20.10.2022.

[79] *Blue Book 2021. EU-ASEAN Development Cooperation in 2020*, p.33.

[80] *European Union launches a Green Team Europe Initiative in partnership with South East Asia*, European Commission, News Announcement, 18 November 2021, https://international-partnerships.ec.europa.eu/news-and-events/news/european-union-launches-green-team-europe-initiative-partnership-south-east-asia-2021-11-18_en, access 20.10.2022.

plastics, and marine litter.[81] As a part of the cooperation with ASEAN members, EU joined in 2021 the International Coral Reef Initiative (ICRI) to extend assistance in protecting marine ecosystems of coral reefs, sustainably managing coral reefs and associated ecosystems,[82] being aware that seas and oceans in Southeast Asia contain 32% (91 700 km2) of the world's shallow coral reefs.[83]

Conclusion

Blue economy, with its complexity in terminology and dynamic development of conceptual framework in the twenty-first century, constitutes one of the most intricate elements of maritime governance. Its horizontal and vertical interconnectedness and interdependence with security, legal, and environmental issues are critical. In this context, vital are:

- the role of securitization of Sea Lines of Communication carrying 80% of the world trade[84];
- rule-based order implemented in the governance of the economically critical parts of the maritime domain under and beyond the jurisdiction of states through UNCLOS;
- sustainable development with socio-economic development decoupled from environmental degradation.

European Union and the Association of Southeast Asian Nations have served as raw models of the two most significant global maritime regions in terms of institutionalization of cooperation, role in implementing rules-based order based on UNCLOS, and impact on implementation of sustainable issues at sea and coastal areas. Despite differences in environmental and security conditions, the two most integrated regional organizations—the EU and ASEAN—experienced in the first two decades of the twenty-first century, the growing convergence of approaches and interests in the blue economy. The awareness of the maritime vitality of ASEAN among the EU countries increased significantly after 2013 and the implementation of China's Belt and Road Initiative. They recognized the necessity of deeper engagement in Southeast Asia, losing gradually in the twenty-first century their position as

[81] *ASEAN, EU to enhance cooperation on protection of the Environment and Climate Change*, ASEAN Secretariat News, Jakarta, July 9, 2019, https://asean.org/asean-eu-to-enhance-cooperation-on-protection-of-the-environment-and-climate-change/, access 02.02.2024.

[82] *Ocean governance: EU joins the International Coral Reef Initiative to protect marine ecosystems*, European Commission, 5 February 2021, https://oceans-and-fisheries.ec.europa.eu/news/ocean-governance-eu-joins-international-coral-reef-initiative-protect-marine-ecosystems-2021-02-05_en, access 10.02.2024.

[83] T. Spencer, M.D. Spalding, *Coral Reefs of Southeast Asia* in A. Gupta, *The Physical Geography of Southeast Asia*, Oxford University Press 2005, pp. 402–427.

[84] *Review of Maritime Transport 2021*, UNCTAD, https://unctad.org/publication/review-maritime-transport-2021, access 02.02.2024.

the number one investor and trade partner for ASEAN countries to China. The situation in the South China Sea influenced both ASEAN and the EU's understanding of the vitality of cooperation in the context of rules-based order at sea and the security of SLOCs. The impact of the war in Ukraine on Black Sea SLOCs and the Israeli-Palestinian conflict on Red Sea SLOCs on bilateral trade made the comprehension of the convergence of interests between EU and ASEAN even deeper. The EU countries invested in the blue economy in Southeast Asia, increasing the existing mechanisms of development assistance and cooperation in fisheries and aquaculture. They transferred and promoted environmentally sound modern technologies in the blue economy to preserve and conserve the ecosystems in Southeast Asia.[85] The joint efforts contributed to the significance of ASEAN in the blue economy in Asia and the Pacific and the increase of the role of the EU in the Indo-Pacific Region and built up the economic competitiveness of the EU and ASEAN.

[85] *ASEAN Tourism Agreement*, ASEAN Secretariat News, Jakarta May 11 2012, https://asean.org/asean-tourism-agreement/, access 02.11.2022.

Chapter 7
Hook, Line and Cooperate: A Three-Staged Approach to Regional Fishery Cooperation

Gilang Kembara

It's widely understood that fish stocks and marine biodiversity within the South China Sea continue to face unprecedented challenges throughout the span of modern history.[1] attributed the decline in fish stocks due to three main reasons: (1) active building and reclamation of islands and features, causing permanent damage; (2) large-scale fishing activities; (3) subsidies to sustain offshore fishing in the South China Sea area.[2] The environmental destruction left within the wake of all these activities has rendered the area uninhabitable for fish, and other marine biota to live. This is exacerbated by an increasing demand of marine products from the neighbouring Southeast and East Asian regions, home to almost two billion population.

The most cited loss of marine biota in the South China Sea came from the widespread poaching of giant clams in the area. Demand from giant clams has grown in recent years, owing to the belief of the meat as an aphrodisiac and delicacy, and the high value of its shell, which served as an unfortunate substitute for the banned elephant ivory. An article by Larson showcased the village of Tanmen on Hainan Island, which harboured over 460 shops that sell giant clam carvings, providing a livelihood for over 100,000 residents.[3] Aside from that, the dramatic changes brought forward by the construction of various man-made facilities and island reclamation

G. Kembara (✉)
S. Rajaratnam School of International Studies, Nanyang Technological University, Singapore, Singapore
e-mail: isgilangkembara@ntu.edu.sg

[1] Nguyen, C. H., and Vu D. H. 2018. "Environmental Issues in the South China Sea: Legal Obligation and Cooperation Drivers." *International Journal of Law and Public Administration* 1 (1): 8–23. https://doi.org/10.11114/ijlpa.v1i1.3260.

[2] Nguyen, C. H., and Vu D. H. 2018. "Environmental Issues in the South China Sea: Legal Obligation and Cooperation Drivers." *International Journal of Law and Public Administration* 1 (1): 8–23. https://doi.org/10.11114/ijlpa.v1i1.3260.

[3] Larson, Christina. 2016. "Shell Trade Pushes Giant Clams to the Brink." *Science* 323–324. https://doi.org/10.1126/science.351.6271.323.

N. Hung Son and N. Thi Lan Anh (eds.), *The South China Sea: The Geo-political Epicenter of the Indo-Pacific?*, https://doi.org/10.1007/978-981-97-8209-3_7

have caused a runoff of pollution. Such pollution not only came from reclaimed lands within the area but also from South China Sea coastal states.

Despite all these, provisions do exist under UNCLOS on the obligations to protect and preserve the Marine Environment. Article 123 of the United Nations Convention on the Law of the Sea[4] describes "states bordering an enclosed or semi-enclosed sea should cooperate with each other in the exercise of their rights and in the performance of their duties under this Convention." Therefore, there is an obligation by all claimant parties, as well as South China Sea littoral states to exercise cooperation in good faith within the South China Sea. The article went on to state that there are four areas where states must cooperate on (1) management of living resources; (2) protection of marine environment; (3) joint scientific research; and (4) cooperate with external states and other international organisations. This is relevant, owing to the fact that the South China Sea is considered as a semi-enclosed sea, with outlets over at its south and northeast.[5]

Moreover, three articles under UNCLOS stipulate responsibility to all states to conduct maritime environmental protection. First, Article 192 recognises a general obligation of all States to protect and preserve the maritime environment. Second, to undertake this obligation, Article 194 stipulates that States shall take all measures to prevent, reduce and control pollution from any source and to ensure that activities under their jurisdiction or control are so conducted as not to cause damage by pollution to other States and their environment. Third, Article 197 imposes an obligation of cooperation for the protection and preservation of the marine environment. It requires states to cooperate on a global basis and, as appropriate, on a regional basis, directly or through competent international organisation. Under these two articles, it is clear that UNCLOS extends the purpose of cooperation for countries to responsibly manage their shared marine environment.[6]

This article will attempt to find a balance between the need to exploit the fish for economic and social needs, with the obligation that states have to preserve and protect their maritime environment. Noting the political volatility of the South China Sea, it would strive to examine "low-hanging" cooperation, before advocating a more formal and wide-reaching multilateral cooperation. A three-staged approach is therefore offered to effectively bridge, and create a mutual recognition that the protection of fish stocks and its environment are of the utmost importance to preserve the livelihoods of the coastal communities of the South China Sea littoral states. The article will first look into the issue of trust deficit that is most apparent between the littoral states. It will address ways in which trust could be enhanced and establish a threshold on which trust level shall not dipped to ensure a minimum level of cooperation. Secondly, the article will explore aspects of joint maritime research and

[4] UN. 1982. "United Nations Convention on the Law of the Sea." *UNCLOS.* Accessed February 6, 2024. https://www.un.org/depts/los/convention_agreements/texts/unclos/unclos_e.pdf.

[5] UN. 1982. "United Nations Convention on the Law of the Sea." *UNCLOS.* Accessed February 6, 2024. https://www.un.org/depts/los/convention_agreements/texts/unclos/unclos_e.pdf.

[6] UN. 1982. "United Nations Convention on the Law of the Sea." *UNCLOS.* Accessed February 6, 2024. https://www.un.org/depts/los/convention_agreements/texts/unclos/unclos_e.pdf.

surveillance to provide a shared understanding of the fundamental condition of the South China Sea. Improving the collective knowledge of the maritime domain will provide a similar understanding of the condition of the sea, and allow claimant states to ensure that adequate levels of protection and cooperation are conducted. Finally, the article establishes the tenets of an efficient fisheries management organisation and pursues the creation of such organisation in the South China Sea. This part will endeavour upon the opportunities and challenges on regions establishing regional maritime fish organisations (RFMO) to help maintain a healthy level of fish stocks and ensure a robust maritime biota that supports it.

Managing the Trust Deficit

Before we delve into the cooperation sides and best practices to develop a nexus between sustainable fishing and marine environmental protection, we need to acknowledge the problem at hand that has hindered further progress to practical cooperation. In April 2016, *Foreign Policy* published an article entitled "Fishing disputes could spark a South China Sea crisis." This report highlighted a "large number of fishing fleets from all South China Sea coastal states are at the front lines over the fight to control tiny rocks [i.e. Mischief Reef, Fiery Cross and Scarborough Shoal].[7]" Truly at that time, there was a growing number of maritime incidents involving regional fishermen, including Chinese fishermen in particular. Bateman and Hongzhou mentioned that mainstream media and a substantial body of academic literature attribute these fishing incidents, and the growing presence of Chinese fishermen in the South China Sea, to China's strategic and political motives, arguing that these fishermen are actually fishing militia. Despite the fact that fishing militia may have been thrown into the mix of the civilian fishing fleet, Bateman and Hongzhou argued that this fishing militia narrative has the potential to be misleading, as it fails to situate the growing fishing disputes within the context of the development of regional fishery sectors. Furthermore, they highlighted the fact that fishery issues are highly securitised within the region, degrading the level of trust needed between South China Sea littoral states to work together towards a common good.[8]

The fishing militia narratives have, when seen through the lens of the Copenhagen school, fallen into the concept of "tactical securitisation." This refers to when lower-level political issues, such as fishing, are linked with the high political issues of national survival. By attaching resource scarcity with security raises the profile of the issue and increases public awareness, importance and urgency in mobilising

[7] Keith, Johnson, and Dan De Luce. 2016. "Fishing Disputes Could Spark a South China Sea Crisis." *Foreign Policy*.

[8] Bateman, Sam, and Zhang Hongzhou. 2017. "Fishing Militia, the Securitization of Fishery and the South China Sea Dispute." *Contemporary Southeast Asia 39* (2): 266–314.

resources and funds.[9] By designating all Chinese fishermen involved in fishery disputes and maritime incidents as militia, the fishing militia narrative effectively links fishery incidents with highly sensitive military operations, and the ongoing territorial and jurisdictional disputes in the South China Sea.

Developing actions that will increase the other side's trust must be strongly motivated by a state's leadership to transform their relationship with the adversary and expect that their propositions will be reciprocated.[10] According to Snyder and Diesing, a state that wants to induce the adversary to cooperate on security issues may use some combination of persuasion, coercion and/or accommodation.[11] A state might try to force other states to cooperate by issuing threats, mobilising or increasing its defence budget. The application of coercive policies may be effective in the short run but will increase the other side's mistrust and further suspicion. Alternatively, the use of concessions by policymakers to another state may be seen as a sincere sign of a desire to improve relations especially if the concession is relatively costly. Social convention indicates that individuals might be more willing to reciprocate gifts and favours marked by the giver's level of sacrifice because such noble gestures are less apt to have ulterior motives. Similarly, a state can begin to prove its good intentions by making a costly concession.[12]

Given the complexity of the South China Sea issue, the fishery and environment sectors have long been considered by politicians and researchers as an ideal field for regional maritime cooperation, which would have a "spill over effect" towards the area.[13] Nonetheless, low level of trust between South China Sea claimant states has made it difficult to conduct essential and obligatory civil maritime cooperation to proceed. The increasing securitisation of fishery issues in the South China Sea could result in reduced cooperation between states. This could be seen by the lack of will littoral states have to follow the Declaration on the Conduct of Parties in the South China Sea (DoC), whereby parties are required to exercise restraint to resolve their disputes, without resorting to threats or the use of force.[14] Hence, having a low level of trust sets a very dangerous condition that could alleviate risk coming from possible incidents, accidents, criminal activities and matters that may threaten

---

[9] Fischhendler, Itay. 2015. "The Securitization of Water Discourse: Theoretical Foundations, Research Gaps and Objectives of the Special Issue." *International Environmental Agreements* 245–255.

[10] Webb, W.M., and P. Worchel. 1986. "Trust and Distrust." In *Psychology of Intergroup Relations*, by William G Austin and Stephen Worchel, 213–228. Chicago: Nelson-Hall.

[11] Snyder, G.H., and P. Diesing. 1977. *Conflict Among Nations: Bargaining, Decision Making and System Structure in International Crises*. Princeton: Princeton University Press.

[12] Abraham Tesser, Robert Gatewood, and Michael Driver. 1968. "Some Determinants of Gratitude." *Journal of Personality and Social Psychology* 233–236.

[13] Wang, and Kuan Hsiung. 2015. "Peaceful Settlement of Dipustes in the South China Sea Through Fisheries Resources Cooperation and Management." *Maryland Series in Contemporary Asian Studies* 1 (3): 1–60.

[14] ASEAN. 2012. "Declaration on the Conduct of Parties in the South China Sea." *Association of Southeast Asian Nations*. May 14. Accessed February 8, 2024. https://asean.org/declaration-on-the-conduct-of-parties-in-the-south-china-sea-2/.

regional cohesion. As such, a minimum level of trust, especially at the operational level, needs to be developed between partners to follow through with any agreements. Bateman and Zhang wrote that trust allows essential and obligatory civil maritime cooperation to proceed without prejudice to sovereignty claims.[15]

Sam Bateman's work on building trust and maritime cooperation rests upon the notion of both operational and strategic trust. His argument on strategic trust was that it is a crucial element for which "cooperation on matters of high politics, and maritime disputes in particular" are solved. Strategic trust is built through effective cooperation in matters often seen as "low politics"; these include fisheries management, environmental protection and social exchanges. Sam Bateman's notion of operational trust underlines the most basic level of trust between actors. Operational trust is the fundamental element for "essential and obligatory civil maritime cooperation to proceed without prejudice to sovereignty claims." He further explained that operational trust is a necessity for epistemic communities to conduct activities, such as marine navigation, scientific observation, or weather monitoring. It allows them to "pursue common interests in a cooperative manner free of the constraints that arise from strategic distrust." As such, a higher level of maritime cooperation between states is essential in maintaining and building both operational and strategic trust.

Joint Maritime Research and Surveillance

To assess the current condition of maritime biota in the South China Sea, a thorough study must be conducted to map out the level of migratory and straddling fish stocks between South China Sea coastal states. It is within the law of nature that fish doesn't possess a single nationality, unlike its human counterparts. As such, fish stocks are highly mobile, and those that ended up in the South China Sea would've likely come from outside of the area. Meltzer[16] and Van Dyke[17] highlighted an argument that calls for compatibility between conservation and management measures in EEZs and on the High Seas. Be that as it may, many coastal states thought this perspective could erode their sovereign rights over the living resources within the EEZ as provided

[15] Bateman, Sam, and Zhang Hongzhou. 2017. "Fishing Militia, the Securitization of Fishery and the South China Sea Dispute." *Contemporary Southeast Asia 39* (2): 266–314.

[16] Meltzer, Evelyne. 1994. "Global Overview of Straddling and Highly Migratory Stocks: The Non-Sustainable Nature of High Seas Fisheries." *Ocean Development and International Law* 255–344.

[17] Van Dyke, and Jon M. 1996. "The Straddling and Migratory Stocks Agreement and the Pacific." *International Journal of Marine and Coastal Law* 406–429.

under.[18,19,20] The argument put forth was later included under the 1995 Agreement (Conservation and Management of Straddling Fish Stocks and Highly Migratory Fish Stocks), which was adopted on 4 August 1995. Five ASEAN member states have signed the 1995 Agreement, with Indonesia being the first on 28 September 2009 and the other four (Philippines, Thailand, Vietnam and Cambodia) during the 2010s. In regards to the South China Sea, Brunei, Malaysia and China have not signed the agreement.[21]

Nonetheless, joint maritime research to observe the condition and assess the fish stocks must be thoroughly conducted. Focusing solely on the differences between each claimant country would only brew more discontent. Instead, each party must concentrate upon their common interests to foster solidarity. It is without doubt that each coastal state relies upon an ample stock of marine biota to ensure the prosperity and sustainability of their coastal communities. Through data collection and surveillance activities can maximum sustainable yield (MSY) be calculated and total allowable catches (TACs) be set. Wang Kuan-Hsiu listed four datasets that are necessary for fishery management[22]:

Biological information: such as status of stocks, trends in catches per unit of fishing effort;
Technical information: such as numbers and kinds of fishing vessels and gear;
Economic information: such as trends in fish prices, fishermen's incomes; and
Social information: such as trends in numbers of fishermen, and mobility into and out of fisheries.

Once the necessary dataset is collected, it is imperative to set up a quota allocation among the coastal states. Without establishing quotas, fishing vessels would compete with each other in order to maximise their share of the TAC. As coastal states agree to put quotas in place, coastal states can plan their development, as they have a guaranteed share of the TACs.[23] Furthermore, every relevant instrument concerning natural resources acknowledges that while coastal states shall determine the allowable catch of resources in its jurisdiction, this right to utilise resources is always coupled with the

[18] UN. 1982. "United Nations Convention on the Law of the Sea." *UNCLOS.* Accessed February 6, 2024. https://www.un.org/depts/los/convention_agreements/texts/unclos/unclos_e.pdf.

[19] Meltzer, Evelyne. 1994. "Global Overview of Straddling and Highly Migratory Stocks: The Non-Sustainable Nature of High Seas Fisheries." *Ocean Development and International Law* 255–344.

[20] Van Dyke, and Jon M. 1996. "The Straddling and Migratory Stocks Agreement and the Pacific." *International Journal of Marine and Coastal Law* 406–429.

[21] UN DOALOS. 2023. "Chronological Lists of Ratifications of, Accession and Successions to the Convention and the Related Agreements." *Oceans & Law of the Sea United Nations.* October 25. Accessed February 12, 2024. https://www.un.org/depts/los/reference_files/chronological_lists_of_ratifications.htm.

[22] Wang, and Kuan Hsiung. 2001. "Bridge Over Troubled Waters: Fisheries Cooperation as a Resolution to the South China Sea Conflicts." *The Pacific Review* 14 (4): 531–551.

[23] Churchill, Robin R., and Daniel Owen. 2010. "External Aspects of Fisheries Management." In *The EC Common Fisheries Policy*, by Robin R. Churchill and Daniel Owen, 300–398. Oxford: Oxford University Press.

duty to give due regard to the duty to preserve and protect the environment and where relevant, the needs of the local population.[24] In exercising these rights and duties, the coastal state may allow the participation of other states in spaces under the former's jurisdiction in the form of information-sharing where relevant, access to surplus of allowable catch, cooperation and coordination surrounding shared resources.

Although the potential for joint maritime research, especially on natural resources mapping, conservation and joint research within South China Sea's maritime boundaries seems to be a rational choice of cooperation between South China Sea littoral states, there remains a strong sense of nationalism and regional security in wide perceptions shared by all stakeholders with regards to region-wide cooperation on fisheries. After all, fisheries activities are related to the domestic political economy structure since its development can help national efforts to mitigate poverty impact and build economic resilience, especially those in remote areas.

Governance of Living Resources and Developing an Inclusive Fishery Mechanism

Considering that marine animals' natural habitat and migration patterns do not conform to the artificial, man-made territorial boundaries ascribed by states, it is essential for South China Sea littoral states to adopt norms and standards that balance common intergovernmental interests in areas of, among others: sovereign rights, scientific basis, economic interests and community rights, especially to govern living resources in areas adjacent to other states' territories or the high seas.

Pertaining to the governing of living resources, the key instruments are the UNCLOS, its subsequent 1995 United Nations Fish Stock Agreement (Fish Stocks Agreement), the 1992 Convention on Biological Diversity (CBD) and its 2010 Nagoya Protocol on Access to Genetic Resources and the Fair and Equitable Sharing of Benefits Arising from their Utilisation (Nagoya Protocol), details of which can be seen on Table 7.1.

In general, we can categorise the norms contained in the applicable instruments to those governing:

Geographic entitlements over marine spaces;
Right to utilise resources based on said entitlements;
Duty to preserve and protect the environment and
International trade in said resources.

[24] See for example, *Articles 56, 61, 63, and 64* of UN (1982) couple the rights to exploit and the duty to conserve; Article 6 of the Convention on Biodiversity adopts the term 'sustainable use' to refer to parties' obligation; the Fisheries and Agriculture Organisation of the United Nations (FAO) established the 1995 FAO Code of Conduct in accordance with the 1995 UN Fish Stocks Agreement as well.

Table 7.1 International norms on fisheries

Subject matter	Instrument
General	UNCLOS Geographic entitlements over marine spaces Exploration, exploitation and management of marine resources Protection and preservation of the marine environment Cooperation on a transboundary, global and regional basis Marine scientific research Shared fish stocks Living resources beyond national jurisdiction
	Fish Stocks Agreement Implementation of UNCLOS with regard to straddling fish stocks and highly migratory fish stocks beyond areas under national jurisdiction, applying mutatis mutandis to the same category within national jurisdiction for the purpose of exercise of sovereign rights
Protection of marine animals	CBD General cooperation National strategies, plans, programmes Identification and monitoring Incentives Research and Training Public education Exchange of information Technical and scientific cooperation
	Nagoya Protocol Fair and equitable benefit-sharing Global and multilateral benefit-sharing mechanism Transboundary cooperation

UNCLOS lays out that marine spaces are categorised into areas within national jurisdiction and beyond national jurisdiction, thus distinguishing the scope of rights and duties of coastal states that flow from each geographic entitlement. In turn, this affects both the scope of authorities and stakeholders.

Areas within national jurisdiction are further categorised into two; the first category of areas within national jurisdiction confers *territorial sovereignty* upon the coastal state, consisting of internal waters, territorial sea and archipelagic waters. Meanwhile, the second category of areas within national jurisdiction confers *sovereign rights*, but not sovereignty, upon the coastal state: the contiguous zone, exclusive economic zone and continental shelf.

The distinction between territorial sovereignty and sovereign rights lies in the fact that while territorial sovereignty grants comprehensive authority to the coastal state, quite akin to sovereignty over land, sovereign rights are limited by subject matter. For example, the sovereign rights associated with the EEZ are limited only to the management and conservation of natural resources. The concept of EEZ itself was born as a compromise between the freedom of the seas, the desire to rectify geographical inequities in access to resources and protection of interdependence between marine living resources and coastal state populations.

Therefore, the discussion of cooperation grounds in fisheries shall not only rely on international law but also on the domestic laws of the coastal state—herein Indonesia—which enjoys prescriptive jurisdiction over a portion of the relevant marine spaces. Such domestic law framework is as discussed *infra.*

Secondly, every instrument concerning natural resources acknowledge that while coastal states shall determine the allowable catch of resources in its jurisdiction, this right to utilise resources is always coupled with the duty to give due regard to the duty to preserve and protect the environment and where relevant, the needs of the local population. In exercising these rights and duties, the coastal state may allow the participation of other states in spaces under the former's jurisdiction in the form of:

Information-sharing where relevant
Access to surplus of allowable catch
Cooperation and coordination surrounding shared resources

In addition, to ensure that each coastal state would comply with the quota allocation based on the data collection and surveillance, the region should aspire to create a regional fisheries management organisation (RFMO). The South China Sea region is actually included within two different RFMOs. First, the South Pacific Regional Fisheries Management Organisation (SPRFMO), which is considered as a general RFMO. Second, the Western and Central Pacific Fisheries Commission (WCPFC), which is considered as a Tuna RFMO. However, the immense geographical scope and the fact that not all South China Sea coastal states are members of these two RFMOs. The complexity of ensuring the compliance of all members within an RFMO that covers the size of the Pacific Ocean causes inefficiency and slow-moving progress.

Therefore, a more tailor-fit mechanism must be planned and rolled out to cater to the specific condition of the South China Sea. Referring to an example made by the CSIS Expert Working Group on the South China Sea, SCS coastal states should agree to establish a Fishery and Environmental Management Area with implementation and enforcement drawing from successful precedents, such as the Great Barrier Reef Marine Park and the OSPAR Convention. What is suggested, is to designated different areas of the South China Sea as ecosystem-based fisheries zones covering the reefs that are vital to regional fish stocks. The mechanism does not impose a total ban on fishing throughout the South China Sea. Rather, it will consist of a patchwork of tailored fisheries zones. The range of which, would go from no-catch zones to allow fish stocks to completely replenish, limited-catch zones where only a certain type of fish could be caught, and non-restrictive zones.[25]

The condition for the establishment of such mechanism rests on the involvement of all parties without prejudice to existing territorial and maritime claims. All parties must be equally involved in the creation and management of the zones. This means that all South China Sea coastal states are to take part in it, including Taiwan. It is to

[25] Poling, Gregory, B., Michael J. Green, Christopher K. Johnson, Murray Hiebert, Matthew P. Funaiole, Bonnie S. Glaser, and Amy Searight. 2018. *Defusing the South China Sea Dispute: A Regional Blueprint.* Expert Working Group Report, Washington D.C. : CSIS.

Table 7.2 Limits of rights and duties on maritime domain

Aspect	Area		Explanation
	High seas	EEZ	
Right to fish	Free for all with limitations	Exclusive sovereign right of coastal state	Art. 116 UNCLOS limits the right to fish in the high seas by provisions on the EEZ (Arts. 63 and 64 which relate to fish stocks occurring across areas (straddling) or migratory)
Duty to conserve resources	By all states	By coastal state	Art. 117 provides the duty of states to cooperate in the conservation and management of living resources on the high seas
Duty surrounding living resources	Scientific evidence is required regarding species exploited and dependent species Duty is owed by the States concerned	Duty is owed by the coastal state, subject to the duty of cooperation in some conditions	Note—the Authority/ISA does examine scientific evidence, but it only calls into question the standards of scientific evidence if the research pertains to deep-sea drilling in the Area (seabed subjacent to the high seas). (see instead below)
Duty to cooperate	All states + states whose nationals exploit said/ identical resources	Duty is owed by the coastal state, subject to the duty of cooperation in some conditions	The states concerned are encouraged to form regional or subregional bodies instead to address (among others) concerns of exploitation and conservation

be advised that the final goal of the cooperation here is to strike a balance between the need to source fish sustainably and to preserve the delicate balance of the South China Sea maritime environment. Furthermore, it has to be remembered that the duty to cooperate is central to the regime governing the utilisation of marine resources in spaces beyond national jurisdiction. The limits of rights and duties can be compared in the following table 7.2:

Conclusion

This article sets out the argument to establish a structured fishery cooperation among the South China Sea littoral states as a way to diffuse tension and build trust between the claimant countries. Noting that the South China Sea area serves as a vital lifeline to millions of people through its abundant living resources, it is imperative that this critical living resource in the form of fish and other marine products is mapped, conserved and sustainably exploited to ensure the livelihood of future generations. However, it should also be noted that ongoing disputes that result in heightened sensitivities over the area have to be taken into account and to shape future cooperations in ways that could bridge the differences between these claimant states. Hence, a three-staged approach to fishery cooperation is offered to allow for an inclusive, and constructive joint collaboration to ensure a sustainable level of living resources in the South China Sea area.

First, understanding that there is currently a trust deficit present between the South China Sea claimant states. This lack of trust may erode even the most basic of cooperation, which allows littoral states to take matters into their own hands, and find no benefits in sharing valuable information between other littoral states. This, coupled with increasing securitisation of perceived sovereign violations, has caused fishery to be categorised as an issue of national security. Allowing joint fishery cooperation would require a minimum level of trust and transparency between these states to allow for the discussion of joint fishing cooperation and how to fairly share the benefit between the relevant stakeholders.

Second, joint maritime research and surveillance. Once an adequate level of trust is achieved between the littoral states, a collaborative maritime research and surveillance should be conducted to assess the level of fish stocks and other living resources within the South China Sea area. This would allow states to calculate a maximum sustainable yield of catches, which would be later followed by a quota of total allowable catches. This will ensure that the number of fish stock is kept at a sustainable level to allow them to replenish back to their habitat. In doing so, states must remember their duty to give due regard to the duty to preserve and protect the environment and where relevant, the needs of the local population.

Third, management of living resources. Once the adequate level of information on fish stocks and quota of catch is established, South China Sea littoral countries could begin to enact joint management of living resources through the creation of a fisheries management control or organisation within the area of the South China Sea. Pertaining to the existing international regulations, states must strive to fulfil their duty to cooperate to form regional bodies that could conserve the level of resources within the area. This stage could be deemed to most sensitive level of cooperation and could only be pursued once an adequate level of cooperation in previous stages has been duly achieved.

The purpose of this three-stage approach is to induce low-hanging cooperation that is present for the littoral states. A successful implementation of a fishery cooperation would not only lead to an increase in confidence between the claimant states, but would also ensure the economic viability of the coastal communities that relies on the South China Sea for their day-to-day activities. It would also ensure a sustainable level of marine habitat that provides positive benefits to the maritime domain in the South China Sea, as well as to those surrounding it.

Chapter 8
Chips on the Deck: US-China Rivalry and Reorganizing the Supply Chains of Semiconductors

Yongwook Ryu

Introduction

The US-China strategic rivalry is arguably the most important structural change in contemporary international affairs affecting all aspects of interstate relations in the region and beyond. As the focus of this rivalry has shifted from a trade war during the Trump administration to tech competition under Biden, the semiconductor sector has come to dominate much of policy attention and debate. Thinner than a hair and smaller than a coin, semiconductors, also known as integrated circuits (hereafter chips), go into almost everything that empowers our lives. They are necessary for all IT products and operations as well as the modern-day digital economy, and are at the core of tech superiority and hegemony. This chapter examines the geopolitics of semiconductors between the US and China, and analyzes its impact on the supply chains. In particular, it argues that the US is purporting to force China to decouple from the chips supply chains by utilizing its market dominance in the front segment of chip production (softwares, EDAs, IPs, etc.) as well as its extensive network of tech capable allies and partners. The US effort manifests in its own industrial policy such as the Chips Act and the American Foundaries Act and its diplomatic effort to partner up with its allies such as Japan, South Korea, Taiwan, and European countries, to curtail China's advancement in the chip sector, especially advanced chips. The paper concludes with a discussion on the implications for the US chip pressure on China for the US-China strategic rivalry.

Y. Ryu (✉)
Lee Kuan Yew School of Public Policy, National University of Singapore, Singapore, Singapore
e-mail: sppyry@nus.edu.sg

N. Hung Son and N. Thi Lan Anh (eds.), *The South China Sea: The Geo-political Epicenter of the Indo-Pacific?*, https://doi.org/10.1007/978-981-97-8209-3_8

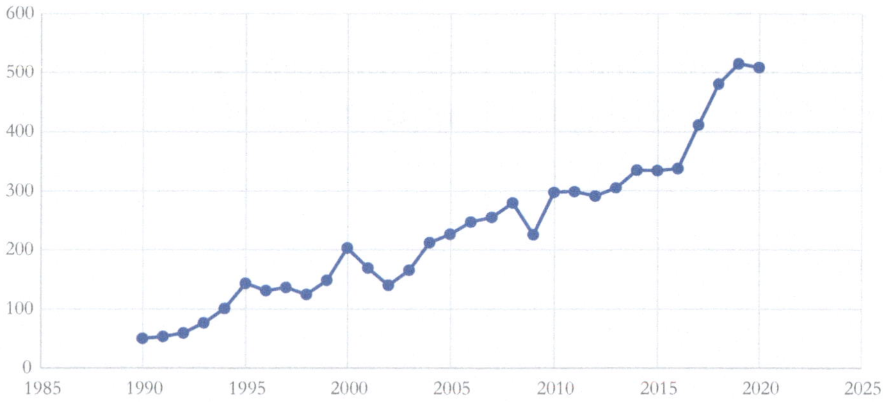

Fig. 8.1 Global chip sales (US$, billion) (*Source* Semiconductor industry association at https://www.semiconductors.org/)

The Global Supply Chains of Semiconductors

As shown in Fig. 8.1 the chip sector has steadily grown over the years surpassing the 500 billion mark in global sales for the first time in 2019,[1] and is set to grow by more than 10% per annum in the next 3 years. While it is a robust growth, however, the chip industry still constitutes a minuscule fraction of global trade, which is estimated to be approximately 20 trillion dollars (as of 2019).

Despite occupying such a tiny fraction of global trade, chips are arguably the most important and fundamental among all IT products, for they are necessary components for almost everything that enables our modern-day life and for the operation of more advanced technologies such as 5G/6G, AI, quantum computing, etc. Hence chip dominance will ensure tech superiority, which will in turn shape the contest for global power and hegemony.[2] If a country loses its competitiveness in the chip sector, it will not be able to compete effectively due to tech lag, and this effectively eliminates any possibility of becoming a global hegemon. It is no wonder, then, why the two most powerful states, the US and China, that increasingly perceive each other as their number one enemy, aim to secure a stable supply of chips while making sure that the other does not end up gaining chip dominance.

The semiconductor industry today has one of the most complex and highly integrated supply chains with different tasks being performed by different actors in

---

[1] SIA (Semiconductor Industry Association), *2020 Factbook; 2019 Factbook; 2018 Factbook; 2017 Factbook; 2016 Factbook; 2015 Factbook; 2014 Factbook*, retrieved from http://go.semiconductors.org/ on Oct 1, 2021.

[2] Chris Miller, *Chip War: The Fight for the World's Most Critical Technology* (2002, New York, Simon & Schuster Ltd).

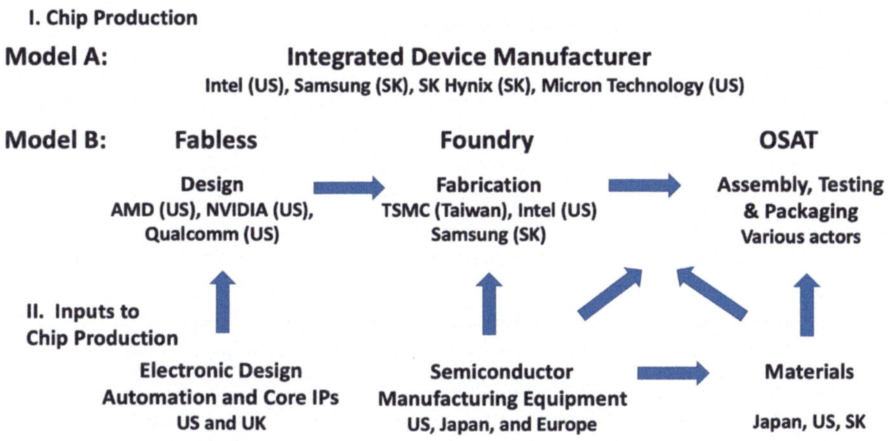

Fig. 8.2 The supply chain of chip production (*Source* modified from CSET issue brief (January 2021) by Khan, Mann and Peterson)

different locales. Figure 8.2 below shows the supply chains and leading companies/countries in each segment.[3]

Chip production involves three main stages of designing, manufacturing, and assembly, testing, and packaging. Despite China's fast rise in tech sectors, China's standing in the chip sector is nowhere near a position to challenge the US. Chinese chip manufacturing firms such as SMIC are generally assessed to be roughly 5 years behind TSMC and Samsung in terms of capacity and tech advancement. Similarly, China does not capture a meaningful market share in the equipment, IPs/softwares, and design. Her best standing is in the OSAT segment where China captures roughly 20% of the market, but this segment can be easily replaced.

Until the advent of US-China strategic rivalry in the late 2010s, the US was content to include China as part of the global chip supply chain, to take advantage of China's cheap and relatively skilled labor, and this highly integrated system worked very efficiently by exploiting the comparative advantages of different firms and locales. However, the situation started to change, as both the US and China began to perceive each other as their arch-enemy. Chips have increasingly become mired with national security issues, and as a result doing business as usual suddenly carried security risks.

[3] Saif Khan, Alexander Mann, and Dahlia Peterson. 2021. "The Semiconductor Supply Chain: Assessing National Competitiveness" CSET Issue Brief Jan 2021. Url at https://cset.georgetown.edu/publication/the-semiconductor-supply-chain/.

The Geopolitics of Semiconductors

The US has long been concerned with its tech superiority over other nations, including chip sector, and would like to strengthen its dominance in this critical technology. The Biden administration has sought to reorganize the chip supply chains by strengthening its relationship with European and Asian allies on the one hand and by either removing China from the supply chain or significantly reducing China's place in global chip production on the other hand, as a way to curtail China's tech rise and challenge.

There are two main goals in the US semiconductor policy. First, it seeks to establish a secure supply chain at home mainly by increasing its manufacturing capacity. Following the development of global chip supply chains, US chip firms have increasingly outsourced manufacturing to foreign firms such as TSMC and Samsung, while focusing on chip design that commands most value in the supply chain. Such specialization has resulted in the declining US manufacturing capacity. According to the Semiconductor Industry Association, the US manufacturing capacity stood at 37% of global capacity in 1990, but decreased to a mere 13% in 2010, and is expected to further decline to 10% by 2030. In the same period, China's capacity is expected to increase from 0% in 1990 to 24% by 2030.[4] The Chips for America Act in 2020 aim to establish a stable and steady supply chain in the US by giving tax incentives to chip firms if they invest in manufacturing factories or chip equipment in the US. In addition, the American Foundries Act of 2020 links the chip sector with national security, and enables the Department of Defense to have an input in capex investment and R&D through the "Buy American" requirement to use domestic outsourcing whenever possible.

Second, the US aims to reorganize the supply chain by removing China from the global supply chains of advanced chips, including AI chips, or reducing her place in chip production to the extent that China will not be in a position to challenge US tech superiority. Even though China is currently nowhere near a position to challenge US hegemony in the chip industry, the US government is deeply concerned with the rate of development of the Chinese chip industry and any potential adverse security implications. China's continued development in the chip industry, coupled with its advancement in other tech areas such as 5G/6G, AI and quantum computing, could pose a significant security threat and challenge to US hegemony in the future, and hence the Biden administration seeks to weaken China's capabilities by curtailing China's role and participation in the supply chains of chip production.

In 2012 the US House of Representatives initiated an investigation on whether Huawei had put backdoors into its equipment, and recommended that no government or contractor systems include Huawei systems. In 2015, the US government blocked a potential M&A deal by Tsinghua Unigroup to acquire Micron Technology for US$23 billion. In 2019 the US Department of Commerce added Huawei to its

---

[4] SIA, 2020, "Government Incentives and US Competitiveness in Semiconductor Manufacturing", Policy Reports. Url at https://www.semiconductors.org/resources/?fwp_resource_types=policy-reports.

entity list, effectively limiting the sale or transfer of American technology to the company and prohibiting the sale of products that use such American technology to Huawei, thereby affecting TSMC's chip sale to Huawei. As a result, TSMC cannot manufacture chips below 14 nm for Huawei. In addition, ASML is prohibited from selling its EUV lithography equipment to any Chinese company, and Chinese chip companies such as HiSilicon and SMIC are also on the US entity list and are subject to US sanctions.

The US restrictions on chips export to China have only expanded since the restrictive measures began. Initially targeting only logic chips, the US government later included memory (NAND and DRAM) chips as part of its restrictions. From then on, the export control has also expanded the range of restricted chips from advanced chips to medium chips as part of its target. For example, in February 2023, DRAM and NAND chips below 13 nm or above 200-layer were to come under export control, but the policy changed to bring chips under 18 nm or above 128-layer under export control within a month.[5]

The other side of the US effort to reorganize the supply chain is to strengthen its cooperation with European and Asian partners. Friendshoring suggests the US partnership with its close allies—South Korea, Taiwan, Japan, the UK, the Netherlands, and Germany.[6] In particular, both Korean and Taiwanese chip manufacturers—Samsung and TSMC—have committed the construction of fabs in Texas and Arizona, respectively, at the request of the Biden administration, which will significantly boost US manufacturing capex in two or three years. At the same time, the US and EU have set up the Trade and Technology Council (TTC) to promote bilateral cooperation on a range of areas, including securing a stable chip supply chain.[7]

China's Response

After what was largely an unsuccessful attempt at indigenous development until the mid-2010s, that aimed to achieve chip advancement through its own investment and innovation backed by government financial support, China switched its model of advancing the chip industry to a mix of indigenous growth and aggressive outbound M&A. The new policy resulted in a considerable increase in the number and volume of M&A deals in China. M&A agreements increased dramatically in 2014, reaching

[5] Gregory Allen. "The Post-October 7 World", 28 September, 2023. url at https://www.csis.org/analysis/post-october-7-world.

[6] Peter Coy, "'Onshoring' is So Last Year. The New Lingo is 'Friend-Shoring" Bloomberg Businessweek, 24 Jan 2021. Url at https://www.bloomberg.com/news/articles/2021-06-24/-onshoring-is-so-last-year-the-new-lingo-is-friend-shoring.

[7] For a different and pessimistic assessment of US effort to set up an entire chip supply chain in the US, see "TSMC founder chides US plan for full chip supply chain onshore" Nikkei Asia, 27 Oct 2021. Url at https://asia.nikkei.com/Business/Tech/Semiconductors/TSMC-founder-chides-U.S.-plan-for-full-chip-supply-chain-onshore.

51 billion yuan, compared to 26 billion yuan in 2012.[8] Prominent examples include Changdian's acquisition of STATS ChipPAC in 2014, Tianshui Huatian's acquisition of FlipChip International (US) in 2015, and Nantong Fujitsu's joint venture agreement with AMD in 2015.[9]

Since 2014, there has been a major shift in China's semiconductor industry policy. In June 2014, the Chinese Government released *Guidelines to Promote National Integrated Circuit Industry*.[10] This is a systematic outline aimed at maximizing the chip industry's critical strategic opportunity and promoting its development. The Chinese government sought to promote integrated development of design, manufacturing, packaging, and testing as well as equipment and materials. The creation of a National Industrial Investment Fund (the so-called "The Big Fund") was meant to enhance financial and tax support and increase talent training and acquisition.

One year later, the Chinese State Council issued the now widely known *Made in China 2025*,[11] and issued a *Roadmap for Technological Innovation in Key Areas of Made in China 2025*. The Chinese government has set the goal for the chip industry to be within one generation away from the advanced level by 2020, and to be at the world's advanced level by 2030.[12] In the 13th Five-Year Plan (2016–2020), the Chinese government has restated its emphasis on the chip sector and put dynamic random access memory (DRAM) as a key national project as well.[13] All this clearly demonstrates that Beijing is fully cognizant of the critical importance of chips—what it calls a "choke point technology" (*qiabozi jishu*).

The chip sector is identified as one of ten strategic industries in *Made in China 2025*, and the Chinese government set up the Big Fund of $20 billion state-backed financing scheme to promote R&D and increase manufacturing capacity. In 2019, the second round of state funding totaled more than $35 billion. Xi Jinping also announced $100 ~ 150 billion investment in the semiconductor industry. The goal is to end the country's dependence on foreign suppliers, to bring China's chip self-sufficiency to about 70%, and to achieve technological parity with the world's leading firms in design, fabrication, and packaging by 2030.

---

[8] Fu Shengbin, When the Stars Shine: The Path of M&A for Semiconductor Industry, *NewFortune*, 2020 Vol.6, 1.

[9] There were some unsuccessful acquisition attempts as well. For example, Tsinghua Unigroup almost acquired 15% of Western Digital (US) in 2015, but gave up on the deal after the US authorities announced that it would investigate into the deal. Tsinghua Unigroup sought to acquire Micron Technology (US) in 2015, but the deal was blocked by the US government.

[10] Cyberspace Administration of China, Ministry of Industry and Information Technology officially announced the *Guidelines to Promote National Integrated Circuit Industry*, retrieved from http://www.cac.gov.cn/2014-06/26/c_1111325916.htm on Oct 5, 2021.

[11] Chinese State Council, *On the Issuance of Made in China 2025*, retrieved from http://www.gov.cn/zhengce/content/2015-05/19/content_9784.htm on Oct 5, 2021.

[12] National Manufacturing Strategy Advisory Committee, *Roadmap for Technological Innovation in Key Areas of Made in China 2025 (2017 Edition) Conference Held in Beijing*, retrieved from http://www.cm2025.org/show-15-166-1.html on Oct 7, 2021.

[13] Chinese State Council, *The Outline of the 13th Five-Year Plan*, retrieved from http://www.gov.cn/xinwen/2016-03/17/content_5054992.htm on Oct 5, 2021.

However, despite its declared ambitions and extensive state funding, China faces several major weaknesses in its effort to attain sufficient self-sufficiency and to bring its national competitiveness to the level comparable to the US. First, except for manufacturing and back-end processes (assembly, packaging, and testing), where Chinese firms have some global standing, China's competitiveness generally lags far behind the US and other countries. Its critical weakness is in the inputs side. China lacks EDA and core IPs, and hence must rely on the US or UK for softwares. China lacks equipment production capacity, and hence must import foreign equipment. In particular, for the production of advanced chips that are below 7 nm, it needs to purchase ASML's EUV equipment, but currently the ASML is under moratorium and therefore cannot sell EUV equipment to any Chinese firms. While it is not impossible to manufacture advanced chips at 7 nm or below using DUV equipment, it is highly doubtful if the yield rate can be high to make production commercially viable. Consequently, China's chip fabrication capabilities today remain at the 14 nm-level and above, and it is here China's competitiveness exists vis-à-vis Taiwan and Samsung.

In addition, China's growth in the chip sector came through its aggressive acquisition of foreign companies rather than from its own endogenous innovations. Hence it is questionable if Chinese firms have the depth of knowledge and experience to advance toward chip self-sufficiency based on its own innovation and R&D especially in the face of growing US pressure and interference. This is critical for the Chinese government's effort to satisfy its growing appetite for chips. China's chip consumption has been a key aspect of chip sales in the Asia–Pacific, which grew from $39.8 billion in 2001 to $300 billion in 2023. Figure 8.3 below shows chip sales by region from 2015 to 2023.

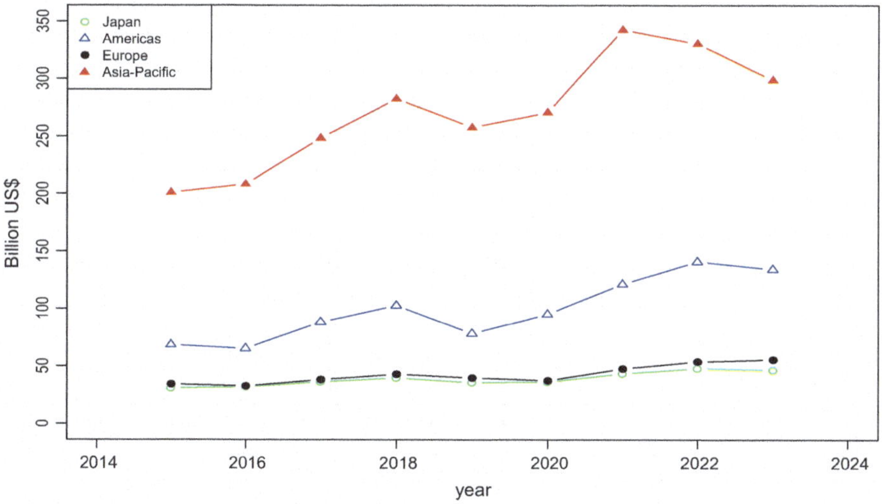

Fig. 8.3 Chip sales by region (*Source* The author's own graph. The data are from world semiconductor trade statistics)

China's share of the Asia–Pacific regional consumption ranges from 50 to 60%. For instance, in 2021, China occupied 56% of the Asia–Pacific chip consumption, excluding Japan. It is important to note that much of the chip demand emanating from China is not for China's own indigenous consumption but for the consumption of global firms doing final manufacturing in China. Hence, as global production lines shift out of China for both economic and political reasons, China's chip demand will necessarily decline. Simply stated, the current level of China's indigenous chip production is insufficient to meet its own internal demand.

Furthermore, Beijing faces a lack of trust from other countries, a key element to create and sustain steady and stable supply chains involving multiple actors. Hence, if other players from Europe and Asia ended up siding with the US in the latter's effort to reorganize the supply chains, China's competitiveness would dramatically decrease, as Beijing would effectively have to do everything on its own. That is a very tall task that even the US would struggle to accomplish.

However, Beijing is unlikely to give up its fight to gain competitiveness in the chip sector, as it knows fully well that losing the chip sector could derail its effort to achieve a "modernized strong country" (*xiandaihua de qiangguo*) and would be tantamount to giving up its quest for global hegemony. Indeed there is more than chip self-sufficiency at stake. Its political ambitions, both domestic and foreign, hinge on whether or not Beijing can successfully achieve self-sufficiency and compete with the US in the global chip sector and, by extension, in advanced technologies at large.

Implications of US-China Rivalry for the Chip Supply Chains

The competition for chip dominance between the US and China will likely intensify. As the ability to either produce on your own or secure a stable supply of chips will influence the capacity of nations in economic, industrial, and military advancement, the contest for chip dominance will intensify accordingly. Simply stated, it is tantamount to a contest for global tech superiority and hegemony. All this is an omen for greater conflict over chips between the US and China in the near future. There are three major implications of this chip contest.

First, chip competition will increasingly take on similar dynamics as an arms race, as both powers are concerned about relative gains, thereby turning the dynamics into a zero-sun game. Both powers will invest more in the sector to advance their own capabilities and take measures to restrict the other's development in the chip sector. Here, the US has a clear advantage over China. Unlike China, the US has a network of allies and partners that command strengths in different segments of global chip production. This will reduce the costs of reorganizing the supply chains for the US and permit the US to better achieve the economies of scale through its tech network. On the other hand, there will be more costs for China, as it is increasingly isolated from the global supply chains. China can seek to drive a wedge between the US and its allies and partners, and at the same time promote self-sufficiency as much as it can. In the process, much of its investment will be wasted and inefficiencies be created, all of which will drain Chinese resources.

Second, despite the view that in the long run the US chip pressure on China will ensure the competitiveness of the US and its allies and partners, there will be significant short-term costs for everyone during the adjustment period. And the management of this painful transition from the current supply chains to the new supply chains that exclude or limit China's role, will be the key to the success of the US effort. For various national governments that join the US effort of reorganizing the global supply chains of chip production, how they balance the interests of national security and the commercial interests of firms is going to be critical, as those two sets of interests do not necessarily align. Hence, countries such as Japan, South Korea, Taiwan, and European countries must make greater efforts to align the interests of firms with those of the national government.

And lastly, despite the geopolitics of semiconductors, who gets to dominate the chip sector—and by implication global hegemony—depends on who is able to innovate and increase productivity. It is a contest not only for capability but also for efficiency and productivity. Hence, national governments must continue with R&D in the chip sector in close policy consultation and coordination with various firms. As Intel has discovered, the dominant position it enjoyed once could quickly disappear within a short span of time, and playing the catch-up game can be exceedingly difficult and costly. Therefore, nations must take on a long-term perspective in formulating its strategy and approach to the chip industry for economic and national security concerns, socio-economic development, and digital transformation toward a tech-based advanced economy.

Appendix

See Figs. 8.1, 8.2, 8.3.

Chapter 9
ASEAN: Important Broker for Marine Scientific Research Cooperation in the South China Sea

Vu Hai Dang

Introduction

The South China Sea is well-known in the world media for being a hotspot for territorial and maritime disputes between China, Philippines, Brunei, Malaysia, Indonesia, Vietnam and Taiwan.[1] However, the regional sea is also a global centre for biodiversity, possessing 12% of the world's mangrove forest, 34% of the world's coral reef and about 8600 species of plants and animals.[2] These characteristics call for greater marine scientific research to be undertaken to understand its marine environment and resources. The Association of Southeast Asian Nations (ASEAN), a regional body established in 1967 to promote stability and prosperity in Southeast Asia,[3] has been actively trying to manage the South China Sea disputes. The Association has done so in particular through the promotion of cooperative activities between claimants, including both ASEAN Member States and China. At the same time, ASEAN has also been a strong promoter of cooperation in science and technology, including in marine science and technology in the region and beyond.

The inspiration for ASEAN cooperation in science and technology was mentioned in the very founding instrument of ASEAN. The ASEAN Declaration, 1967 stipulates one of the aim and purpose of ASEAN is to "provide assistance to each other in the form of training and research facilities in the educational, professional, technical

[1] For details of the South China Sea disputes, see Raul Pedrozo, China versus Vietnam: An Analysis of the Competing Claims in the South China Sea (August 2014) CNA Occasional Paper and Ashley Roach, Malaysia and Brunei: An Analysis of their Claims in the South China Sea (August 2014) CNA Occasional Paper.

[2] Vu Hai Dang, "Biodiversity and Conservation", in Routledge Handbook of the South China Sea, ed. Keyuan Zou (London: Routledge, 2021): 278–294 at 278.

[3] About ASEAN, https://asean.org/about-asean, November 17, 2024.

V. H. Dang (✉)
Diplomatic Academy of Vietnam, Hanoi, Vietnam
e-mail: vuhaidang@dav.edu.vn

N. Hung Son and N. Thi Lan Anh (eds.), *The South China Sea: The Geo-political Epicenter of the Indo-Pacific?*, https://doi.org/10.1007/978-981-97-8209-3_9

and administrative spheres".[4] Recognizing that science and technology are necessary and indispensable tools towards achieving ASEAN's mission, an Ad hoc Committee on Science and Technology was established and met for the first time on 27–29 April 1970. The said meeting agreed that ASEAN cooperation in science and technology should be guided by the objectives of initiating and intensifying regional cooperation in scientific and technological activities; generating and promoting development of scientific and technological expertise and manpower in the ASEAN region; facilitating and accelerating the transfer of scientific developments and technologies among ASEAN countries and from the more advanced industrialised countries to the ASEAN region; providing support and assistance in the application of the results of research and development, and in the more effective use of natural resources in the ASEAN region; and providing support towards the implementation of present and future ASEAN programmes.[5]

This Chapter suggests that ASEAN could use its existing cooperative mechanisms and relations with its Dialogue Partners to improve the marine scientific research cooperation in the South China Sea. Such an endeavour not only contributes to a better understanding of the natural characteristics of the body of waters, and hence facilitating to the resolution of its current environmental challenges, but can also help decrease tension and build trust between South China Sea claimants.

It first reviews the ASEAN Plans of Action on Science and Technology, ASEAN and ASEAN plus mechanisms to promote cooperation in science and technology, then focusing on current ASEAN priorities in marine scientific research. Finally, the Chapter provides concrete suggestions on how ASEAN could help improve marine scientific research cooperation in the South China Sea.

ASEAN Plans of Action on Science and Technology

The cooperation in science and technology in ASEAN is implemented through ASEAN Plan of Action on Science and Technology. So far, five of such plans have been adopted:

The first ASEAN Plan of Action on Science and Technology was adopted in 1985 and then updated in 1989. The objective of the Plan of Action was to strengthen and enhance the capability of ASEAN in science and technology so that it can promote economic development and help achieve a high quality of life for the peoples of ASEAN.[6] Strategic plans and actions to achieve this objective include intensifying cooperation in science and technology; widening involvement and increasing

---

[4] The ASEAN Declaration (Bangkok Declaration), Bangkok, Thailand, 8 August 1967, s4.

[5] ASEAN Plan of Action on Science, Technology and Innovation 2016-2025, adopted at the 16th AMMST Joint Press Release, Vientiane, Lao PDR, 6 November 2015, s2.

[6] 4th Meeting of the ASEAN Ministers for Science and Technology Joint Press Release, Manila, Philippines, 30–31 January 1989.

participation and cooperation among the scientists and researchers of member countries; maintaining a high level of scientific and technological expertise and, in the process, develop an intelligent workforce in a rapidly changing and highly competitive world; promoting technology transfer and the commercialization of research results; ensuring human resources development for promoting scientific, technological and economic development; and providing an overall awareness in ASEAN on the strategic role that science and technology plays in economic development.[7]

The 2nd Plan of Action on Science and Technology was adopted in 1994. It contains five objectives and six strategies. The five objectives are to achieve:

- A high level of intra-ASEAN cooperation in science and technology that is synergistic and self-sustaining and having the active participation of the private sector;
- A network of science and technology infrastructure and programmes for public and private sector human resource development;
- An active economically beneficial institution-industry technology transfer;
- An enhanced state of public awareness of the importance of science and technology to ASEAN's economic development; and
- An expanded science and technology cooperation with the international community.
- The six strategies are: supporting regional science and technology programmes that are economically and socially beneficial to ASEAN; providing close coordination and management of science and technology activities; developing science and technology human resources; information networking of centres of excellence; promoting institution-industry technology transfer; and promoting S&T awareness.[8]

ASEAN Plan of Action on Science and Technology 2001–2004 (extended to 2006): The ASEAN Plan of Action on Science and Technology 2001–2004 was adopted in Brunei in 2001.[9] The objectives to be achieved under the Plan of Action include:

- An intensified cooperation on science and technology development and R&D between the public and private sector, that has a strong thematic focus, and is interdisciplinary and cross-sectoral;
- An expanded scope of regional programmes leveraging on national experiences and resources and ASEAN-Help-ASEAN initiatives that will enable the newer ASEAN Members to move up the learning curve and become economically competitive;
- A highly mobile, intelligent and creative S&T Community that thrives on knowledge creation and application;

---

[7] 4th Meeting of the ASEAN Ministers for Science and Technology Joint Press Release.

[8] 6th AMMST Joint Press Release, Manila, Philippines, 2–3 February 1994, para. 10.

[9] 9th AMMST Joint Press Release, Bandar Seri Begawan, Brunei, 17–18 September 2001, Darussalam.

- A system of rewards and incentives to encourage innovation and technology commercialisation and attract talent to a lifelong career in science and technology;
- A means of seeding and sustaining science and technology programmes through innovative ways of investing in S&T endeavours and generating revenue; and
- An enhanced system of management of the future enterprise that is innovative, bold and entrepreneurial.[10]

In order to achieve these objectives, the following thrust for actions were provided:

- Networking of science and technology centres of excellence and programmes so as to optimise resources and achieve maximum results;
- Developing policy for programme selection, design and management in a new science and technology enterprise, taking into consideration sectoral needs and the needs of newer member states;
- Intensifying research and development collaboration in strategic and enabling technologies and promoting technology commercialisation;
- Developing human resources to meet the needs of e-ASEAN, newer members and the knowledge economy;
- Developing science and technology infrastructure and content for e-enabling research, human resource development, technology foresighting and intelligence gathering, technology commercialisation and venture development;
- Generating revenue through innovative management systems and enterprise formation;
- Engaging dialogue partners in a focused manner in major programme areas and flagship projects; and
- Managing the science and technology enterprise in the new millennium.[11]

The ASEAN Plan of Action on Science and Technology 2007–2011 (extended to 2015) was adopted in 2006.[12] The objectives to be achieved under APAST 2007–2011 include to:

- To foster science and technology as a key factor in sustaining economic growth,
- enhancing community well-being and promoting integration in ASEAN through human resource, research and technology development and provision of technical services to
- meet the needs of economic integration;
- To apply science and technology tools and methodologies to enhance economic and industrial planning;
- To formulate a systematic approach in the implementation of the ASEAN-Help-ASEAN programmes to address the science and technology needs and strengthen the science and technology infrastructure of less developed Member countries;
- To use science and technology as a major tool for ASEAN to move forward in a unified and cohesive manner; and

[10] ASEAN Plan of Action on Science, Technology and Innovation 2016–2025, 8.

[11] ASEAN Plan of Action on Science, Technology and Innovation 2016–2025, 15.

[12] 4th IAMMST Joint Press Release, Kuantan, Malaysia, 29 August 2006.

- To build on the accomplishments of ASEAN Plan of Action on Science and Technology 2001–2004 extended until 2006.[13]
- In order to achieve these objectives, the following thrust for actions was provided: intensifying research and development collaboration and promoting technology commercialisation; developing science and technology human resources; networking of science and technology centres of excellence and programmes; strengthening science and technology infrastructure and support systems; and forging closer cooperation with dialogue partners and other relevant organisations on regional projects.[14]

The ASEAN Plan of Action on Science, Technology and Innovation 2016–2025 was adopted in 2015.[15] The goals set by ASEAN Plan of Action on Science, Technology and Innovation 2016–2025 are:

- ASEAN Science, Technology and Innovation addressing the grand challenges of the new millennium;
- Economically integrated ASEAN involving active collaboration between the public & private sectors especially SMEs and enhanced mobility of talents;
- Deep awareness of Science, Technology and Innovation & the beneficial impacts of Science, Technology and Innovation on the bottom of the pyramid;
- An innovation-driven economy with a deep Science, Technology and Innovation enculturation and a system of seeding and sustaining Science, Technology and Innovation by leveraging Information and Communication Technology and the resources of our talented young, women and private sectors;
- Active research and development collaboration, technology commercialisation and entrepreneurship and network of centres of excellence; and
- An enhanced Science, Technology and Innovation management system in the new AEC so as to support ASEAN innovation reaching global markets and that promotes innovation, integration and narrowing of development gaps across ASEAN Member States.[16]

To achieve these objectives, the following thrusts of actions are provided:

- Strengthening strategic collaboration among academia, research institutions, networks of centres of excellence and the private sector to create an effective ecosystem for capability development, technology transfer and commercialisation;
- Enhancing the mobility of scientists and researchers, people-to-people connectivity and strengthen engagement of women and youth in Science, Technology and Innovation;

[13] ASEAN Plan of Action on Science, Technology and Innovation 2016–2025, 8.

[14] ASEAN Plan of Action on Science, Technology and Innovation 2016–2025, 15.

[15] ASEAN Plan of Action on Science, Technology and Innovation 2016–2025, adopted at the 16th AMMST Joint Press Release, Vientiane, Lao PDR, 6 November 2015.

[16] ASEAN Plan of Action on Science, Technology and Innovation 2016–2025, adopted at the 16th AMMST Joint Press Release, Vientiane, Lao PDR, 6 November 2015, 41.

- Establishing innovative system and smart partnership with dialogue and other partners to nurture science, technology and innovation enterprises to support Micro, Small and Medium Enterprises, nurture knowledge creation and science, technology and innovation applications to raise competitiveness; and
- Raising public awareness and strengthen science, technology and innovation enculturation to enhance ASEAN science and technology cooperation.[17]

ASEAN and ASEAN Plus Mechanisms to Promote Cooperation in Science and Technology

ASEAN cooperation in science and technology has become a sectoral under the ASEAN Socio-Cultural Community.[18] As such ASEAN mechanisms established to promote cooperation in science and technology include: the ASEAN Ministerial Meeting on Science and Technology, ASEAN Committee on Science and Technology, ASEAN Sub-Committee on Marine Science and Technology and ASEAN Science Fund.

- ***ASEAN Ministerial Meeting on Science, Technology and Innovation***: The ASEAN Ministerial Meeting on Science and Technology (AMMSTI) met the first time in Thailand, 1980.[19] It sets the policies for ASEAN cooperation in science and technology.[20]
- ***ASEAN Committee on Science, Technology and Innovation***: The Ad hoc Committee on Science and Technology established in 1971 was later renamed ASEAN Permanent Committee on Science, Technology, then ASEAN Committee on Science and Technology and ASEAN Committee on Science, Technology and Innovation (COSTI). COSTI is responsible for setting directions, coordinating activities of its subsidiary bodies, creating public awareness of regional S&T activities and their contribution to economic development and reviewing overall progress of collaboration, including the progress of its relations with the ASEAN's Dialogue Partners as well as other external collaborators.[21]

Individual Sub-Committees were established to oversee the management, coordination, evaluation and implementation of regional programmes and projects. The Sub-Committees are expected to assess the effectiveness and impact of their projects

---

[17] ASEAN Plan of Action on Science, Technology and Innovation 2016–2025, adopted at the 16th AMMST Joint Press Release, Vientiane, Lao PDR, 6 November 2015, 41

[18] The ASEAN Socio-Cultural Community is one of three ASEAN Communities (the two others being ASEAN Political-Security Community and ASEAN Economic Community) which focus on improving the life of ASEAN citizens, see "ASEAN Socio-Cultural Community", ASEAN, https://asean.org/our-communities/asean-socio-cultural-community/, September 26, 2022.

[19] First Meeting of the ASEAN Ministers of Science and Technology Joint Press Release, Pattaya, Thailand, 27–28 October 1980.

[20] ASEAN Plan of Action on Science, Technology and Innovation 2016–2025, 32.

[21] ASEAN Plan of Action on Science, Technology and Innovation 2016–2025, 32.

in strengthening the regional Science and Technology capabilities. Advisory bodies were also set up to make policy recommendations to COSTI on matters related to the implementation of the ASEAN Plan of Action on Science and Technology as well as the management of the ASEAN Science Fund. Thus, the subsidiary bodies of COSTI include the following:

- Sub-Committee on Biotechnology;
- Sub-Committee on Food Science and Technology;
- Sub-Committee on S&T Infrastructure and Resources Development;
- Sub-Committee on Meteorology and Geophysics;
- Sub-Committee on Microelectronics and Information Technology;
- Sub-Committee on Marine Science and Technology;
- Sub-Committee on Materials Science and Technology;
- Sub-Committee on Sustainable Energy Research;
- Sub-Committee on Space Technology and Applications;
- Advisory Body of the ASEAN Science Fund; and
- Advisory Body on the ASEAN Plan of Action on Science and Technology.

Among those, the Sub-Committee on Marine Science and Technology's purpose is to promote sustainable development of marine living and non-living resources while increasing the potential of these resources to meet the requirements of ASEAN. It also seeks to increase the number of qualified personnel in marine science and technology.[22]

- ***The ASEAN Science Fund***: The ASEAN Science Fund (ASF) was adopted by the 4th AMMSTI in 1989 for the purpose of implementing research and development programmes as may be identified by ASEAN COSTI. At the time it was named ASEAN Trust Fund for Science and Technology. The initial voluntary contribution to the Fund was USD 50.000 for each ASEAN Member State.[23]

At the ASEAN plus level, ASEAN has established cooperative mechanisms with China, Japan, Republic of Korea, ASEAN plus Three, India, EU, Russia, the United States and the United Kingdom. These are:

- ***ASEAN-China Joint Science and Technology Committee***: The ASEAN–China Joint Science and Technology Committee was established in 2012 to advance ASEAN–China cooperation in the area of science and technology. Committee is composed of senior officials representing the State Science and Technology Commission of China and the ASEAN's COST. The Committee meets normally every two years, alternately in China and ASEAN. The meetings shall be co-chaired by China and ASEAN. The Committee plan, approve, coordinate,

[22] ASEAN Plan of Action on Science, Technology and Innovation 2016–2025, 30.

[23] 4th Meeting of the ASEAN Ministers for Science and Technology Joint Press Release, Manila, Philippines, 30–31 January 1989, 3.

monitor and evaluate joint cooperative programmes and activities in science and technology.[24].

- ***ASEAN-Japan Cooperation Committee on Science and Technology***: The ASEAN-Japan Cooperation Committee on Science and Technology was established in 2009 to promote cooperation in science and technology between ASEAN and Japan. The Committee has so far met once per year.[25]
- ***ASEAN-Republic of Korea Joint Science and Technology Committee***: The ASEAN-Republic of Korea Joint Science and Technology Committee was established in 2011 to advance cooperation in science and technology between ASEAN and South Korea. So far, it has met twice per year.[26] At its 4th meeting, a centre for science and technology partnership to promote exchanges and policy sharing programme between ASEAN and South Korea was established.[27]
- ***ASEAN Committee on Science and Technology Plus Three***: The ASEAN Committee on Science and Technology Plus Three (COST + 3) was established in 2006[28] to discuss recent developments on cooperation in science, technology and innovation as well as note updates on science, technology and innovation policies of the Plus Three countries (China, Japan and South Korea). Regular activities under COST + 3 include the APT Junior Science Odyssey, ASEAN + 3 Centre for the Gifted in Science Board of Directors Meeting and ASEAN + 3 Teachers' Workshop and Students' Camp for the Gifted in Science.[29]
- ***ASEAN-EU Dialogue on Science and Technology***: The ASEAN-EU Dialogue on Science and Technology was established by the ASEAN-EU Ministerial Informal Meeting on Science and Technology in 2008. This is a Senior Official level mechanism between ASEAN COST and the European Commission that would conduct regular consultations to seek ways on how to conduct cooperative activities in science and technology between ASEAN and EU.[30] Areas of

[24] Meeting of the ASEAN-China Joint Science and Technology Committee (JSTC) : Terms of Reference, 14th May 2012, online: ASEAN <https://asean.org/?static_post=meeting-of-the-asean-china-joint-science-and-technology-committee-jstc-terms-of-reference>

[25] 13th AMMST Joint Press Release, Singapore, 6 November 2009, 4.

[26] "The 3rd Meeting of ASEAN-ROK Joint Science and Technology Committee held" (30 May) online: <https://english.msit.go.kr/eng/bbs/view.do?sCode=eng&mId=4&mPid=2&pageIndex=&bbsSeqNo=42&nttSeqNo=255&searchOpt=&searchTxt=>. See also 14th AMMST Joint Press Release, Ho Chi Minh City, Viet Nam, 26 November 2011, 9; 16th AMMST Joint Press Release, Vientiane, Lao PDR, 6 November 2015, 14.

[27] Jung Min-kyung, "S. Korea, ASEAN to launch science center for cooperation" (28 June 2019) online: The Korea Herald <http://www.koreaherald.com/view.php?ud=20190628000453>.

[28] Chairman's Press Statement for the Informal Ministerial Meeting on Science and Technology between ASEAN and Australia, China, India, Japan, Korea and New Zealand, Kuantan, Malaysia, 29 August 2006.

[29] Overview of ASEAN Plus Three Cooperation (April 2020), online: ASEAN <https://asean.org/storage/2016/01/APT-Overview-Paper-24-Apr-2020.pdf>.

[30] 5th IAMMST Joint Press Release, Manila, Philippines, 07–08 July 2008, 12–13.

cooperation in science and technology between ASEAN and EU are health, food, nanotechnology, ICT, water, maritime transport and mobility of researchers.[31]

- ***ASEAN-India Working Group on Science and Technology***: At the first meeting of the ASEAN-India Joint Cooperation Committee in New Delhi, 1996, an ASEAN-India Working Group on Science and Technology (AIWGST) was established.[32] In 2008, India set up the ASEAN-India Science and Technology Development Fund to support R&D projects and associated project development activities.[33] Project and scientific activities supported and implemented under ASEAN-India Science and Technology programme include: ASEAN-India Collaborative Research and Development on Thermally Sprayed Ceramic-Based Coatings; Research and Development project on Extent of Transfer of Alien Invasive Organisms (Nuisance) in South/Southeast Asia Region by Shipping; Training Course on Analysis of Chemicals and Biological Contaminants in Raw and Processed Products for ASEAN Countries; The Indian Ocean Dipole Mode; El Nino Southern Oscillation and Monsoon Interactions and their Socio-Economic Impacts on India-ASEAN Nations; ASEAN-India science and technology Digital Library; and Training program on Quality System in Manufacturing.[34]
- ***ASEAN-Russia Working Group on Science and Technology***: The ASEAN-Russia Working Group on Science and Technology was established by the Plan of Action of the ASEAN-Russia Working Group on Science and Technology 2007–2011. The Plan of Action provides for enhanced cooperation between ASEAN and Russia in science and technology including in the promotion of dialogues among science and technology officials, scientists and researchers and encouragement of technology transfer and exchange.[35] According to the ASEAN-Russian Federation Plan of Action on Science, Technology and Innovation (2016–2025), ASEAN and Russia will strengthen and develop joint research and development activities in the following areas: biotechnology; food security and sustainable agriculture; water resources and water treatment technology; clean and nuclear technologies and power generation; oil and gas technologies; microelectronics and information technology; meteorology and geophysics; nanotechnology; geoinformatics; environmental management; energy technology and renewal energy; material science; and space technology and application.[36]

---

[31] European Commission, Roadmap for EU–ASEAN S&T cooperation, online: EU <https://ec.europa.eu/research/iscp/pdf/policy/asean_roadmap_2018.pdf>.

[32] 1st ASEAN—India Joint Cooperation Committee Meeting Joint Press Release, New Delhi, 14–16 November 1996, 10.

[33] "ASEAN-India Science, Technology & Innovation Cooperation", online: Ministry of External Affairs <https://www.aistic.gov.in/ASEAN/HomePage>.

[34] "ASEAN-India Science, Technology & Innovation Cooperation", online: Ministry of External Affairs <https://www.aistic.gov.in/ASEAN/HomePage>.

[35] "ASEAN and Russian Federation", online: ASEAN Learning Centre <http://asean.dla.go.th/public/article.do;jsessionid=7908B7C4039BEC28C2D692A9E4AED239?menu2Id=86&countryCode=9&lang=en&cmd=goViewByCountry>.

[36] ASEAN Plan of Action on Science, Technology and Innovation 2016–2025, adopted at the 16th AMMST Joint Press Release, Vientiane, Lao PDR, 6 November 2015, 62.

- ***ASEAN-United States Consultation on Science and Technology***: The ASEAN-United States Consultation on Science and Technology was inaugurated in 2011.[37] Under its framework, a ASEAN Science and Technology Fellows Pilot Program was implemented since 2014 to strengthen scientific and technical input into ASEAN Member States strategic priorities by enabling ASEAN scientists to work directly with policymakers in ASEAN Member States while also increasing science capacity in the region. The Program provides the opportunity for Ph.D. scientists who are citizens and residents of any of the ASEAN Member States to learn about policymaking while contributing their knowledge and analytical skills to their national governments in support of ASEAN science and technology priorities.[38]
- ***ASEAN—United Kingdom Dialogue on Science, Technology and Innovation***: ASEAN—UK Dialogue on Science, Technology and Innovation met for the first time in 2023. It provides a platform to promote and intensify cooperation in the scientific, technological and innovation activities between ASEAN and the United Kingdom. Areas of cooperation between the two sides in science and technology include climate change adaptation, developing clean energy solutions, improving health systems and increasing resilience to natural disasters.[39]

Goals, Objectives and Priorities of ASEAN Cooperation in Marine Scientific Research

The priorities of ASEAN cooperation in marine scientific research are provided in the provisions of the ASEAN Plan of Action on Science, Technology and Innovation 2016—2025, relating to the goals, objectives and priority areas of the Sub-Committee on Marine Science and Technology.[40] Pursuant to the Plan of Action, the general goal of the Sub-Committee for this period is to seek to promote sustainable development of marine living and non-living resources while increasing the potential of these resources to meet the requirements of ASEAN and to increase the number of qualified personnel in marine science and technology.[41] The objectives of the Sub-Committee are:

- Implementing cooperation activities in scientific projects that maximise mechanisms for enabling country participation in accordance with current and potential capabilities;

[37] 14th AMMST Joint Press Release, Ho Chi Minh City, Viet Nam, 26 November 2011, 10.

[38] "ASEAN-U.S. Science & Technology Fellows Pilot Program", online: US Mission to ASEAN <https://asean.usmission.gov/innovasean_20131022/>.

[39] The First ASEAN-UK Dialogue on Science, Technology and Innovation Opens, 20 October 2023, online: ASEAN https://asean.org/the-first-asean-uk-dialogue-on-science-technology-and-innovation-opens/.

[40] ASEAN Plan of Action on Science, Technology and Innovation 2016–2025, 44.

[41] ASEAN Plan of Action on Science, Technology and Innovation 2016–2025, 44.

- Establishing increased interactions between marine scientists and private sector in order to strengthen the outcome of scientific cooperation, and promote higher level of intra-ASEAN collaboration;
- Developing cooperation with international dialogue partner(s) in priority areas of marine science and climate change; and
- Facilitating data sharing and publications for the exchange of information and enhance technology transfer.[42]

Its priority areas of action include trans-boundary aquatic pollution/marine debris, risk management and mitigation from climate change; and renewable energy and marine biodiversity.[43]

According to the ASEAN Plan of Action on Science, Technology and Innovation 2016–2025 Implementation Plan, the following cooperation projects are to be implemented during the period 2016–2025[44]:

- Extent of transfer of nuisance organisms between South and South East Asia by shipping;
- ASEAN-India cooperative research and development for mariculture, biomining and bioremediation technologies;
- Carbon sink and sequestration in aquatic ecosystems;
- Ocean acidification and its ecological impacts;
- Conservation of migratory marine mammals and other endangered marine organisms;
- Response to cross border oil spill incidents;
- Capacity building and networking on biofuels from aquatic algae;
- Extent of transfer of alien invasive organisms in South/SE Asia by shipping. Phase II. Towards an ASEAN-India ballast water management exemption zone;
- Joint ASEAN-India Oceanographic Cruise;
- ASEAN-Russia project on Advancing Sustainable Development and Protection of Marine Environment in ASEAN Member States;
- ASEAN Tropical Marine Ecosystem Network;
- Climate change impacts and coastal adaptation of coastal community within the South China Sea; and
- ASEAN-Russia project on developing of informative platform for innovative wastewater treatment technologies for industrial enterprises in ASEAN Member States.

[42] ASEAN Plan of Action on Science, Technology and Innovation 2016–2025, 44.

[43] ASEAN Plan of Action on Science, Technology and Innovation 2016–2025, 44.

[44] APASTI 2016–2025 Implementation Plan, adopted at the 9th IAMMST, 29 October 2016, Siem Reap, Cambodia, Annex 6 at 89.

Suggestions for ASEAN to Improve Marine Scientific Research Cooperation in the South China Sea

ASEAN could consider undertaking the following measures to improve marine scientific research in the South China Sea: creating a working group on marine scientific research in the South China Sea, establishing a shared database of scientific research implemented relating to the South China Sea, supporting a network of South China Sea research institutions and building partnership with other regional marine scientific cooperation mechanisms.

i) ***Creating a Working Group on Marine Scientific Research in the South China Sea***

A working group on marine scientific research in the South China Sea could be established under the Sub-Committee on Marine Science and Technology[45] to promote cooperation in marine scientific research in the South China Sea. Such a working group would allow representatives from all ASEAN Member States to meet regularly to exchange information, data and research relating to the South China Sea and in particular, to provide ideas and suggestions for undertaking more cooperative marine scientific research projects on this body of water. The participants to the working group should comprise both government officials in charge of science and technology from ASEAN Member States and well-known scientists in Southeast Asia and beyond the region who have an interest and expertise relating to the South China Sea.

ii) ***Establishing a Shared Database of Scientific Research Implemented Relating to the South China Sea***

Over the years, there has been many marine scientific research and surveys undertaken in the South China Sea and new ones being developed and implemented every now and then. However, so far, there is no comprehensive database which collects and stores information relating to these research as well as the data collected, and results achieved. Such a database could help people and experts to know what have been researched in the South China Sea and what we know so far about this marine region. It would help scientists who intend to develop new projects of marine scientific research in the South China Sea avoid repeating what have been done, leading to a waste of resources. ASEAN has developed different types of databases so the Association would have no difficulty to undertake this endeavour for the South China Sea.

iii) ***Supporting a Dialogue Network of South China Sea Research Institutions***

There are a number of research institutions both from ASEAN Member States and other States which have experiences in conducting marine scientific research in the South China Sea such as the Institute of Oceanography (Viet Nam), Institute of Oceanography and Maritime Studies (Malaysia), Tropical Marine Science Institute

---

[45] See above ii) ASEAN Committee on Science, Technology and Innovation.

(Singapore) and the 3rd Institute of Oceanography (China). ASEAN could facilitate the creation of a dialogue network between these institutions, allowing them to meet each other, exchanging experiences and activities and discussing on the undertaking of possible joint marine scientific research projects. Experiences for this dialogue network could be learned from the Track II Network of ASEAN Defence and Security Institutions Meeting.

iv) ***Building Partnership with Other Regional Marine Scientific Cooperation Mechanisms***

There are a number of other regional mechanisms which also have a mandate in undertaking marine scientific research in the South China Sea such as the UNESCO's Intergovernmental Oceanography Sub-Commission of the Western Pacific (IOC WESTPAC),[46] Southeast Asian Fisheries Development Center (SEAFDEC),[47] and the Scientist Working Group under the Center for Humanitarian Dialogue (HD Centre).[48] Among those, ASEAN has only established partnership with SEAFDEC by creating a ASEAN-SEAFDEC Fisheries Consultative Group in 1999.[49] ASEAN could also consider establishing similar partnership with IOC WESTPAC and HD Centre to promote cooperation in marine scientific research in the region. These partnerships could enhance the effectiveness as well as provide more resources for the implementation of marine scientific research projects in Southeast Asia in general and in the South China Sea in particular.

[46] The IOC WESTPAC was established in IOC in 1989 to promote international cooperation and to coordinate programs in marine research, ocean observations and services, as well as capacity building in the Western Pacific and adjacent seas. The IOC WESTPACT has implemented a number of marine scientific research projects to study the natural conditions of marine regions in the Western Pacific, including in the South China Sea. For details, see IOC WESTPAC, https://iocwestpac.org/, September 27, 2022.

[47] The SEAFDEC was established in 1967 as an autonomous inter-governmental body to promote and facilitate concerted actions to ensure the sustainability of fisheries and aquaculture in Southeast Asia. SEAFDEC has implemented many research projects relating to the fisheries in Southeast Asia, including in the South China Sea. For details, see SEAFDEC, http://www.seafdec.org/, September 27, 2022.

[48] The HD Centre is a non-governmental organisation specialising in the prevention of conflicts. The Centre has been implementing a number of projects to strengthen confidence-building between South China Sea States. A Fisheries Scientific Working Group with scientists from China, Philippines, Malaysia, Indonesia and Vietnam and international advisers, established the HD Centre, has just completed a joint research project on the situation of skipjack tuna (Katsuwonus pelamis) in the South China Sea. For details, see South China sea Fish Stocks at Risk Without Regional Cooperation, Five-Country Scientific Report Warns (2 September 2022) see HD Centre, https://www.hdcentre.org/updates/south-china-sea-fish-stocks-at-risk-without-regional-cooperation-five-country-scientific-report-warns/#:~:text=Donor%20Relations-,South%20China%20Sea%20fish%20stocks%20at%20risk%20without%20regional,five%2Dcountry%20scientific%20report%20warns&text=MANILA%20%E2%80%93%202%20Sept%202022%20%E2%80%93%20Despite,from%20the%20risk%20of%20collapse, September 27, 2022.

[49] The ASEAN-SEAFDEC Strategic Partnership—Fisheries Consultative Group Mechanism, see SEAFDEC, http://www.seafdec.org/documents/2016/11/19fcg_ref01.pdf, September 27, 2022.

Conclusion

ASEAN has been playing an important role in developing cooperation in science and technology, including in marine scientific research, both between Southeast Asian countries and between Southeast Asia and the world. Leveraging on this experience, ASEAN could serve as a broker for promoting cooperation in marine scientific research in the South China Sea to better understand its marine environment and resources and to contribute to manage the South China Sea disputes. This paper provides some concrete suggestions for ASEAN to take up this role, namely by creating a working Group on marine scientific research in the South China Sea; establishing a shared database of scientific research implemented relating to the South China Sea; supporting a dialogue network of South China Sea research institutions; and building partnership with other regional marine scientific cooperation mechanisms. The successful promotion of cooperation in research in the South China Sea would help ASEAN to affirm its role as the central mechanism for peace, stability and cooperation in the wider Indo-Pacific region.

Chapter 10
The Case for Autonomy: A Military, and Legal, Option for Creating Capacity to Handle Challenges in the South China Sea

Caroline Tuckett

Introduction

The number and type of disputes emerging in the South China Sea are many and complex. However, there are two key challenges, faced by many littoral States in the South China Sea which are consistent, and interlinked. Firstly, attempted restrictions on the freedom of navigation as provided for under the UN Convention on the Law of the Sea (UNCLOS).[1] Secondly, the need to build capacity to increase Maritime Domain Awareness, which in turn, will assist in upholding the freedom of navigation. This paper will approach these challenges through a legal lens. It will be proposed that the use of autonomous systems and vessels is a possible option for handling such challenges. The freedom of navigation through a particular area for example, can be asserted using an autonomous vessel. Equally, an autonomous vessel or system can be used to enhance Maritime Domain Awareness. The paper will outline the practical advantages of the use of this developing technology, including reduced cost and reduced risk to life. It will also focus on how, in international law, the use of autonomy is a credible option for enhancing the legal position of those States who feel threatened by such challenges. The pervasive theme throughout is that the classification of the autonomous asset is vital to understanding how it can be used in accordance with international law.

[1] https://www.un.org/depts/los/convention_agreements/texts/unclos/unclos_e.pdf.

C. Tuckett (✉)
Royal Navy, Portsmouth, UK

N. Hung Son and N. Thi Lan Anh (eds.), *The South China Sea: The Geo-political Epicenter of the Indo-Pacific?*, https://doi.org/10.1007/978-981-97-8209-3_10

Novel and Hybrid Maritime Threats and Challenges—The Legal Context

Before approaching these challenges, it is worth setting out the legal context. While militaries from different States regularly encounter one another in the South China Sea, this has not translated into a state of open conflict, with the one notable exception being the Battle of the Paracels in 1974. This seemingly obvious point is key when looking at the legal context: the law to be considered is the law of peacetime operations, not the Law of Naval Warfare. Owing to the maritime environment in which this dispute is being played out, the guiding reference is UNCLOS.[2] However, it should also be remembered that the customary international law principles of State responsibility are also in play: and this applies just as much in the operation of autonomous systems by a State organ, as it does for crewed vessels.[3] In other words, States have an obligation to ensure the operation of their autonomous assets is lawful. The lack of crew does not equate to a lack of legal responsibility.

From a practical perspective, there have been examples of breaches of other international agreements, such as the harassment at sea by Chinese militia vessels against Philippine fishing vessels within the South and East China Sea, as well as some very close encounters between Chinese vessels and warships from other States. Such incidents could be construed as breaches of international obligations under International Regulations to Prevent Collisions at Sea (COLREGS, also known as the Rules of the Road).[4] Indeed, in some cases, there has been a definitive legal assessment that these breaches have occurred, such as in the *South China Sea Arbitration.* In that instance, the Tribunal held that the actions of the Chinese Coast Guard against the Philippine fishing vessels around Scarborough Shoal had breached a number of the Rules of the Road.[5]

International legal obligations aside, these incidents also highlight an increased physical risk to personnel at sea. Clearly, at times it will be essential to have a crew onboard a vessel, such as for fishing. However, particularly when it comes to upholding the freedom of navigation or increasing Maritime Domain Awareness—both areas of focus which often fall within the military domain—the presence of personnel onboard is not as essential as has been in the past.

---

[2] See fn1.

[3] Draft Articles on State Responsibility, see https://legal.un.org/ilc/texts/instruments/english/draft_articles/9_6_2001.pdf.

[4] http://www.mar.ist.utl.pt/mventura/Projecto-Navios-I/IMO-Conventions%20(copies)/COLREG1972.pdf.

[5] See The Republic of the Philippines v The People's Republic of China PCA Case No 2013–19, 12 July 2016 para 1109 for incidents involving Philippine fishing vessels.

Challenge 1: Upholding the Freedom of Navigation

The most well publicised method for enforcing freedom of navigation rights is a State endorsed Freedom of Navigation Operation (FONOP). A FONOP is an operation most usually conducted by a Navy, aimed to support the freedom of navigation by "protesting and challenging attempts by coastal States to unlawfully restrict access to the seas."[6] The US has a formally established Freedom of Navigation Program, which has been running since 1979, while other States are more ad hoc.[7] Generally, two different types of operation come under the umbrella of a directed FONOP: one which challenges jurisdiction; for example, a Navy may challenge the insistence that warships "obtain advance approval from or give prior notification" to China before conducting innocent passage through territorial waters, without seeking permission in advance.[8] The second challenges a stated excessive maritime claim. An example here would be to sail within the straight baselines claimed by China around the Paracel Islands, but in a manner that is not consistent with the innocent passage, such as pausing briefly to conduct a man overboard drill or launching the helicopter. This kind of FONOP therefore emphasises the right to the freedom of navigation (including in that freedom, the right to launch an aircraft or conduct a military exercise) on the high seas.[9]

It is tempting to think of FONOPs in terms of large warships sailing through a contested zone—because by and large this is what has been publicised, and has happened, so far. But the freedom of navigation encompasses many other areas, such as hydrographic survey work, rights of overflight or even the simple act of sailing on the high seas.[10] By way of example, the passage of a warship through the Taiwan Strait often attracts media attention, however despite its name, the Taiwan Strait is

---

[6] USA, *Annual Freedom of Navigation Report Fiscal Year 2017*, page 2.

[7] Ibid, page 2. The UK has conducted FONOPs in the Indo-Pacific with two Royal Navy warships in recent years, the actions of *HMS Albion* being the most prominent in the press.

[8] Reservation lodged with the UN upon ratification of UNCLOS on 25 August 2006, available at United Nations Treaty Collection Depositary (*United Nations*), < https://treaties.un.org/Pages/ViewDetailsIII.aspx?src=TREATY&mtdsg_no=XXI6&chapter=21&Temp=mtdsg3&clang=_en#EndDec > accessed 2 September 2019.

[9] John Hemmings, "Charting Britain's Moves in the South China Sea" (*rusi.org*, 6 February 2019). < https://rusi.org/commentary/charting-britains-moves-south-china-sea > accessed 25 May 2020.

[10] Kraska, p10. Art. 38(1) (b) Statute of the International Court of Justice refers to "international custom, as evidence of a general practice accepted as law". In *Federal Republic of Germany v Denmark Federal Republic of Germany v Netherlands* ICJ 20 February 1969 (*North Sea Continental Shelf*), para 71, the ICJ considered when a treaty rule could pass into customary international law. This would apply here: the treaty rule is the freedom of navigation enshrined in UNCLOS. The Court held that for a rule to pass into customary international law, "State practice, including that of States whose interests are specially affected, should have been extensive and virtually uniform in the sense of provision invoked;—and should moreover have occurred in such a way as to show a general recognition that a rule of law of legal obligation is involved".

an area of high seas.[11] In summary, every time a vessel leaves port and proceeds to sea, it is exercising the right to the freedom of navigation as provided by UNCLOS.

Crucial, therefore, is to consider *how* to exercise that freedom of navigation, in a way which is competitive, both legally and practically. Putting the legal arguments to one side, the sheer.

mass of some of the competitors in the Indo-Pacific region means that many Navies will struggle to catch up. It has also been noted in the US that while there is no actual metric for defining how many FONOPs would satisfy the legal element of state practice, the current number of an average no more than two US FONOPs per year is not likely to be sufficient, noting that China is making daily assertions of sovereignty.[12] This is where autonomous vessels could help.

Challenge 2: Increase Maritime Domain Awareness

The co-operation of littoral States in sharing information is always going to be of value. Maritime Domain Awareness is achieved through numerous forms, but often, it will again come down to a question of mass. The more assets a State has at sea, the more situational awareness it will gain. But, assets, and the people to crew them, are expensive. Here, autonomous systems can play a role. Out in the Middle East, the US Task Force 59, as part of the 5th Fleet, is conducting trials with a fleet of Sail Drones, precisely to enhance maritime domain awareness.[13] The UK Royal Navy has been working with the National Oceanographic Centre to use gliders for military data gathering in the North Atlantic.[14] Trials have also been conducted using those same gliders to assist in anti-submarine operations.[15] In both cases, the overriding aim is to increase Maritime Domain Awareness.

[11] The high seas are often referred to as "international waters", a term which is not in UNCLOS but is used to refer to all waters beyond 12 nautical miles, and so the freedom of high seas apply.

[12] https://www.reuters.com/world/us-navy-says-uss-john-finn-conducted-transit-taiwan-strait-2024-01-24/.

[13] https://sldinfo.com/2021/10/task-force-59-creating-maritime-capabilities-for-the-5th-fleet-area-ofoperations/.

[14] https://noc.ac.uk/facilities/marine-autonomous-robotic-systems/gliders and https://www.royalnavy.mod.uk/news-and-latest-activity/news/2019/june/14/190614-enterprise-trialsunderwater-gliders.

[15] https://www.royalnavy.mod.uk/news-and-latest-activity/news/2020/april/30/300420-glider-trials

Autonomous Systems and Vessels

Why use an autonomous system? The first advantage is a reduced cost: a US Navy (USN) Arleigh Burke is estimated to cost $700,000 a day to run, whereas Sea Hunter, a USN LUSV, costs $15–20,000.[16] The rough cost of a Sail Drone is $2500 a day, compared to $30,000 a day for a crewed research vessel.[17] The reduced cost can then translate into an ability to generate a higher mass.

The increased risk to manpower in the increasingly frequent tense encounters that occur can also be mitigated. It is not unusual for warships conducting FONOPS to find themselves at very close distances to the PLA(N), and as a result, with an increased risk of collision. Collisions at sea are always going to be dangerous, but when the collision is between two warships, both carrying ammunition, it is even worse. Such an encounter could arguably escalate the situation in the South China Sea even further.

There are of course, still some disadvantages. An autonomous system may be easier to apprehend by another State, as has now been seen in both the South China Sea, and the Middle East.[18] It should also be acknowledged that a smaller autonomous vessel may not have the same bold reputational impact as that of the use of a crewed warship.

Unmanned or Uncrewed or Autonomous?

If autonomous systems are to be used, however, they need to be classified correctly. To add to the already complex debate, there is a lack of consensus as to whether "unmanned" should be used, or "uncrewed" as the gender-neutral alternative. This is a debate which affects both civilian and military operators. Recent guidance from the International Organisation for Standardisation (ISO) has stated that uncrewed means "no crew onboard", whereas "unmanned" means "no humans onboard", thereby making a distinction between those who will be passengers, and those who will actively pilot the vessel.[19] Not all have adopted this view as an absolute, and the UK, by way of example, will often use "autonomous" as an umbrella term.[20]

---

[16] Kraska, Disruptive Technology and the Law of Naval Warfare, p83.

[17] https://www.science.org/content/article/fleet-sailboat-drones-could-monitor-climate-change-S-effectoceans.

[18] https://news.usni.org/2016/12/16/breaking-chinese-seize-U-S-navy-unmanned-vehicle and https://www.theguardian.com/us-news/2022/aug/30/us-navy-drone-iran-persian-gulf.

[19] See Maritime Autonomous Systems Regulatory Working Group https://www.maritimeuk.org/priorities/innovation/maritime-uk-autonomous-systems-regulatory- working-group/masrwg-conferences/, or alternatively House of Lords International Relations and Defence Committee 2nd Report of Session 2021–22: *LOSC, the law of the sea in the 21st Century* Chapter 6, available at https://publications.parliament.uk/pa/ld5802/ldselect/ldintrel/159/159.pdf.

[20] https://www.imo.org/en/MediaCentre/HotTopics/Pages/Autonomous-shipping.aspx.

As if the debate about nomenclature was not already complicated enough, the word "autonomous" also has several different meanings. It does not, for example, automatically mean a ship which is entirely capable of independent operation without human intervention. Perhaps with this in mind, the International Maritime Organisation (IMO) has issued guidance as to the different "degrees of autonomy".

The four degrees have been defined as follows:

> ***Degree one****: Ship with automated processes and decision support: Seafarers are on board to operate and control shipboard systems and functions. Some operations may be automated and at times be unsupervised but with seafarers on board ready to take control.*
> ***Degree two****: Remotely controlled ship with seafarers on board: The ship is controlled and operated from another location. Seafarers are available on board to take control and to operate the shipboard systems and functions.*
> ***Degree three****: Remotely controlled ship without seafarers on board: The ship is controlled and operated from another location. There are no seafarers on board.*
> ***Degree four****: Fully autonomous ship: The operating system of the ship is able to make decisions and determine actions by itself.*[21]

We will now turn to the two options available for classification: equipment, or vessel.

What's in a Name?

UNCLOS states that all *ships* or *vessels* have the right to the freedom of navigation, including innocent passage, transit passage, and archipelagic innocent passage, and archipelagic sea lane passage.[22] Therefore, if a State wishes to exercise the freedom

---

[21] UNCLOS Articles 17, 38, and 87 respectively. The UK position is that the right of innocent passage, afforded to "ships of all States" also therefore applies to warships.

[22] See for example: the Convention On The Prevention Of Marine Pollution By Dumping Of Wastes And Other Matter (London Mexico City, Moscow and Washington 29 December 1972 as amended), the United Nations Convention on Conditions for Registration of Ships (Geneva 7 February 1986), the Nairobi International Convention on the Removal of Wrecks (Nairobi 18 May 2007) art 1.2, the 1989 Salvage Convention, the Convention for the Unification of Certain Rules of Law with respect to Collisions between Vessels (Brussels 23 September 1910), the Convention for the Unification of Certain Rules of Law respecting Assistance and Salvage at Sea (Brussels 23 September 1910), the International Convention Relating to the Arrest of Sea-Going Ships (Brussels 10 May 1952), the International Convention on the Arrest of Ships (Geneva 12 March 1999), the International Convention on Maritime Liens and Mortgages (Geneva 6 May 1993), the Convention on Limitation of Liability for Maritime Claims 1976 (London 19 November 1976), the Convention on the Contract for the Carriage of Goods by Inland Waterways (Budapest 22 June 2001), the International Convention for the Unification of Certain Rules of Law relating to Bills of Lading (Brussels 25 August 1924), the International Convention Relating to Intervention on the High Seas in Cases of Oil Pollution Casualties 1969 (Brussels 29 November 1969 as amended) art II.2.

of navigation rights as provided for by UNCLOS with an autonomous system, it needs to be formally classified as a vessel or a ship.

UNCLOS uses both the terms ship and vessel interchangeably and notably, in the French version, the single word *navire* is used, and in Spanish, *buque*. Thus, the consensus on the international stage is that the words "ship" and "vessel" are synonymous. UNCLOS does not however, provide a definition of ship or vessel, and there are at least 13 different definitions of ship in international treaties.[23] By way of example, a "vessel" is defined in the COLREGs as: "every description of water craft, including non-displacement craft, Wing-In-Ground craft and seaplanes, used or capable of being used as a means of transportation on water."[24]

The International Convention for the Prevention of Pollution from Ships (MARPOL) defines a "ship" as "a vessel of any type whatsoever operating in the marine environment and includes hydrofoil boats, air-cushion vehicles, submersibles, floating craft, and fixed and floating platforms."[25] In the 2005 Suppression of Unlawful Acts At Sea (SUA) Convention the ship is "a vessel of any type whatsoever not permanently attached to the sea-bed, including dynamically supported craft, submersibles, or any other floating craft".[26] UK domestic law has perhaps tried to encapsulate all of these: the Merchant Shipping Act 1995 states that a "ship" includes "every description of vessel used in navigation".[27] This ambiguity is a legal freedom—which we can use, not misuse, to achieve the aim of classifying, and formally registering, autonomous systems as vessels. The UK Royal Navy has 23 different "vessels" on its Defence Shipping Register, all of varying descriptions and uses.[28]

The Importance of the Word "Vessel"

There are three specific reasons, related to privileges afforded to vessels by international law, why use of the word "vessel" has important legal implications. Firstly, and as a shared concern with the civilian industry, is the exercise of the freedom of navigation. Naval vessels need to be able to sail independently and with some caveats, freely, all over the globe.

UNCLOS provides for this, for example by allowing for vessels to exercise the right of innocent passage through the territorial sea of another State, as well as to

---

[23] Rule 3(a) COLREGS.

[24] Article 2(4) MARPOL.

[25] Article 1(1)(a) Convention for the Suppression of Unlawful Acts against the Safety of Maritime Navigation (SUA Convention) (Rome 10 March 1988 as amended).

[26] Section 313 Merchant Shipping Act 1995, available at: https://www.legislation.gov.uk/ukpga/1995/21/contents.

[27] See fn 11, House of Lords International Relations and Defence Committee 2nd Report of Session 2021–22: *UNCLOS, the law of the sea in the 21st Century.*

[28] LOSC Articles 17, 38 and 87 respectively.

conduct transit passage through international straits, or indeed simply to navigate freely on the high seas.[29] The UK's position is that the right of innocent passage, afforded to "ships of all States" also therefore applies to warships. Of note with regards to the South China Sea, this is not a position supported by China.[30] In a conflict, the situation is slightly different. Under the Law of Neutrality, belligerent Parties may not use the territorial seas of a Neutral State for belligerent action. They are, however, entitled to use each other's territorial seas under the regime of the Law of Naval Warfare.[31]

The second area of concern is the principle of sovereign immunity. By virtue of UNCLOS Articles 32, 95, and 96, warships and government vessels on non-commercial service have sovereign immunity, which excludes the effects of certain international treaties around issues such as the application of jurisdiction by other states. Therefore, if a warship is suspected of.

non-compliance with the laws of another State while in its territorial seas, it can only be asked to leave, it cannot be seized.[32]

UNCLOS does not define government ships on non-commercial service. The term is often used, however, synonymously with "auxiliary vessels". The San Remo Manual and the UK define auxiliary vessels as: "…a vessel, other than a warship, that is owned by or under the exclusive control of the armed forces of a State and used for the time being on government non-commercial service".[33] Auxiliaries therefore are considered to have sovereign immunity, in the same way warships do. Autonomous vessels currently being trialled within the UK RN are registered as government ships

[29] See China's declaration made when ratifying UNCLOS, https://treaties.un.org/Pages/ViewDetailsIII.aspx?src=TREATY&mtdsg_no=XXI-6&chapter=21&Temp=mtdsg3&clang=_en. China made the following declaration on 25 August 2006: "The People's Republic of China reaffirms that the provisions of the United Nations Convention on the Law of the Sea concerning innocent passage through the territorial sea shall not prejudice the right of a coastal state to request, in accordance with its laws and regulations, a foreign state to obtain advance approval from or give prior notification to the coastal state for the passage of its warships through the territorial sea of the coastal state." For a recent example of where the UK has used a warship to assert the right of innocent passage see media reporting of the passage of HMS DEFENDER in the territorial seas off the coast of Crimea in 2021, for example: https://www.naval-technology.com/news/uk-and-russia-in-diplomatic-row-after-british-ships-innocent-passage/.

[30] See fn 21, Part I paras 14–22.

[31] UNCLOS Article 30.

[32] The UK has previously accepted that auxiliaries, not being warships, cannot legitimately conduct attacks. While enjoying sovereign immunity as Government-owned or operated vessels (a status useful only outside armed conflict), auxiliaries lack the ability lawfully to conduct strike actions unless or until their status is amended to that of a warship. On the other hand, an auxiliary (or, for that matter, a merchant ship) can be armed in order to protect itself—and the use of such weapons in selfdefence is not an act of hostility. They can carry warlike stores, military personnel and equipment such as helicopters, encrypted communications systems and electronic countermeasures. They are liable to lawful attack at any time, because by their very nature, purpose and use they are making a contribution to military operations.

[33] Article 18, Chinese Coast Guard Law 2021, available at http://politics.people.com.cn/n1/2021/0123/c1001-32009344.html.

on non-commercial service, affording them the ability to assert the rights of both sovereign immunity and passage.

Again, of relevance to operating in the South China Sea, the China Coast Guard Law 2021 has authorised the Chinese Coast Guard to use force to remove foreign vessels from "Chinese waters". The legislation also contains an express provision which gives that same authorisation to be used for foreign military vessels.[34]This arguably strengthens the case for using autonomous vessels: the reduced risk to manpower in light of increasing assertiveness on the part of China to disregard the principle of sovereign immunity.

Finally, and perhaps most importantly in the context of military operations, is the provision of belligerent rights. As a matter of customary international law, only a warship is entitled to exercise belligerent rights.[35] There is no defined list of these rights, but broadly they cover: kinetic strike, visit board search and seizure (VBSS), laying mines, amphibious operations against enemy held coast, and blockade enforcement.[36] The definition of a warship in UNCLOS will be looked at in more detail below, but as a starting point, the definition begins with "..warship means a ship…"[37] It is axiomatic therefore that piece of equipment, or a device, cannot be a warship.

Autonomous Equipment or Systems

While there are distinct advantages to an autonomous system being classed as a vessel, that does not mean that all autonomous systems need to be classified as vessels; far from it. The gliders that the UK has used for data gathering, for example, are not vessels, they are pieces of equipment and thus do not have navigational rights.

In contrast to the plethora of definitions regarding ships, there is no definition of "vehicle", or indeed "device" in international shipping law, and yet this term is often used to refer to systems with an autonomous capability. The references to such "equipment" are limited in UNCLOS, they are used mainly in the context of marine scientific research.[38] However, what can be gleaned from UNCLOS and supporting treaties is that a ship or vessel operates independently, whereas a "device" is "launched" or "landed".[39] Therefore, as alluded to above, even though such operations are not badged as "FONOPS", the operation of these systems is still a way of upholding some of the principles of the freedom of navigation. They are being operated in pursuit of the rights and privileges afforded under UNCLOS.

---

[34] Manual of the Laws of Naval War, Oxford 1913, Articles 3 and 12. See also San Remo Manual, fn 24 para 13.21.

[35] San Remo Manual on the Law of Naval Warfare, Part IV, p25–29.

[36] UNCLOS Article 29, my emphasis.

[37] UNCLOS Part XIII, Sect. 10.4.

[38] UNCLOS Article 19(2)(f).

[39] Royal Navy to test underwater gliders in North Atlantic (naval-technology.com), and Updated: Chinese Seize U.S. Navy Unmanned Vehicle—USNI News.

It can also be used as a means or method of naval warfare, as will be outlined below. Commonly used examples of such equipment are the gliders operated by both the USN and the RN, often for military data gathering purposes, and in the case of the US Navy, infamously seized by the People's Republic of China (PRC) People's Liberation Army (Navy) in the South China Sea.[40] Provided the equipment is being used in exclusively governmental non-commercial purposes, then the operating State can claim sovereign immunity under customary international law. The United States indeed claimed that the glider seized was a piece of sovereign immune equipment, and ultimately this led to the return of the glider.[41]

What if There is a Conflict?

Clearly, the intent is to avoid escalating any tensions into a state of conflict. However, from events seen in Black Sea, autonomous systems are now being used in conflict at sea.[42] Although at the time of writing, no Navy has declared the operation of an autonomous warship, the UK has made a public statement to say that UNCLOS Article 29 does encompass the concept of autonomous warships.[43] Article 29 states that a warship is:

> a ship belonging to the armed forces of a State bearing the external marks distinguishing such ships of its nationality, under the command of an officer duly commissioned by the government of the State and whose name appears in the appropriate service list or its equivalent and manned by a crew which is under regular armed forces discipline.[44]

Under International Humanitarian Law (IHL), there is an obligation to ensure distinction between combatants and non-combatants. UNCLOS as an instrument of peacetime law is clearly separate and distinct from IHL, including the Law of Naval Warfare. However, Article 29 provides a crucial link to IHL, because of the definition of a warship contained within.[45] The intent of the wording of Article 29 is to attach state responsibility to the activities of a "vessel" capable of acting in a belligerent manner and therefore allow non-belligerents to understand the extent of lawful conduct by vessels of different types. Further, this ensures that the effects of warfare are limited to only legitimate targets.

---

[40] https://news.usni.org/2016/12/20/china-returns-U-S-navy-unmanned-glider.

[41] https://www.bbc.co.uk/news/world-europe-63437212.

[42] House of Lords International Relations and Defence Committee 2nd Report of Session 2021–22: UNCLOS, the law of the sea in the 21st Century Chapter 6, available at https://publications.parliament.uk/pa/ld5802/ldselect/ldintrel/159/159.pdf.

[43] UNCLOS Article 29. The crew of a warship (including any civilians onboard) are entitled to Prisoner of War status if captured during an international armed conflict.

[44] It is worth noting that the wording of Article 29 is a direct lift from the Law of Naval Warfare, namely the 1907 Hague Convention VII, Conversion of Merchant Ships to Warships. Available at: https://ihldatabases.icrc.org/ihl/INTRO/210.

[45] Vienna Convention on the Law of Treaties, Article 31(1).

Opponents to this position may argue that at the time of the UNCLOS III negotiations, the Conference did not consider autonomous vessels because of the technology available at the time. The UK takes the view that this does not mean the Convention is not capable of application to new technology and has sought to rely on the Vienna Convention on the Law of Treaties:

> A treaty shall be interpreted in good faith in accordance with the ordinary meaning to be given to the terms of the treaty in their context and in the light of its object and purpose.[46]

Further, case law since the ratification of UNCLOS has established that the Treaty can be interpreted in the light of new technology rather than ignoring it.[47]

Therefore, it is the UK's position that the "commanding officer" of an autonomous warship would be ashore. Equally, there would be a "crew": namely the team acting in support of the commanding officer, to assist in the planning and conduct of operations, as well as maintenance of the vessel. Clearly, for Article 29 to have effect, the commanding officer would still need to be a commissioned officer, and the crew would be serving members of the Royal Navy.

Since the UK's assertion, the only other State to make a public declaration on the matter has been the United States, in the amendment to the Commanders' Handbook to the Law of Naval Operations, which stated:

> There is no requirement the commanding officer or crew be physically on board the warship. warships may be remotely commanded, crewed, and Operated;

and

> When flagged as a ship, a UMS may exercise the navigational rights and freedoms and other internationally lawful uses of the seas related to those freedoms. Unmanned systems may be designated as USS if they are under the command of a commissioned officer and manned by a crew under regular armed forces discipline, by remote or other means.[48]

In the same vein, an autonomous system which is not a vessel, such as an autonomous maritime drone laden with explosives, can still be used as a lawful means or method of warfare. If these assets are to be used as weapons systems, several legal obligations result, primarily *before* use and then *during* use. In the *before* category, if the maritime asset is a new weapon, or at least a revised means or method of warfare, then States party to Additional Protocol I to the Geneva Conventions must conduct a weapon review under Article 36.[49] According to this provision, any new means or

---

[46] For example, with reference to the application of new technology to the principles of hot pursuit under UNCLOS Article 111, see Arctic Sunrise Arbitration para 259–260.

[47] NWP 1-14 M *The Commander's Handbook on the Law of Naval Operations* March 22 Edition, 2.2.1 and 2.3.5.

[48] 1977 Additional Protocol I to the Geneva Conventions, Article 36. Available at https://www.icrc.org/en/doc/assets/files/other/icrc_002_0321.pdf The list of State signatories is available at https://ihl-databases.icrc.org/en/ihl-treaties/api-1977/state-parties.

[49] The format for a weapons review is not fixed, it is a matter for individual States. For an example of one State's approach see https://assets.publishing.service.gov.uk/government/uploads/system/uploads/attachment_data/file/507319/20160308-UK_weapon_reviews.pdf, which is the published UK policy on Article 36 Weapon Reviews.

method of warfare should not be "prohibited by this protocol" or "any other rule of international law" applicable to that party.

This weapons review is the process by which a government must assess the potential use for a new means or method of warfare, against the requirements set in international law.[50]

During use, regardless of the classification of weapon system (mine, torpedo, missile, or other), the weapon system must be deployed against a lawful target in accordance with the Law of Naval Warfare.[51] While this legal regime is not governed directly by Additional Protocol I, and specifically the conduct of hostilities rules contained within, it is widely accepted that customary law counterparts of the rules do apply at sea.

The key, however, is that the same practical reasons highlighted above which exist for the use of autonomous vessels and systems in peacetime, would still apply in conflict. Namely, a reduced daily operating cost and a reduced risk to life to personnel within a State's Armed Forces.

Conclusion

Autonomous systems and vessels are in no way the complete answer to meeting novel threats and challenges in the South China Sea. However, they can be of real value. Not only do they provide a possible practical solution to building mass and capacity, but they can also be used to uphold the principles enshrined in UNCLOS, most notably the freedom of navigation. Although UNCLOS does not specifically refer to the operation of autonomous systems, it nevertheless provides a sound legal construct within which to operate them. Key to this is ensuring they are classified correctly. While it is sincerely hoped that the situation will not escalate that far, they are also a viable option for operations in conflict as well, provided they are used in accordance with international law.

[50] As articulated in: International Institute of Humanitarian Law, San Remo Manual on International Law Applicable to Armed Conflicts at Sea (Cambridge University Press 1994); hereafter referred to as "San Remo Manual". The San Remo Manual is a contemporary restatement of the law of armed conflict at sea, collated by an international group of specialists in international law and naval expert.

[51] Ibid, see Part IV, para 78.4 in the Commentary, in particular.

Chapter 11
Emission Reduction from Shipping and Net-Zero Shipping: Institutional Deficiencies and the Way Forward

Michael Tsimplis

Introduction

A relatively small number of states dominate the shipping market. There are three major shipbuilding states[1] and four ship-recycling states.[2] Thirty-five states owned ninety-five percentage of the deadweight tonnage with Greece, China, and Japan, owning more than 42%.[3] The top eight ship registers have more than 5% of the global tonnage each, and collectively account for 66% of the global tonnage.[4]

The small number of states involved with international shipping has not, however, guided the shipping sector towards consensus in relation to decarbonisation. The shipping sector, buttressed behind its international regulator, the International Maritime Organisation,[5] argued its way out of the Kyoto Protocol in 1997[6] and succeeded in not being formally referred to under the 2015 Paris Agreement.[7] Its initial strategy for decarbonisation has been developed in 2018, 26 years (or a generation of ships) after

[1] China, the Republic of Korea and Japan. These three countries account for 93% of the global number of ships built in 2022 (UNCTAD, Review of Maritime Transport 2023) 31.

[2] Bangladesh, India, Pakistan and Turkey. These four countries accounted for 92.7% of the recycled tonnage in 2022. (n 1) 37.

[3] (N 21) 34. Ships of 1000 grt or larger are counted in the ownership statistics.

[4] Panama, Liberia, Marshall Islands, Bahamas, Malta, Hong Kong (SAR), Singapore, China, (n 1) 35.

[5] The Convention on the Inter-Governmental Maritime Consultative Organization Adopted by the United Nations Maritime Conference in Geneva on 6 March 1948 9 U.S.T. 621, 289 U.N.T.S. 48.

[6] The Kyoto Protocol to the United Nations Framework Convention on Climate Change, 11th December 1997 entry into force 16/02/2005 (2303 UNTS 148).

[7] The Paris Agreement, Paris 12/12/2015, in force 4/11/2016, UNTS Registration 54113.

M. Tsimplis (✉)
City University of Hong Kong, Kowloon, China
e-mail: mtsimpli@cityu.edu.hk

N. Hung Son and N. Thi Lan Anh (eds.), *The South China Sea: The Geo-political Epicenter of the Indo-Pacific?*, https://doi.org/10.1007/978-981-97-8209-3_11

the United Nations Framework Convention on Climate Change 1992[8] established the objective of avoiding dangerous anthropogenic climate change in international law and policy. A revised IMO Strategy was adopted in July 2023. The plan to provide a carbon price in some form of a market-based mechanism did not materialise and has been delayed further. Because of the lack of efficient shipping policies during the past three decades, ships have continued to emit greenhouse gases, undisturbed and indifferent to efforts to reduce emissions. Ship engine technology has not improved, and, as a result, it is unlikely that the IMO's strategy will significantly contribute to global efforts to control the greenhouse gas concentrations in the atmosphere.

Two statements highlight the problems involved. The first is the Marshall Islands' characterisation of the IMO's Secretary-General's views expressed in 2015 as "a danger to the planet".[9] This statement was made days before the beginning of the negotiations that led to the Paris Agreement. The second is the statement by the shipping industry concerning greenhouse emission reduction that "... the commercial development of relevant technologies, fuels, propulsion systems and related infrastructure are the responsibility of other out-of-sector stakeholders rather than shipowners".[10] The first statement indicates that the IMO, the very efficient UN body established to harmonise the operation of international shipping, was, in 2015, isolated from, arguably, the most important global environmental challenge. The second statement indicates that the sector, is unwilling to invest in technology, leaving the initiative to the rest of society. These characteristics result from the legal and institutional approaches adopted over the past 50 years. They show that the standardisation of ships and the command-and-control policy through certification which the IMO has developed has removed innovation and competitiveness from the sector. Shipowners see themselves as users of ready-made and certified ships which they expect to run for 20–30 years without having to spend money into improving the environmental performance of the ship. Various reasons have led to this unsatisfactory position.

[8] The United Nations Framework Convention on Climate Change, adopted May 9, 1992.

[9] "His call is not just a danger to the planet, but as the research points out, also to the shipping industry's future prosperity, and therefore the future stability of world trade", RMI's Foreign Affairs Minister Tony de Brum said in a statement. See: https://www.offshore-energy.biz/marshall-islands-sekimizus-view-on-co2-emissions-danger-to-the-planet/) (accessed June 21, 2022).

[10] ISWG-GHG 10/5/2 3 September 2021 submitted by the International Chamber of Shipping and Intertanko.

The International Law of the Sea Constraints

Internationally trading ships do so by exercising rights available to their flag state. Because the LOSC[11] supports the freedom of navigation on the high seas, a ship outside jurisdictional areas is under the exclusive jurisdiction of the flag state.[12] Freedom of navigation for the ships of all states without interference by foreign states are conditions supportive of international trade. However, they are not helpful for environmental protection because polluting actions on the high seas cannot be controlled unless a naval ship of the flag state is present. Navigational rights are further supported by the requirement that the laws of coastal states concerning the Construction, Design, Equipment, and Manning of ships on innocent passage cannot exceed those adopted in the IMO. It is only where a ship comes into the port of a state that the powers of the coastal state can be exercised in full.

However, the customary international law powers have been curtailed by the LOSC. The supremacy of the flag state has been used to develop the trading of ships through a certification system.[13] The certification system operates as follows. The flag state confirms that the ship is compliant and issues a corresponding certificate which then forms the basis of the entitlement to trade at the ports of foreign states. The control of the ship is based, at first instance, on the inspection of the relevant certificate. The reliance on the certification system is supportive of international trade. However, it also means that the coastal state is restricting its rights to survey the ship thoroughly to the situations where specific conditions are satisfied.

This control system originated in the 1914 SOLAS Convention[14] and was later adopted by the IMO. The LOSC which was agreed after the development of this system, had no choice but to endorse it. Doing otherwise would undermine the IMO efforts to ensure minimum regulatory standards for ships. Thus, the LOSC expressly supports the IMO by referring several issues for resolution to the "competent international organisation".[15] The IMO is the only organisation which can be described as a competent international organisation for shipping matters so it is clear that the IMO-based regulations are adopted under the LOSC arrangements.

---

[11] Convention on the Law of the Sea, Dec. 10, 1982, Entry into force, 1st November, 1994, 1833 U.N.T.S. 397.

[12] LOSC Art. 92(1). An exception exists under Art. 110 and on emergency situations involving a need for intervention under International Convention Relating To Intervention On The High Seas In Cases Of Oil Pollution Casualties, Brussels, 29 November 1969, entry in force 6 May 1975, 970 UNTS 211; 9 ILM 25 (hereinafter 1969 Intervention Convention); Protocol relating to Intervention on the High Seas in Cases of Pollution by Substances other than Oil (Intervention Protocol 1973), London, 2/11/1973, entry in force, 30 March 1983 and its further amendments. The freedom of navigation is also available to states in the EEZ of other states and the coastal state has to have "due regard" to the rights of foreign states when exercising its rights in the EEZ.

[13] LOSC Art. 217(3) and 226(1)(a).

[14] See Tsimplis M. (2021), Environmental Norms in Maritime Law. Edward Elgar.

[15] See LOSC Arts. 41(4), 53(9), 211(1), 211(2), 217(1), 217(5), 218(1), 220(7). However, the IMO is expressly referred to once in the context of Special Arbitration. See LOSC Annex VIII Art.2(2).

The International Maritime Organisation

The Inter-governmental Maritime Consultative Organization (IMCO) was established by International Convention in 1948 and renamed in 1975 as the International Maritime Organisation (IMO). The IMO is the central negotiating forum[16] for shipping.[17] The IMO is a forum concerned with technical cooperation, not one where principles, political, and economic issues are discussed. As a result, technical approaches dominate its operation. The adoption of uniform technical rules creates a framework of minimum regulatory standards for ships irrespective of the flag each ship flies. Thus, assuming uniform enforcement, all externalities arising from the operation of ships are the same for all flag states and differ only between ship generations. Because the minimum standards are sufficient for trading across the world and there are no rewards for adopting higher standards, innovation, and competition on the environmental quality of the ships are rendered irrelevant. Because of this arrangement, the shipping sector collectively has defended its privileges and has resisted change. One of the privileges is the use of grandfathering clauses, i.e. exemptions from new standards granted to existing ships. Thus, the adoption of new standards is usually restricted to new-built ships. By excluding existing ships from new environmental measures, the reaction of shipowners with vested interests disappears, and consensus at the IMO is easier to achieve. However, these exemptions delay the beneficial effect of regulatory improvements and make the use of older ships more attractive as, in addition to having cost less than the new ships, the older ships have to comply with lower standards. Furthermore, in many IMO instruments, there is a prioritisation of the ship's operational and commercial needs over environmental compliance.[18]

The sectoral interests are prioritised partly due to the decision-making dynamics at the IMO:

1) Most delegations come primarily from national governments' trading and shipping departments or ship registers. They do not have interests or mandates from

[16] The IMO has been argued to have law-making powers under the tacit amendment procedure (see, for example, Churchill R.R.and G. Ulfstein, (2000), Autonomous Institutional Arrangements in Multilateral Environmental Agreements: A Little- Noticed Phenomenon in International Law, The American Journal of International Law, Vol. 94(4), 623–659. Tsimplis M. (2013), Shipping and the Marine Environment in the 21st Century, In Maritime Law Evolving. Clarke, M. (ed.). 1st ed. UK: Hart Publishing, p. 95–128 suggests that these are restricted powers of amendment of technical or quantitative details granted to the IMO bodies by the contracting states of the relevant convention, and subject to an undergoing negotiating process and do not lead to the creation of legislative powers to any of the IMO bodies.

[17] For the way the IMO operates, see Balkin R. P., (1999), The Establishment and Work of the IMO Legal Committee, in Current Maritime Issues and the International Maritime Organisation, (Nordquist M.H. and Moore J.N. editors), Martinus Nijhoff Publishers,291–308; Gaskell, N., (2003), Decision Making and the Legal Committee of the International Maritime Organization, The International Journal of Marine and Coastal Law, 18(2), 155–214; Harrison, J., (2011), Making the law of the Sea, Cambridge Studies in International and Comparative Law, Cambridge University Press, in particular Chapter 6, pp 154–199.

[18] Ibid.

environmental departments. To the extent that the leadership and the management of the IMO and the various committees are agreed upon from the pool of delegates, it is unsurprising that the sector's interests lead the proceedings.
2) The preference for technical solutions applicable to all ships makes the interventions of environmental NGOs ineffective, because the environmental effects of the selected technical solutions are rarely considered at the merchant fleet level.
3) Sectoral NGOs have the technical knowledge and the links with the governmental departments to argue their way through.

With a small group of classification societies instrumental in shipbuilding and controlling ships as recognised organisations, there is a closely knit mentality of protecting the sector from what is perceived as costly and potentially destabilising exposures to change. The dominance of the commercial sector's interests means that regulations are designed to reduce the financial risks for invested capital in shipping and avoid competition in environmental standards. The resulting regulatory framework is then considered to be a problem-solved approach where delays in implementation and bad practices are blamed, but the correctness of the approach is not questioned.

Decarbonisation

Within this context, it is unsurprising that the IMO has delayed action in decarbonisation (Fig. 11.1).

GHG emissions from ships only comprise a small contribution to the global emissions problem.[19] Nevertheless, shipping is a wealthy sector, not a state; thus, the delays in action are difficult to justify. The estimates of the social cost put on CO_2 emissions vary between states, but for the sake of argument, the value set by the US Administration is adopted—$51 per tonne.[20] In 2018, it was estimated that GHG emissions from shipping were 1,076 million tonnes,[21] corresponding to a social cost of around $55 billion per year. The Initial IMO Strategy on Reduction of GHG Emissions from ships[22] has, at the highest level of ambition, a reduction of 50% by 2050 with reference to 2008 values, estimated to be 790 million tonnes of GHG emissions.

[19] About 2.7%. See Olmer N, Comer B, Roy B, Mao X, Rutherford D. Greenhouse gas emissions from global shipping, 2013–2015. In: ICCT, editor, The International Council on Clean Transportation; 2017. p. 1–38.

[20] The Trump Administration estimated the same cost to be in the range of $1–7 per tonne by excluding impacts outside the USA see: Cost of Carbon Pollution Pegged at $51 a tonne, by Jean Chemnick, E&E News on March 1, 2021, available at https://www.scientificamerican.com/article/cost-of-carbon-pollution-pegged-at-51-a-tonne/#:~:text=That's%20after%20the%20Biden%20administration,EPA%20regulations%20and%20government%20spending accessed on 8/4/2021.

[21] Faber J et al. (2020), Fourth IMO GHG Study 2020, IMO Publications.

[22] Resolution MEPC.304(72), Adopted on 13 April 2018. For a commentary see Chircop, A. (2019). The IMO Initial Strategy for the Reduction of GHGs from International Shipping: A Commentary, The International Journal of Marine and Coastal Law, 34(3), 482–512.

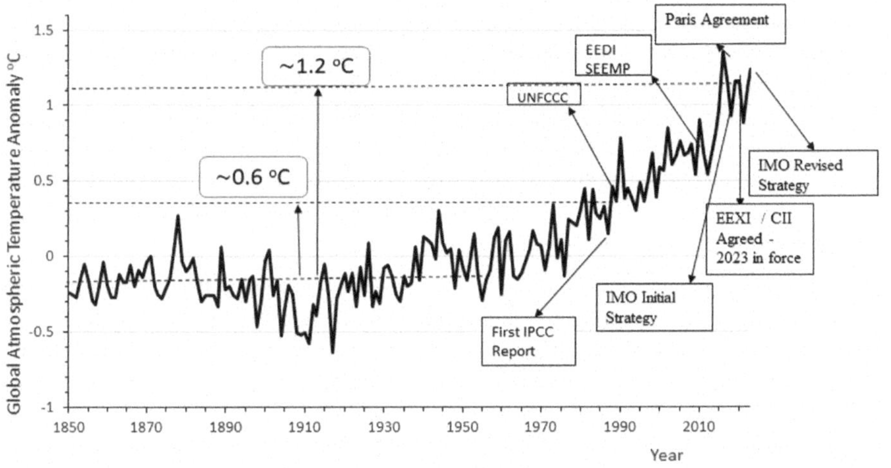

Fig. 11.1 Global temperature change (from NOAA) with respect to the period 1990–2000. The timeline of the first Intergovernmental Panel for Climate Change Report (1990), the United Nations Framework Convention for Climate Change (UNFCCC, 1992) and the 2015 Paris Agreement are used as milestones of reaction to the Climate Change challenge by the international community. The time of adoption of a number of IMO instruments is also shown. Thus the Energy Efficiency Design Index (EEDI), for new ships, the Ship Energy Efficiency Management Plan (SEEMP), The IMO Initial and Revised Strategies and the agreement on the Energy Efficiency Existing Ship Index (EEXI) and the Carbon Intensity Index (CII) are also marked. Notably, the first IMO resolution was adopted in 1997 (MP/CONF. 3/35) but was not acted upon for a long time

Assuming this highest level of ambition is achieved by the IMO strategy, the social cost of GHG emissions from shipping would be reduced to about $20 billion per year, assuming that the social cost of $51 per tonne remains unchanged with time.

The Revised IMO Strategy[23] increased the targeted reductions by 20%–30% by 2030 and 70%–80% by 2040. Net-zero emissions are to be achieved by or around 2050. In adopting the net-zero target, the IMO defined emissions as well-to-wake GHGs (including CO_2, methane (CH_4), and nitrous oxide (N_2O)). Net zero does not necessarily mean that there will be no GHG emissions by ships. Instead, it means that when the whole cycle of fuel production and consumption is considered, the emissions produced will be balanced by the absorption of CO_2 in the production process or the capture and storage of CO_2 after emission with onboard Carbon Capture and Storage Systems.[24] However, the cost of production of e-fuels depends on the cost of renewable energy available for that production,[25] and the costs for onboard Capture and Storage of CO_2 estimated at $220–290/ton$CO_2$ in the most suitable ship and

[23] 2023 IMO STRATEGY ON REDUCTION OF GHG EMISSIONS FROM SHIPS, RESOLUTION MEPC.377(80), Adopted on 7 July 2023. MEPC 80/WP.12,

[24] See for example REDUCTION OF GHG EMISSIONS FROM SHIPS, Submitted by RINA, MEPC 80/INF.14.

[25] See The Potential of E-fuels to Decarbonise Ships and Aircraft, Submitted by OECD, MEPC 80/INF.12.

effective CO_2 emission reduction of 74–78%[26] it is difficult to see how the sector will be incentivised without a carbon tax high enough to make these alternative ways of getting to net-zero possible.

A market-based mechanism is under discussion, but according to the work plan in the revised strategy, it will not, if agreed, start applying before 2027. The form of the market-based mechanism has yet to be specified with the shipping sector resisting a carbon-trading mechanism and preferring a flat tax, determined through the IMO, with rebates for better performers. Over the past four years (2019–2022), the total fuel consumption by reporting to the IMO ships has remained constant with a very small improvement in energy efficiency.[27] As the fuel consumption has not reduced and there has not been any significant increase in the use of cleaner fuel, the conclusion must be that there has not been any emissions reduction so far with respect to ships which have submitted a report. It is unknown what the position is for the non-reporting ships, but it would be unreasonable to expect it to be any better.

GHG Emissions Reduction for the Highest Polluters and in the Busiest Regions?

Notably, the adopted IMO's approach of regulating all ships uniformly is not the most efficient because not all ships are equally polluting. LNG carriers, cruise ships, and containerships are the highest GHG emitting ships. However, because some sectors involve more ships than other, the bulk carrier sector is the higher GHG emitter, with container ships and tankers following. Two approaches can work better than the IMO strategy. One would be to focus on the more polluting ships, with container ships being the highest priority. An alternative approach could focus on implementation in states where most ships go and which can control their GHG emissions. Imposing immediate and efficient GHG emission reductions in the major trading states will significantly reduce GHG emissions for the merchant shipping sector.[28] It is not suggested that parts of the shipping industry should be left unregulated or that states should be allowed to avoid the necessary due diligence in performing their duties. It is indicated that differentiation between types of ships and areas of operation and selective enforcement may lead to a quick reduction of GHG emissions from shipping.

---

[26] (N 25).

[27] Report on annual carbon intensity and efficiency of the existing fleet (Reporting years: 2019, 2020, 2021 and 2022). Note by the Secretariat, MEPC 81/6/1.

[28] Within this context, efforts by the USA and the European Union to implement early or in excess of the IMO requirements, the so-called "gold plating", are likely to increase the regulatory benefits and reduce the environmental impacts of shipping.

European Union's Regional Intervention

The inclusion of shipping under the European Union's Emissions Trading Scheme (EU ETS)[29] from January 1st, 2024, is likely to be more efficient than the IMO's complicated and inefficient system. The application of the EU ETS to shipping includes a phase-in period during which emission allowances for 40%, 70%, and 100% of the emissions will be required for 2024, 2025, and 2026. Currently, the EU ETS only applies to ships larger than 5000 gt and covers 100% of emissions for intra-EU voyages and 50% of emissions for voyages outside the EU. An expansion for offshore ships is planned for 2027, as well as the potential inclusion of ships between 400gt–5000gt after an evaluation. A crucial point is that the EU's ETS includes several sectors; thus, it supports uniform carbon pricing, which is independent of the IMO's procedures and subject to progressive capping by the EU. Whether the reality of the EU ETS system will break the sector's resistance in the IMO and lead to an efficient global alternative or an additional tax payable by all ships in addition to the EU's ETS remains to be seen.

Is the IMO Moving Away from Grandfathering Clauses?

There are also some slight indications that the IMO is moving away from the grandfathering clauses. The Energy Efficiency Existing Ship Index (EEXI) and the Carbon Intensity Indicator (CII), which were agreed upon in June 2021 and entered into force on 1 January 2023[30] apply to existing ships larger than 400 gt.

The Energy Efficiency Ship Index

The EEXI is an estimator of the carbon dioxide emissions per transport work. The more efficient a ship is, the lower the emissions are for the same amount of transport work. In theory, the EEXI is based on the ship engine's characteristics, power and consumption, which determine the CO_2 emissions and the ship's characteristics, cargo capacity, and reference speed, which determine the transport work. The numbers used in the EEXI calculation are the ship's design characteristics; therefore, there is no monitoring involved. Of course, a ship can improve its energy performance by, for example, changing the fuel consumed or installing sails. The way an indicator like the EEXI is to be used as a policy instrument is to require that it does not go above

[29] Directive (EU) 2023/959 of the European Parliament and of the Council of 10 May 2023 amending Directive 2003/87/EC establishing a system for greenhouse gas emission allowance trading within the Union and Decision (EU) 2015/1814 concerning the establishment and operation of a market stability reserve for the Union greenhouse gas emission trading system (Text with EEA relevance).

[30] See Resolution MEPC.334(76) adopted 17 June 2021.

a maximum value and progressively lower this maximum value, thus forcing the less efficient performers to consider improvements or drive them out of the market.

However, the way the EEXI is implemented includes several adjustments requested by various sub-sectors of the industry, which reflect the particularities of different ships. This differentiation also includes propulsion systems. Thus, the standard does not prefer the more efficient propulsion systems but the more efficient ship designs that have adopted a specific ship propulsion system. Thus, higher and lower emitters are all treated equally as if the purpose of the arrangement is not to exclude the more polluting systems and reduce emissions but rather to give the impression of doing so. Furthermore, the baseline for setting the EEXI is calculated on the statistics of existing ships. Because smaller ships have higher EEXI than larger ships of the same type, the reference baseline for smaller ships is much higher. Thus, there is no objective standard for the EEXI.

Using the statistical interpolation of existing ships as the baseline and allowing for the different ship sizes, propulsion systems, and types means that the legal framework is indifferent to the absolute energy efficiency and treats high and low-emitting ships the same. This encourages the attempts to obtain adjustments for particular engine or ship designs, resulting in compromises and adjustments which are difficult to assess for efficiency,

Using the statistical status quo as the baseline means that, on average, half of the ships of every category and every size will have an EEXI better than the average at the starting point. They will need to do nothing to improve efficiency until the progressive reduction of the maximum allowed EEXI applicable to the specific type of ship becomes lower than their current EEXI. Thus, the progressive capping of the EEXI will affect the worst performers in each ship category, propulsion type, and ship size, who will need to do something to improve their energy efficiency. All the others will be compliant irrespective of the fact that they are neither energy-efficient nor "green" and may have done nothing to improve the ship's efficiency.

Perhaps more surprising is that the required EEXI improvements can be achieved, for many ships, by simply reducing fuel consumption, which itself can be achieved by limiting the engine's power, in essence, slowing down the ship. Speed limitations were advocated for over a decade and could have been done easily and quickly. However, to consider it to work as a design factor of the ship and thus affect the EEXI, an Energy Power Limitation (EPL) or Shaft power limitation (SHaPoLi) system must be installed on the ship. This can be overridden by the master in cases of emergency.[31] Because several ships do not utilise the engine's full power to travel large distances, the power limitation will be minimal in terms of actual energy efficiency. These ships will continue emitting as much as they did, but they will have a lower EEXI and a certificate from the flag state to show for this. Moreover, even when a ship improves its energy efficiency, it does not follow that the ship will emit less CO_2, because the ship may operate for longer periods. Thus, the EEXI, as a measure, is deficient in its design due to its non-uniformity; it cannot deliver real improvements in energy

[31] In which case it needs to be reported.

efficiency, and in terms of emissions, better results would have been achieved by simply reducing the speed of ships.

The Carbon Intensity Indicator

While the EEXI is a ship design indicator, the Carbon Intensity Indicator (CII) is a performance indicator based on the annual ship emissions estimated on the basis of the type and quantity of bunkers used divided by the product of the distance travelled and the carrying capacity of the ship. The CII is not based on the actual cargo transported but on the cargo that could have been transported on the particular ship. This was done because of the lack of data on cargoes transported. It does create, however, some peculiarities. Voyages on ballast burn less fuel than laden voyages. Thus, two identical ships, one continuously on ballast and the other fully loaded, will have different CII, with the wastefully travelling on the ballast ship being considered a better performer than the loaded ship.[32] Thus, shipowners can reduce the ship's consumption by having the ship party laden or on ballast. The bigger picture would be that for a given cargo, a partly loaded ship would require another ship to carry the rest of the cargo, thus increasing the overall emissions. Thus, the selected CII may increase inefficiencies in the global transportation system.

The baseline CII is calculated on the basis of median statistics of the CII of existing ships on the basis of 2019 data and by using different adjustments for the ship's type and size. This forms the reference CII for the specific ship. As it is based on median statistics, half of the ships in each category should be above the reference CII. The required CII will be calculated each year after 2023 by reducing the reference CII by 5%, 7%, 9%, and 11% for 2023, 2024, 2025, and 2026. Thus, the regulatory objective for each year will be set, and then the actual energy efficiency, the attained CII, will be compared with the required for that year's CII. One would have expected that since the CII is calculated per ship type and by reference to the size, there would be uniform treatment in the characterisation of the CII. This is not, however, the case. For each ship category, four numbers are used as the boundaries between the 5 performance categories. For example, for a bulk carrier, the numbers are 0.86, 0.94, 1.06, and 1.18, corresponding to the CII attained. These correspond to an attained CII being 14% and 6% smaller and 6% and 18% higher than the required CII. By comparison, the numbers for a RO-RO cargo ship are 0.66, 0.9, 1.11, 1.37 putting the outer limits of the best performer at 34% less than the CII and the worse performers at 37% worse than the required CII, more than double the boundaries for the bulk carriers. All this complexity will result in the certification of the ship by the flag state in performance level A (Major superior), B (Minor superior), C(moderate), D(Minor Inferior), or

[32] All the different types of emission indicators concerned by the IMO produce such peculiarities. See: Wang S., H. N. Psaraftis, J. Qi,(2021), Paradox of international maritime organization's carbon intensity indicator, Communications in Transportation Research, 1, 100005, .https://doi.org/10.1016/j.commtr.2021.100005.

E(Inferior). However, currently, there are no penalties for underperformance; the only requirement is that ships with a grade of E or D for three consecutive years must develop a plan to improve their score as part of the SEEMP and have it approved by the flag state.

The Impact of the CII and EEXI

The adoption of these two indicators has shifted the attention away from whether these will, in fact, contribute to the reduction of emissions from ships and towards the problems the measures will introduce in the operational and commercial aspects of shipping. The CII is determined by how the ship will be operated over the reporting year in terms of the bunkers and the speed used. Where the ship is time-chartered, the decision-making for the contractual performance is passed to the charterers, who bear the risk of delays and may recover paid hire under off-hire clauses. Voyage charters are normally under an obligation of due or utmost despatch. Thus, the sector focuses on contractual arrangements that can resolve these and other difficulties and protect the shipowner from having a ship with a reduced CII at the end of the charterparty.[33]

Will the EEXI and the CII Contribute to Decarbonization?

The IMO's approach has been to regulate emissions from each ship. This is evidenced by the EEDI and the Ship Energy Efficiency Management Plan (SEEMP), in 2013, measures designed to improve energy efficiency for new and existing ships, respectively and which have failed to produce any noticeable reduction in shipping emissions. The Initial Strategy in 2018 was the first time emissions reduction of the whole fleet by reference to the total emissions of all the trading ships benchmarked against emissions over a previous period are considered. Still, the selected measures, the EEXI and the CII are energy efficiency indicators for each ship. Improving them for each ship does not mean that the ship emits less, as it may work more, let alone lead to emission reductions when the number of ships may increase. Note also that the referencing for emissions reduction is set by reference to the highest emissions point in 2008. The reference point does not matter if zero emissions are the target, but it does matter when partial reductions are considered.

The IMO promotes the view that the EEXI and the CII, by increasing energy efficiency, reduce the emissions from the same ship if these indices have not been introduced, the business-as-usual scenario. However, GHGs stay in the atmosphere

---

[33] See for example CII OPERATIONS CLAUSE FOR TIME CHARTER PARTIES 2022 and the CII CLAUSE FOR VOYAGE CHARTER PARTIES 2023, the EEXI TRANSITION CLAUSE FOR TIME CHARTER PARTIES 2021. In addition, 5 other clauses have been developed in response to the EU ETS extension to cover ships visiting EU ports. All clauses are available at https://www.bimco.org/contracts-and-clauses/bimco-clauses accessed 8/22024.

for several decades or centuries; for example, the CO_2 concentration naturally reduces by half over 120 years. Thus, suggesting that reductions by reference to the business-as-usual scenario can ever be a sufficient response to climate change is false. Nor can it be argued that allowing time for the sector to move is reasonable. Even if the 2 decades of inaction by the sector, under the protection of the IMO's shield, is ignored, what is the justification for allowing one of the wealthier sectors to profit by burdening the ability of future generations to live sustainably?

The EEXI and CII standards will be met for many existing ships by simply slowing down. So, a cynic could say that the whole regulatory framework is much ado about nothing. There are serious doubts that these measures will be of much benefit[34] and by the time this is confirmed, the current ships would most likely have run their useful life. Perhaps that is the objective.

With ships having twenty-five to thirty years of life, the ships ordered today will still be in circulation in 2050. Today's ships will not have zero emissions but, for LNG-fueled ships, reduced emissions of about 30%. Thus, the net-zero policy is unachievable without a much faster replacement of ships or their engines. It is clear, however, that unless the current generation of ships is wholly withdrawn, there is little chance of achieving greenhouse gas reductions, let alone net-zero emissions in shipping.

The pessimistic outlook is a consequence of the sector's refusal to take action and the industry's unwillingness to invest in cleaner ships over the past two decades. This unwillingness continues to be expressed in the statement mentioned above by the International Chamber of Shipping (ICS) and Intertanko, eminent shipowner associations.[35]

The shipping industry refuses to take the lead in innovation because the dominant interests are those of existing shipowners worried about the diminution of value of their investments if cleaner ships are developed fast. Establishing incentives to reward efficient ships and make polluting ships pay are as crucial in achieving decarbonisation as removing grandfathering clauses and ensuring compliance by directly monitoring emissions.[36]

Ports and Inter-Sectoral Competition

The effort to decarbonise shipping affects the competition between ports, provides opportunities for increasing market share for some companies, and raises issues with maritime cabotage. These are briefly described below.

[34] Small reductions are likely to be achieved because ships already operate at speeds and engine loads unaffected by the technical efficiency targets set by EEXI. See Rutherford D., X. Mao, and B. Comer, (2020), Potential CO_2 reductions under the Energy Efficiency Existing Ship Index, Working paper, October, 2020, The International Council on Clean Transportation.

[35] ISWG-GHG 10/5/2, September 3, 2021.

[36] See also Psaraftis HN, Kontovas CA. (2021) Decarbonization of Maritime Transport: Is There Light at the End of the Tunnel? Sustainability, 13(1):237. https://doi.org/10.3390/su13010237.

The efficiency of each ship is determined by fuel consumption. Thus, long delays in port increase the emissions without increasing the distance travelled. Such ports may become unfavourable to shipowners. Ports providing electric power to ships while at the port, thus reducing the burning of bunkers may become preferred.

In the liner shipping sector, strategic market alliances have led to a reduction in competition. The formation of shipping alliances occurred simultaneously with an increase in the size of container ships, contributing to fewer ships and significant reductions in connectivity for small island states. Vertical integration is also a trend in this sector, with companies acquiring an interest in terminals, ships, ports, logistics, rail, and air freight. This business model is argued to provide better operational and energy efficiency. The expansion of the liner sector is restricted at the national level by maritime cabotage, restricting foreign operators from providing shipping services between ports in the same state.[37] Thus, a ship can call in two ports of a state and deal with importing and exporting cargo but cannot transport cargo between these two ports. This means local cargo is more likely to be transported by land with larger emissions. The liner sector has argued for open competition for cabotage services on the grounds of efficiency. In contrast, it had argued (unsuccessfully) for an extension of the exemption of alliances from anti-competition laws in the EU after 2024 on the basis of increased load factors and energy efficiency.[38] The business model for liner shipping is in sharp contrast with the business model for tramp shipping where voyages in ballast, short or long, are the norm. Such voyages could be avoided if consolidation similar to that of the liner sector was developed, but this would require a different business model. Thus, it is clear that the route for decarbonisation challenges the commercial status quo.

There are also additional considerations in that green shipping is likely to be based on innovations achieved in technologically advanced states, which will benefit from the adoption of such technologies at the expense of less-advanced states, which will need to buy the technology. However, many states, including the EU states, provide marine fuel subsidies which are inconsistent with emissions reduction policies.[39] These additional factors can, perhaps, help to understand the complexity of the negotiations at the IMO but cannot justify the inefficient regulatory outcomes.

---

[37] UNCTAD, "Rethinking Maritime Cabotage For Improved Connectivity" (2016) page 6.

[38] See the submission by the World Shipping Council, the International Chamber of Shipping, and the Asian Shipowners' Association in response to the European Commission's "Call for Evidence" regarding the evaluation of the Consortia Block Exemption Regulation dated 3 October 2022 available at https://ec.europa.eu/info/law/better-regulation/have-your-say/initiatives/13519-EU-competition-law-evaluation-of-the-Consortia-Block-Exemption-Regulation/F3347045_en accessed 8/2/2024.

[39] International Transport Forum (2019), Maritime Subsidies: Do they provide value for money? Available at https://www.itf-oecd.org/maritime-subsidies-do-they-provide-value-money accessed on 8/2/2024.

Conclusions

The IMO was created to establish minimum safety standards for ships and, later, to develop minimum pollution standards. The technical character of these requirements and the sectoral character of the organisation's leadership and decision-making have led to the IMO becoming a protective shield against demands for cleaning up ship operations in general and for decarbonising the sector in particular. After more than 2 decades of delays, the two versions of the decarbonisation strategy have developed energy efficiency requirements in the design and the operation of ships. These cannot lead to the decarbonisation of shipping and will not be able to stop an increase in the GHG emissions from the sector if the number of ships or the number of voyages increases. In other words, any increase in international trade will likely further increase GHG emissions from shipping.

However, adopting the EEXI and the CII has shifted the focus on their implementation and the operational, technical, and contractual allocation of financial risks. To the extent that the major response for compliance both for the EEXI and the CII would be, at least for the first years, a reduction in the speed of ships, it is indeed surprising how the IMO has produced an elaborate, opaque system of calculating energy efficiency indices full of compromises expressed through adjustment factors. The performance indicators will create misleading impressions by classing a large percentage of the existing ships as energy-efficient. The truth is that shipping has not invested and still resists as a sector, with notable exceptions, the investment in green shipping. This is done to protect the value of the investment in existing ships. The adopted regulations appear to change the long tradition of providing grandfathering protection to existing ships. However, the CII and the EEXI design means that only a small percentage of existing ships in each category will be affected; most ships will continue operating with minor adjustments in performance and with little or no change in their emissions.

What can states do? There are several actions that states can take. The legal framework is quite flexible, and significant powers are available to coastal states, as the EU states have demonstrated by extending the EU ETS system to ships. These powers are not affected by the standards agreed upon at the IMO, which must be considered as what they are: the minimum standards achieved by consensus and de facto insufficient to lead to decarbonisation of the sector.

States can go much further than the IMO measures when ships visit their ports. Ships in a port or within the jurisdiction of a state can be asked to comply with the coastal state's standards imposed as conditions for entry, provided they are not discriminatory against a particular flag. These conditions can include a demand for lower emissions by modifying operational practices, for example, requesting slower speeds and just-in-time arrival. Financial incentives can be developed by introducing lower fees for less-polluting ships or rewarding shipping companies that demonstrate environmental stewardship through fewer inspections or relevant certification.[40] Removal of all marine fuel subsidies for all GHGs should be supported. Port development to provide electricity to ships, while docked, should be encouraged and can be supported by developmental funds by taxing the national shipping industry and the foreign ships using the ports of the coastal state.

Operational options are also available and need to be considered seriously. In addition to slowing down and arriving just in time, reducing the number of voyages in ballast, that is, without cargo, should be targeted. Such optimisation will require the re-organisation of the logistics chain, in particular tramp shipping. However, in the absence of financial incentives for environmental performance or taxation of emissions, the financial benefits of inefficient and environmentally damaging commercial practices will continue.

Establishing a cross-sectoral carbon price is the best option for reducing emissions. If shipping is, as the IMO claims, the most efficient way of transport,[41] the sector should have nothing to fear from such a system. A carbon price determined by a cross-sectoral market will diffuse any efforts by shipping to delay taking measures and remove the IMO's ability to protect shipping from the decarbonisation demands. It will encourage investment in technology and reward first movers. In shipping, the bottom line matters. Allowing shipowners who emit less to profit and push the polluting ships out of the market will make decarbonisation easier. After all, it is the lack of any competitive advantage in developing greener ships that have stalled the sector's development.

[40] It is worth noting that the 1982 LOSC treats atmospheric pollution like marine pollution from ships. However, the inclusion of the GHG, SOx and NOx emissions in MARPOL 1973/1978 Annex VI precluded any possibility of dealing with the regulation or control of these emissions in a different way, and it seems inconceivable that this situation can be changed now.

[41] See the IO statement at https://sdgs.un.org/statements/international-maritime-organization-imo-15585#:~:text=It%20is%20in%20fact%20the,of%20a%20sustainable%20global%20economy accessed 8/2/2024.

Chapter 12
Opportunities and Challenges Associated with Synergy Between the Mekong Sub-Regional Cooperation Frameworks and the ASEAN-Led Mechanisms

Mai Sayavongs

Introduction

The Mekong River, which originates from the Tibet Plateau, China (called the Lancang River in China), is the 12th longest river in the world. The Mekong River plays a critical role in the livelihoods of the peoples in the sub-region since it is one of the main sources of food and water that supports the agricultural industry in most of the Mekong countries. Mekong sub-region is a strategic connecting point between mainland Southeast Asia and China as well as between mainland Southeast Asia and South Asia.[1] The Mekong sub-region is one of the most dynamic and strategic geographies in the world. This sub-region not only experiences a rapid growth but is also able to grab a great attention from major powers in the region and beyond. Currently, there have been many Mekong cooperative mechanisms. These mechanisms can be categorized into two groups: intra-regional mechanisms and cooperation mechanisms with partner countries outside the region. The group of intra-regional mechanisms consists of the Greater Mekong Sub-region (GMS 1992), The Mekong River Commission (MRC 1995), Ayeyawady-Chao Phraya-Mekong Economic Cooperation Strategy (ACMECS 2003-Thailand), cooperation between the four countries: Cambodia-Laos-Myanmar-Vietnam (CLMV), Vietnam-Laos-Cambodia Development Triangle (CLV-1999), the Mekong-Lancang Cooperation (MLC 2016-China),[2] and ASEAN Mekong Basin Development Cooperation (AMBDC-1995); whereas, cooperation

[1] The ISEAS–Yusof Ishak Institute (2020), Why the Mekong Matters to ASEAN: A Perspective from Vietnam', available at < https://www.iseas.edu.sg/wp-content/uploads/2020/06/ISEAS_Perspective_2020_77.pdf>, viewed on 26 Oct 2022.

[2] Diplomat (2019).

M. Sayavongs (✉)
Institute of Foreign Affairs, Vientiane, Laos
e-mail: maisayavongs@yahoo.com

N. Hung Son and N. Thi Lan Anh (eds.), *The South China Sea: The Geo-political Epicenter of the Indo-Pacific?*, https://doi.org/10.1007/978-981-97-8209-3_12

mechanisms with partner countries outside the region includes the Lower Mekong Initiative (LMI-US 2009), Friends of the Lower Mekong (FLM 2011-US and its partners), Mekong-Ganga Cooperation (MGC 2000-India), Mekong-Japan Cooperation (MJC 2007-Japan), Mekong-Korea Cooperation (MKC 2013-ROK), etc.[3] This is just to name a few.

Similarly, at the regional level, for instance, under the umbrella of ASEAN, there have been numerous ASEAN-led cooperation mechanisms such as the East Asia Summit (EAS), the ASEAN Regional Forum (ARF), the ASEAN Plus Three (APT), the ASEAN Defense Ministers' Meeting (ADMM), ADMM-Plus among others.[4]

Over the years, the existing sub-regional and regional mechanisms have presented opportunities to the countries in the region in terms of socio-economic development. However, there has been a concern regarding the benefit maximization that is intertwined with the growing implicit and explicit competition among the mechanisms, which could undermine cooperation and sustainable development in this sub-region and in ASEAN as a whole with a rising influence of major powers advancing their respective political and economic interests. Furthermore, the increasingly intensified power rivalry could also undermine the ASEAN Centrality.

This paper discusses potentials and challenges for the existing sub-regional cooperation frameworks to be synergized with ASEAN cooperation mechanisms for the greater benefits of region and beyond. However, it firstly examines the opportunities that the existing sub-regional cooperation mechanisms have presented to the sub-regional countries and beyond.

Opportunities Presented by the Mekong Sub-Regional Cooperation Mechanisms to the Development of Sub-Regional Countries

The Mekong sub-region, consisting of five countries namely Cambodia, Laos, Myanmar, Thailand, and Vietnam, is a home to 326 million people.[5] It is regarded as one of the greatest development potentials in Asia. Over the past few decades, the existing cooperative mechanisms have brought the opportunities for development to the riparian countries. This includes more prospects for having access to various

---

[3] Organ of Political Theory of Vietnam Communist Party's Central (2022), Cooperation in the Mekong Sub-region and Vietnam's Participation, available at <https://tapchicongsan.org.vn/web/english/international/detail/-/asset_publisher/ZeaSwtFJtMgN/content/cooperation-mechanisms-in-the-mekong-region-and-vietnam-s-participation>, viewed on 27 Oct 2022.

[4] Ibis.

[5] ADB (2022), Greater Mekong Sub-region, available at <https://www.adb.org/what-we-do/themes/regional-cooperation/overview/gms#:~:text=The%20Greater%20Mekong%20Subregion%20(GMS,population%20of%20around%20326%20million.>, viewed on 28 Oct 2022.

sources of funding to better address the need for their national socio-economic development, especially for connectivity infrastructure development.[6] For example, implementing its Mekong-Japan Cooperation Mechanism, Japan through the Japan International Cooperation Agency (JICA) has been one of the largest sources of official development assistance (ODA) to the Mekong countries. Cambodia, Laos, Myanmar, and Vietnam have received more than 50% of Japan's ODA share in Asian region. In just three years, after the Mekong-Japan Partnership was established in 2007, more than 5.5 billion USD was provided by the government of Japan to support development projects in the Mekong countries. Thanks to funds provided by the government of Japan, numerous infrastructure development projects have been completed, bringing tangible benefits to the sub-region and beyond. For instance, in Laos, many connectivity infrastructure projects to fulfill the missing links were funded by Japan. This includes the 2nd Mekong Friendship Bridge (2006), connecting Laos and Thailand via Savannakhet and Mukdahan provinces, and the upgrading of the national Road No.9 in 2003 leading to Vietnamese Lao Boa, Vietnamese border. This is part of East–West Economic Corridor development. Similarly, there have been a number of infrastructure development and improvement projects, such as roads, ports, and airports that were financed by Japan in Vietnam, Cambodia, and Myanmar over the past years.

In addition, the Mekong countries still have gained benefits from the China-led MLC, which aims to enhance cooperation among its member countries based on the 3 + 5 cooperation model. That is cooperation in three pillars: Political and Security, Economic and Sustainable Development, Socio-Cultural and People to People Exchange, focusing on five priority areas namely connectivity, production capacity, cross-border economic cooperation, water resource management, agriculture, and poverty reduction.[7] To put the MLC Five-Year-Action Plan (2018–2022) into implementation, the Mekong-Lancang Cooperation Special Fund (MLCSF) has been established during the 1st MLC Summit in 2016 to which the government of China contributed USD 300 million. As a result, recently there have been more than 700 projects implemented in the Mekong countries with the financial support from the LMC Special Fund, valued at 80 million USD. These projects have played a role in the socio-economic development of MLC member countries. Specifically, the Lao PDR has also obtained tangible benefits through the implementation of MLC projects and programs. Thanks to the MLC Special Fund, 80 projects have been fruitfully implemented in Laos with a total value of over 21 million USD. Remarkably, the Early Harvest Projects, such as the Laos-China Joint Poverty Alleviation Project of 33 million Yuan have been implemented in 2020 in Vientiane capital and Luang Prabang

---

[6] German Institute for International and Security Studies (2019), Connectivity Initiatives in the Mekong Region: Too Many or Too Little, available at < https://www.swp-berlin.org/publications/products/projekt_papiere/BCAS_2019_Leng_Mekong_Countries.pdf>.

[7] China Daily (2018), Five-Year Plan of Action on Lancang-Mekong Cooperation (2018–2022), available at < https://www.chinadaily.com.cn/a/201801/11/WS5a56cd04a3102e5b17374295.html>, viewed on 31 Oct 2022.

province, which has importantly contributed to small-scale infrastructure development of the respective cities, comprising public health centers, teachers' dormitories, garbage management, and training programs on clean and organic farming.[8]

Apart from that, there are still other mechanisms such as the Mekong-ROK, LMI, and Friends of the Lower Mekong including donors like Australia, Japan, New Zealand, the European Union, the Asia Development Bank, and the World Bank that have been playing a critical role in socio-economic development of the Mekong sub-region.[9]

In short, the existing cooperation mechanisms have made a substantial contribution to the development of the region and beyond through providing assistance in various forms such as grants, loans, and technical assistance that enable the need for the development of sub-regional countries to be better addressed. However, it must be acknowledged that the development gap among countries in the sub-region remains an issue.

Potentials for Synergizing the Existing Sub-Regional Cooperation Framework with ASEAN-Led Mechanisms

Even though there are many cooperation frameworks working toward contributing to the overall development of the Mekong sub-region and beyond, specifically in the field of infrastructure development as it is seen as one of the fundamental factors underlying the overall development of a certain country. Over the years, although it is witnessed that there have been numerous strategies being implemented to enhance connectivity within the Mekong sub-region as well as between the Mekong countries and other regions, funding for implementing these connectivity initiatives is still far from being adequate. According to the recent estimates, ASEAN nations will need to annually invest between 5 to 13% of their respective GDPs on infrastructure development as their economies grow stronger. Despite the existence of numerous infrastructure development initiatives, the ongoing investment in connectivity infrastructure is always required to ensure robust economic growth in the region.

Moreover, there is still a huge gap in infrastructure development among the Mekong countries with those of ASEAN as a whole. For instance, the Global Competitiveness Report (2019) by the World Economic Forum has ranked Singapore the 1st, out of 137 countries, for its overall infrastructure development, while some of the

[8] MoFA Lao PDR (2022), Article on the Sixth Anniversary of the Establishment of Mekong-Lancang Cooperation by H.E. Saleumxay KOMMASITH, Minister of Foreign Affairs of the Lao PDR (23 March 2016-23 March 2022), available at <http://www.mofa.gov.la/index.php/activities/state-leaders/4636-article-on-the-sixth-anniversary-of-the-establishment-of-mekong-lancang-cooperation-by-h-e-saleumxay-kommasith-minister-of-foreign-affairs-of-the-lao-pdr-23-march-2016-23-march-2022>.

[9] Mekong-US Partnership (2020), Friends of Mekong, available at <https://mekonguspartnership.org/partners/fom/#:~:text=The%20Friends%20of%20the%20Mekong,Nam%2C%20and%20the%20United%20States.>, viewed on 31 Oct 2022.

ASEAN members, particularly the Lower Mekong countries still lag behind, with Thailand being ranked at 71st, Vietnam at 77th, Laos at 93rd and Cambodia at 106th (Myanmar's data was unavailable as of 2019). These rankings demonstrate that infrastructure development gaps among ASEAN and the Mekong countries remain quite broad. This can be interpreted that there is an urgent need for some Mekong countries to put greater effort on accumulating more investment and resources in infrastructure development.[10] More importantly, countries in the Mekong sub-region should look for a variety of funding sources from the regional and sub-regional cooperation frameworks.[11]

Over the years, sub-regional cooperation has contributed to the mobilization of funds and resources for infrastructure development and the promotion of socio-economic development in the Mekong sub-region.[12] As previously discussed, the Mekong countries have received generous support from various development partners to help fulfill the need for infrastructure development. For instance, with the support from the government of Japan, many infrastructure projects have been accomplished. This includes the 2nd Mekong Friendship Bridge, connecting Laos and Thailand, and other projects surrounding the development and improvement of roads, ports, and airports in Vietnam, Cambodia, and Myanmar.

Similarly, the GMS Program has made an important contribution to the increased integration and prosperity of the region. Infrastructure development has been the core of the program, and a major achievement has been significantly increased physical connectivity in the sub-region as demonstrated by the construction of the three main GMS corridors: the East–West, North–South, and Southern economic corridors.[13] Furthermore, the Pan-Asia Railway Network has been a long time in the making, which includes three important routes with the aim of connecting mainland Southeast Asia with the rest of the world.[14] Under the Belt and Road Initiative (BRI), the Laos-China railway connecting Vientiane, Laos with Kunming, China has been completed and in operation since 2nd December 2021, which plays a critical role in enhancing regional connectivity. Another flagship project under the BRI framework is the China-Thailand high-speed railway, linking Bangkok to Nongkhai, a province adjacent to Laos, and subsequently connects with the China-Laos railway, the railway will travel

---

[10] WorldEconomicForum. (2019). *The Global Competitiveness Report 2019*, available at: <https://www.weforum.org/reports/how-to-end-a-decade-of-lost-productivity-growth>, viewed on 3 Nov 2022.

[11] Sim Vireak (2019), Mapping Mekong Cooperation Complementarities and Policy Implications, available at: <http://www.asianvision.org/archives/publications/avi-perspective-issue-2019-no-9>, viewed on 3 Nov 2022.

[12] German Institute for International and Security Studies (2019), Connectivity Initiatives in the Mekong Region: Too Many or Too Little, available at < https://www.swp-berlin.org/publications/products/projekt_papiere/BCAS_2019_Leng_Mekong_Countries.pdf>.

[13] ADB (2012), the Greater Mekong subregion at 20: Progress and Prospects, available at: < https://www.adb.org/sites/default/files/publication/30064/gms-20-yrs-progress-prospects.pdf> , viewed on 3 Nov 2022.

[14] Maya Majueran (2022), Pan-Asian Railway Boosts Regional Connectivity, available at: < http://www.chinadaily.com.cn/a/202201/08/WS61d8f3aba310cdd39bc7fdd3.html>, viewed on 3 Nov 2022.

from Thailand all the way to Malaysia. The China-Thailand railway is expected to be finished by 2028, with Phase 1 from Nongkhai-Nakhon Ratchasima, is in the process of construction. These aforesaid projects have made a significant contribution to the implementation of the ASEAN Master Plan on ASEAN Connectivity (MPAC 2025), allowing the countries in the sub-region and beyond to be more physically connected.

In fact, the Laos-China railway has already produced impressive tangible benefits to Laos and China as well as the sub-region. It has facilitated domestic and cross-border transport of goods and passengers. This is indicated by the fact that the travel time has been significantly reduced. For instance, it usually takes 10–11 h to travel by bus from Vientiane to the UNESCO world heritage town of Luang Prabang, but by train it takes only 1 h and 45. Likewise, from Vientiane to Kunming it takes around 9–10 h by train. In contrast, if traveling by bus or car, it takes up to 30–36 h. In a nutshell, the Laos-China railway has made land transport between the northern Lao cities and from Kunming, Yunnan, China to Vientiane more convenient, more accessible, more affordable compared to air transport. Evidently, within a year after its opening for services, the railway carried a total of 8.5 million passengers and transported 11.2 million tons of cargo.[15] This growth has boosted trade between Laos, China, and neighboring countries, as well as promoting people to people exchange in the region.

As the Mekong sub-region is an integral part of the ASEAN, the synergy between the existing Mekong sub-region cooperation frameworks with ASEAN-led mechanisms should be explored further as it could potentially provide more opportunities for the Lower Mekong sub-region to mobilize resources ranging from finance, expertise to technologies. With the increasing support, the sub-region could better address the need for comprehensive development and ultimately, concretize the ASEAN Community Vision Blueprints 2025.

Challenges Associated with Synergizing the Existing Sub-Regional Cooperation Framework with ASEAN-Led Mechanisms

Despite the fact that there have been numerous mechanisms and initiatives in the sub-region over the past decades, there are challenges that need to be addressed. Firstly, it seems that there is a lack of coordination among the existing cooperation frameworks both at sub-regional and regional levels to ensure that the mechanisms are implemented in a complementary manner.[16] This could result in overlapping rather than seeking for cooperation among sub-regional cooperation frameworks as

[15] The State Council Information Office, PRC, China-Laos Railway reports robust operation a year after launch, available at http://english.scio.gov.cn/m/beltandroad/2022-12/02/content_78548060.htm, viewed on 5 Nov 2022.

[16] German Institute for International and Security Studies (2019), Connectivity Initiatives in the Mekong Region

well as with other regional cooperation frameworks including ASEAN-led mechanisms. These mechanisms might overlap each other in terms of projects, agendas, and operational models as a result of non-communication among themselves. Each project tends to work on their own separate ways and not complementing the other similar projects which share the same objectives. In other words, it might be a waste of resources, which could otherwise be directed for other new development projects for the member countries.

Moreover, the competition among major powers for the expansion of their political and economic influence in the region through implementing their mechanisms is another prominent challenge that could hinder the synergy among the existing sub-regional and regional cooperation frameworks. Instead of finding ways for synergy among them, they tend to contain one another.[17] Furthermore, scholars are concerned that, for instance, the explicitly intensifying US-China rivalry could undermine ASEAN solidarity and ASEAN Centrality as ASEAN member states might be forced to take sides between the superpowers. China puts its BRI and MLC into implemented whereas the US has its LMI and Indo-Pacific Strategy as well as mini-lateral cooperation frameworks like QUAD and AUKUS, which tend to be countering those of China. This is conceded that it is a threat for regional peace, stability, and security despite the fact that ASEAN as an inter-governmental organization has set its fundamental principles including ASEAN Centrality and ASEAN Consensus as well as making itself the hub of regional cooperation aiming at drawing major powers such as China, the US, Japan among others into ASEAN cooperation frameworks through multiple platforms, including the East Asia Summit, the ASEAN Regional Forum, and ASEAN recently came up with its ASEAN Outlook on Indo-Pacific as an important guidance for cooperation between ASEAN and its dialogue partners.[18]

Nonetheless, in saying that it does not necessarily mean that the existing sub-regional cooperation frameworks have not made any contribution to the ASEAN integration. This is because of the fact that there are various sub-regional cooperation mechanisms that play a role in implementing ASEAN plans and strategies, including MPAC 2025, which enabled the countries in the region to be more physically connected.

: Too Many or Too Little, available at < https://www.swp-berlin.org/publications/products/projekt_papiere/ BCAS_2019_Leng_Mekong_Countries.pdf>, viewed on 1 Nov 2022.

[17] The Diplomat (2022), What Does ASEAN Centrality Mean to China?, available at, <https://thediplomat.com/2022/06/what-does-asean-centrality-mean-to-china/>, viewed on 1 Nov 2022.

[18] The World Scientific Connecting Great Minds, Is ASEAN Centrality Being Undermined by the US-China Institutional Competition? An Analysis Based on ASEAN Regional Forum (ARF), available at <https://www.worldscientific.com/doi/abs/10.1142/9789811242953_0014>, viewed on 31 Oct 2022.

Recommendations

In order to ensure that the existing sub-regional cooperation frameworks and ASEAN-led mechanisms are implemented in a coherent and complementary manner so that they can make more meaningful contribution to the maintenance and promotion of regional peace, stability, security, and prosperity as well as to the process of ASEAN community building, this paper has provided a few recommendations as follows:

1) **Promote and strengthen policy dialogues among ASEAN and dialogue partners.** Both sub-regional and regional cooperation mechanisms' drivers should explore ways or possibilities to promote and enhance the policy coordination and dialogue.
2) **Advocate openness and inclusiveness**. Explore practical cooperation on relevant areas or sectors. Promote coordinated development with other strategies, in proper forms, initiated by relevant sub-regional and regional cooperation mechanisms, such as ASEAN, GMS, ACMECS and MLC, MJC, M-ROK etc. so as to create more opportunities for regional cooperation. Strengthen exchanges and cooperation with various stakeholders and jointly promote the synergy, in order to raise the willingness of all parties to participate and achieve maximum benefits which would be extensively and fairly shared.
3) **Uphold the fundamental principles of ASEAN, especially ASEAN Centrality:** Enhanced the leadership role of ASEAN in promoting sub-regional and regional development cooperation and exploring the way to synchronize sub-regional development strategies and ASEAN development strategies such as the ASEAN Community Vision Blueprints 2025, Initiative for ASEAN Integration (IAI) Work Plan IV and MPAC 2025, ensuring that sub-regional cooperation is complementary to ASEAN's efforts toward regional integration and narrowing down the development gap within ASEAN and ASEAN community building.
4) **Encourage exchange of information among sub-regional cooperation frameworks**, with a view to promoting effective synergy among them.
5) **Promote healthy competition among development partners.** Taking into account that cooperation and complementarity should predominate over a "zero-sum game" mindset or deliberate division and conflict. The Mekong countries are well aware that if Mekong platforms are politicized or used as a platform to advance polarization, the region will unavoidably suffer from geopolitical repercussions.

Conclusion

The South China Sea is a hotspot for complex and enduring sovereignty and maritime disputes between multiple parties. Rich in natural resources and boasting a diverse maritime ecosystem, this region is also crucial for global sea lanes of communication, making it a fiercely contested area. With rising tensions between emerging and established powers, the South China Sea has evolved from a local sovereignty conflict to a broader competition for influence and geo-strategy, serving as a crucial test for *rule by law* or *rule of law* under the current international legal system. As a result, the South China Sea disputes now draw in not just the immediate claimants but also global and regional powers. This heightened involvement underscores the geopolitical stakes, transforming the region into a critical arena for international diplomacy and military maneuvers. The strategic importance of the South China Sea as the hub of the Indo-Pacific cannot be overstated. As tensions rise, the area has become a focal point for both regional and global powers, amplifying its significance on the world stage.

South China Sea Players

Among various players, China is a claimant and dominant player in the South China Sea. As elaborated by Leszek Buszynski, being a rising power, China believed it could dismiss UNCLOS in the South China Sea, attempting to enforce its own resolutions to secure its claims. It rejected the 2016 Arbitral Award, insisting on the legitimacy of its historical rights. In fact, Sarah Kirchberger emphasized that China's strategic intent in the South China Sea extends much further and is largely determined by maritime geography and the significance of the first and second island chains. By escalating geopolitical pressure, Buszynski concluded that China aims to force the US into a compromise and gain ASEAN's acceptance of its maritime claims and dominant position. With such ambitions, it is imperative to establish a geopolitical configuration of power to counterbalance China's ambitions and provide it with an incentive to resolve these issues in accordance with the law. Ultimately, there

N. Hung Son and N. Thi Lan Anh (eds.), *The South China Sea: The Geo-political Epicenter of the Indo-Pacific?*, https://doi.org/10.1007/978-981-97-8209-3

can be no settlement of the South China Sea based on international law without a "strategic equilibrium" that involves the US and its partners and allies upholding and strengthening the international legal system.

As for the US, according to Frank Jannuzi, the US has significantly shifted its stance, moving from an emphasis on peaceful settlement processes to actively rejecting many of China's excessive maritime claims. The US is no longer a neutral party and now aligns with the Philippines, supporting the Tribunal Award that rejects China's maritime claims. This shift has heightened tensions between the US and China in the South China Sea for at least a decade to come. In a similar approach, as highlighted in the strategic equilibrium formula by Buszynski and the analysis of Premesha Saha, India, Japan, Australia, the United Kingdom, Canada, and the European Union have also departed from their balanced approach by continuing to support the Tribunal Award, the rule-based international order, and show commitment by maintaining a military presence in the South China Sea. Amidst such a backdrop, according to Pou Southirak, ASEAN has struggled to maintain its collective duty to deal with one of the most challenging tasks in managing great power relations. As part of maintaining peace, stability, and prosperity in the region, it must also maintain collective strategic autonomy as well as safeguard the independence of each regional bloc.

From a Sea of Competition to a Sea of Connection

Despite increasingly fierce competition, the South China Sea still offers numerous opportunities for cooperation in various fields. Traditional areas such as fishing and marine environment protection remain crucial for regional stability and sustainability. A structured fishery cooperation, as proposed by Gilang Kembara, involving a three-stage approach—(i) understanding the trust deficit, (ii) conducting joint maritime research and surveillance, and (iii) managing living resources—could help diffuse tensions and build trust among the South China Sea littoral states. Marine research, as suggested by Vu Hai Dang, could also be strengthened with the nurturing roles of ASEAN in the form of a working group on marine scientific research in the South China Sea, a shared database of scientific research implemented relating to the South China Sea, a dialogue network of South China Sea research institutions or partnerships between ASEAN and other regional marine scientific cooperation mechanisms. In addition, as suggested by Tomasz Lukaszuk, implementing a sustainable approach and effectively countering illegal, unreported, and unregulated (IUU) fishing by enhancing existing monitoring, control, and surveillance tools, along with vocational training projects, would not only help modernize the fisheries sector but also promote sustainable and legal exploitation of fish stocks tailored to individual needs.

Moving beyond traditional areas, the region possesses the potential for cooperation in fostering green transitions in low-carbon and blue economies, as well as making strides in digital transformations through advancements in maritime surveillance, autonomous and unmanned systems and vehicles, as well as semiconductor supply chains. In the context of blue economies, the intricate connections with security, legal, and environmental issues highlight the lessons learned from effective cooperation models between ASEAN and the EU provided by Lukaszuk. This includes maintaining maritime security of Sea Lines of Communication (SLOCs) through initiatives like CRIMARIO and IORIS, as well as upholding a rule-based order in managing economically vital maritime zones under and beyond national jurisdiction through UNCLOS. Coastal states in the South China Sea, according to Michael Tsimplis, could support the low-carbon shipping industry by implementing a cross-sectoral carbon price and setting stringent entry conditions that demand lower carbon emissions. This would involve removing subsidies for marine fuels contributing to greenhouse gas emissions, reorganizing logistics for optimal efficiency, and creating incentive funds for less-polluting ships and shipping companies. By enforcing these green standards, South China Sea littoral states can promote sustainable shipping practices and contribute to global environmental goals.

In the realm of technology, technology development in autonomous systems and vessels presents both novel threats and challenges, as well as significant opportunities. The potential benefits of these new technologies, as suggested by Caroline Tuckett, can be realized through the cooperation of littoral states, ensuring that operations align with the principles of UNCLOS and international law. In addition, the current geopolitical and global dominance over semiconductors necessitates that countries in the South China Sea, as proposed by Yongwook Ryu, strengthen cooperation in research and development in the chip sector through close policy consultation and coordination with various firms, while also developing a long-term strategy for the chip industry to address economic and national security concerns, socio-economic development, and digital transformation toward a tech-based advanced economy.

As all rivers eventually flow into the sea, cooperation among riparian states along the Mekong River also significantly contributes to the health and stability of the South China Sea. Mai Sayavongs advocated for such cooperation to be effective through the promotion and strengthening of policy dialogues among ASEAN and its dialogue partners. This could be achieved by promoting openness and inclusivity, fostering practical cooperation in relevant areas and sectors, adhering to ASEAN's core principles, especially ASEAN centrality, facilitating information exchange among sub-regional frameworks, and encouraging healthy competition among development partners, rather than engaging in a "zero-sum game" mentality or fostering division and conflict.

As the South China Sea has shifted from a region of sovereign and maritime disputes to a broader arena of strategic competition and confrontation, a new approach is necessary to maintain peace and stability. The region should not be viewed through the lens of competition, but rather through the perspectives of connections. Connections and cooperation are not just potential but also prospective. Highlighting shared interests among littoral states and external powers, in accordance with international law and UNCLOS, should be the cornerstone for promoting cooperation in areas such as maritime security, sustainable fisheries, marine conservation, technological advancements in autonomous and unmanned systems, semiconductors, and the blue economy. Only through cooperation can the sustainable management, peace, prosperity, and security of the South China Sea be achieved.

The manufacturer's authorised representative in the EU is Springer Nature Customer Service Centre GmbH, Europaplatz 3, 69115 Heidelberg, Germany. If you have any concerns regarding our products, please contact ProductSafety@springernature.com

Printed and bound by CPI Group (UK) Ltd, Croydon, CR0 4YY
01/10/2026
02225977-0016